The Rebirth of Area Studies

The Rebirth of Area Studies

Challenges for History, Politics and International Relations in the 21st Century

Edited by
Zoran Milutinović

I.B. TAURIS
LONDON • NEW YORK • OXFORD • NEW DELHI • SYDNEY

I.B. TAURIS
Bloomsbury Publishing Plc
50 Bedford Square, London, WC1B 3DP, UK
1385 Broadway, New York, NY 10018, USA
29 Earlsfort Terrace, Dublin 2, Ireland

BLOOMSBURY, I.B. TAURIS and the I.B. Tauris logo
are trademarks of Bloomsbury Publishing Plc

First published in Great Britain 2015
Reprinted 2019

Copyright © Marilyn Dunn, 2015

Marilyn Dunn has asserted her right under the Copyright,
Designs and Patents Act, 1988, to be identified as Author of this work.

For legal purposes the Acknowledgements on p. vii constitute
an extension of this copyright page.

Cover design: Eleanor Rose
Cover image © Vince Cavataio/Getty Images

All rights reserved. No part of this publication may be reproduced or
transmitted in any form or by any means, electronic or mechanical,
including photocopying, recording, or any information storage or retrieval
system, without prior permission in writing from the publishers.

Bloomsbury Publishing Plc does not have any control over, or responsibility for,
any third-party websites referred to or in this book. All internet addresses given
in this book were correct at the time of going to press. The author and publisher
regret any inconvenience caused if addresses have changed or sites have
ceased to exist, but can accept no responsibility for any such changes.

A catalogue record for this book is available from the British Library.

Library of Congress Cataloging-in-Publication Data
Names: Klemme, Heiner, editor. | Kuehn, Manfred, editor.
Title: The Bloomsbury dictionary of eighteenth-century German philosophers /
edited by Heiner F. Klemme and Manfred Kuehn.
Other titles: Dictionary of eighteenth-century German philosophers
Description: New York: Bloomsbury Publishing Plc, 2016. | Originally
published under title: Dictionary of eighteenth-century German
philosophers: London: Continuum, 2010. |
Includes bibliographical references and index.
Identifiers: LCCN 2015040044 | ISBN 9781474255974 (pb) |
ISBN 9781474256001 (epub) | ISBN 9781474255981 (epdf)
Subjects: LCSH: Philosophers–Germany–Dictionaries. | Philosophy,
German–18th century–Dictionaries.
Classification: LCC B2615.D53 2016 | DDC 193–dc23
LC record available at http://lccn.loc.gov/2015040044

ISBN: HB: 978-1-7883-1434-3
PB: 978-0-7556-3680-8
ePDF: 978-1-7867-3608-6
eBook: 978-1-7867-2636-0

Typeset by Integra Software Services Pvt. Ltd.

To find out more about our authors and books visit
www.bloomsbury.com and sign up for our newsletters.

Contents

Acknowledgements		vi
Contributors		vii
1	Introduction: Area Studies in motion *Zoran Milutinović*	1
2	Twenty-first-century Area Studies: Blurring genres, evolutionary thought and the production of theory *Susan Hodgett*	19
3	How to think about 'area' in Area Studies? *Jan Kubik*	53
4	Eastern Europe, with and without borders *Wendy Bracewell*	91
5	Disciplinarity, interdisciplinarity and the plurality of Area Studies: A view from the social sciences *Mark R. Beissinger*	129
6	Comparative Area Studies without comparisons: What can Area Studies learn from Comparative Literature? *Zoran Milutinović*	151
7	Rethinking Area Studies: Figurations and the construction of space *Claus Bech Hansen*	177
Index		211

Acknowledgements

This volume results from the conference *Area Studies in the 21st Century*, held at UCL on 9 November 2015, and organized by the Centre for East European Language Based Area Studies (CEELBAS) with the support of the three other national Area Studies centres created within the scope of the UK's funding council's Language Based Area Studies initiative (2006–2016): the Centre for Russian, Central and East European Studies (CRCEES), the White Rose East Asia Centre, and the Centre for the Advanced Study of the Arab World (CASAW). We are grateful to the Art and Humanities Research Council and the British Academy for generously supporting the second phase of the LBAS initiative and for funding this conference. We would also like to thank Thomas Stottor, who commissioned this book for I.B. Tauris and patiently made sure that we did not drift away, and Thomasz Hoskins and Nayiri Kendir, who helped us bring it to completion.

Contributors

Wendy Bracewell is Professor of Southeast European History at the School of Slavonic and East European Studies, UCL. She has written about the three-way border between the Habsburg Monarchy, the Ottoman Empire and the Venetian territories in Dalmatia in the sixteenth century, and about the ways travel writers from eastern Europe have used the idea of Europe and its borders to position themselves and their societies from the sixteenth to the twentieth century. She is currently writing a study of centres and peripheries in the production of knowledge in the eighteenth century, and the ways these appear in polemics over travellers' accounts.

Claus Bech Hansen holds a PhD from the European University Institute in Florence/Italy and his work focuses on migration, development and state transformation. Claus has worked as researcher and lecturer at various universities and is currently at UNICEF, where he works on mobility, displacement and the rights of migrants and refugees.

Zoran Milutinović is Professor of South Slav Literature and Modern Literary Theory at the School of Slavonic and East European Studies, UCL, member of *Academia Europaea* and co-editor of Brill's book series *Balkan Studies Library*. He is author of five books, most recently *Bitka za prošlost. Ivo Andrić i bošnjački nacionalizam* (2018) and *Getting Over Europe. The Construction of Europe in Serbian Culture* (2011).

Susan Hodgett is Professor of Area Studies at the University of East Anglia. She has published widely on Area Studies, narratives and the Capability Approach. She is currently Chair of the Area Studies sub-panel in the UK Research Excellence Framework to 2021. She was Principal Investigator of the Arts and Humanities Research Council's Blurring Genres Network to 2018 (https://www.ulster.ac.uk/faculties/

arts-humanities-and-social-sciences/schools/applied-social-policy-sciences/research/blurring-genres) and is currently writing on Politics, Narratives and the Visual Arts with Professor Rod Rhodes (Southampton University).

Jan Kubik is Professor at and former Director of the School of Slavonic and East European Studies, UCL, and the Department of Political Science, Rutgers University, New Brunswick. He is author, co-author or editor of five books, including: *The Power of Symbols against the Symbols of Power, The Rise of Solidarity and the Fall of State Socialism in Poland* and *Twenty Years After Communism: The Politics of Memory and Commemoration* (prepared and edited with Michael Bernhard). Among his research interests are: political culture and the politics of memory; civil society, protest politics and social movements; communist and post-communist politics; populism; and interpretive and ethnographic methods. He received MA from the Jagiellonian University in Kraków and PhD (anthropology, with distinction) from Columbia University.

Mark R. Beissinger is the Henry W. Putnam Professor of Politics at Princeton University. Beissinger's area of study is the former Soviet Union, with a focus on social movements, revolutions, nationalism, state-building and imperialism. He is author or editor of five books, including most recently *Historical Legacies of Communism in Russia and Eastern Europe* (2014). He was founding director of the Center for Russia, East Europe and Central Asia (CREECA) at the University of Wisconsin-Madison, and in 2007 served as President of the American Association for the Advancement of Slavic Studies. At Princeton he served as Director of the Princeton Institute for International and Regional Studies (PIIRS) from 2010 to 2017.

# Introduction: Area Studies in motion

Zoran Milutinović

This volume argues not only that the declaration of Area Studies' death was premature, but that this research field has undergone a series of significant transformations in the last few decades, and currently demonstrates signs of dynamism, vitality and strength quite unusual for the presumed post-mortem state. Instead of being frozen in their Cold War and pre-globalization past – the image frequently recalled by their critics – Area Studies have been in motion all along and presently occupy a place different from the one ascribed to them by those who see Area Studies as redundant. The contributors to this volume trace this trajectory and put forward several proposals for further development. Although they do not share a common perspective on Area Studies' future, appropriate methods and aims – which is already obvious in their different understandings of Area Studies as a field, a discipline or a cluster of disciplines or research fields – they all agree that Area Studies are as necessary, viable and fruitful today as they have been throughout the twentieth century.

Let us recall the main points raised in criticism of Area Studies.[1] It has been claimed that the forces of globalization, which unify and homogenize the world, make the study of specific spaces redundant, and that scholarship should focus on studying global processes instead of place-specific features. Area Studies were characterized as a pseudo-academic research field, too complicit with power and serving its interests.[2] Further, they were compared with well-established academic disciplines, and found wanting for lacking a specific method and a clear and unique object. Moreover, Area Studies were judged to be theoretically and methodologically inferior to the disciplines, incapable of theory-building and merely descriptive. Many Area Studies specialists – most of whom, it is often forgotten, have specific disciplinary backgrounds – disagree with this criticism, and believe that place-specific knowledge is still needed, that all knowledge can be instrumentalized by power, that methodological purity is an outdated requirement in the twenty-first century and that theory-building requires contexts as much as conceptual production. Contrary to the optimism regarding globalization processes in the early 1990s, it is now difficult to deny that globalization works in contradictory ways. Global processes are implemented in place-specific ways: as Chakrabarty maintained, 'the universal concepts of political modernity encounter pre-existing concepts, categories, institutions, and practices through which they get translated and configured differently'.[3] In addition to this, it is now widely accepted that globalization produces integration as well as disintegration – that it causes the disappearance of some borders and divisions, while introducing new ones at the same time.

While the narrative of the expansion of Area Studies research centres, departments, programmes and other units within US and UK academia since the beginning of the Cold War can be convincingly supported by evidence, it is not as clear that the Cold War and the funding offered by various governmental agencies and non- or near-governmental organizations was the sole root of this expansion. It coincided with the post-Second World War expansion of universities worldwide: new academic institutions were established, and already existing ones expanded by opening new programmes and forming research centres, including Area Studies ones. However, all other disciplines expanded in a similar way in that same period, many of them benefiting from various forms of strategic funding. The beginning of the opposite process – the contraction – did coincide with the end of the Cold War, and with the consequent withdrawal of governmental and non-governmental support for Area Studies, but the withdrawal of funding also affected, and continues to affect, many other areas of teaching and research. The explanation for cuts to funding for Music departments may be different, and not at all related to the end of the Cold War, but the general movement is obvious for all to see. The end of the Cold War – if an end it really was – could be just a convenient pretext for what has already been happening in other academic areas, and with different justifications. The undeniable prominence of Area Studies teaching and research during the Cold War should be seen only as one stage in the history of Area Studies as an academic enterprise, and neither as their defining feature, nor as evidence of their origin, nature and purpose.

Area Studies do not trace their genealogy to the early Cold War period, as Timothy Mitchell reminds us.[4] Area Studies institutions – mostly 'Oriental' ones – had already been established in Russia and France at the beginning of the nineteenth century, and similar ones soon appeared in Germany and the Habsburg Empire. The first Area Studies programmes in the USA were established immediately after the First World War: the Oriental Institute of the University of Chicago in 1919, and the Department for Near Eastern Studies at Princeton in 1927. In the UK, the School of Slavonic at King's College in London opened in 1915, consisting of four posts in Russian, Serbian, Slavonic Literature and East European History, and largely financed by foreign governments.[5] Over the years, it began to offer other East European languages, social science and humanities disciplines, and in 1931 became the School of Slavonic and East European Studies (SSEES), since 1999 a part of University College London. In 1916 the School of Oriental Studies in London opened its doors to students, with the remit of teaching languages, histories, customs, laws and literatures of the peoples of Asia. Not only was this remit of researching and teaching knowledge about an area *not* opposed to disciplinary knowledge, but the School of Oriental Studies actually gave birth to the first ever Department of Linguistics in the UK in 1932. The School acquired its present name, School of Oriental and African Studies (SOAS), when a Rockefeller grant in 1938 helped it establish African studies. The establishment of these four significant Area Studies institutions in the UK and USA precede the Cold War by many years: 'knowing the enemy' was certainly not their *raison d'être*.

Knowing the world available for penetration and possession, and later Cold War use of Area Studies' body of knowledge, is quite another matter. Linking political and academic fields is the rule rather than the exception, reserved only for Area Studies institutions. It would not be too difficult to list a number of scholars who left a deep impact on the Cold War world, but did not have an Area Studies background: Henry Kissinger came from Harvard's Department of Government, and Zbigniew Brzezinski from Johns Hopkins University's School of Advanced International Studies. An Area Studies background does not predispose scholars either to serve the aims of power or to oppose them. As scholars, most of them follow the old-fashioned aim of saying and writing what they believe to be truth in their respective fields of knowledge. This can always be put to good use by those in power, but abstaining from compiling a dictionary of an Asian language, simply because those in power could use it to teach their colonial army that language, is hardly what a linguist should do. *Cui bono?* is often a useful question, but if it becomes the only question governing our judgement it may lead to reductionist and even cynical conclusions, and unnecessarily denigrate those who engage the better part of their souls in the process of furthering our knowledge of the world. The relationship between power and Area Studies institutions is a much more complex affair than normally acknowledged by those who, in the wake of Said's *Orientalism*, accuse a whole field of academic inquiry of complicity with imperialist interests. The founder of the School of Slavonic and East European Studies in London explicitly linked the political and academic fields underlying the School's mission, but it was not British imperialism or colonialism that had supported its establishment: rather, it was 'the cause of self-determination for the peoples of Eastern Europe'.[6] In her chapter in the present volume, Wendy Bracewell argues that Area Studies scholars, as all other academics, can very effectively subvert and resist the intentions of those in power, or criticize their aims and approaches, or produce knowledge that undermines their endeavours; to extend our example above, the same Russian dictionaries used by the British intelligence community also helped Kim Philby and Geoffrey Prime learn Russian, as Bracewell reminds us. Some of the most vocal opponents of the US policies in Indo-China were a group of Asian Studies scholars in the Committee of Asian Studies, who published the Bulletin of Concerned Asian Scholars and thus gave public voice to dissenting views.[7] If the question is whether Area Studies scholars help promote the interests of power, the answer can only be: some do, some do not. Like Pascal, many academics also bet on eternity. If, however, this question is asked on a more general level, where – following Foucault – every body of knowledge immediately creates a relationship of power, and there is no relationship of power that does not produce knowledge, we are all in the same position, as David Szanton notes, Area Studies scholars as much as those who work in the disciplines.[8]

The chasm between Area Studies and the disciplines has often been overstated. Several disciplines that contribute to Area Studies are place-bound of necessity: historians, linguists, anthropologists, geographers, and literature and culture specialists all work within disciplines that can only be area-based. Theory-building and a higher level of abstraction, as opposed to description, occur in them without any distinction between knowledge about an area and disciplinary knowledge. Sociology and Political Science are both methodologically diverse, and in addition to formal modelling and rational choice theory also use a plethora of methods that have more in common with interpretation aimed at understanding than with nomothetic approaches aimed at explanation. The former is by no means less rigorous than the latter, and is supported by a rich, complex and self-reflexive theory of understanding and interpretation. However, interpretation does not equal mere description: rather, it is directed towards meaning and significance – Gadamer would say towards *truth* – of the phenomenon under study, and acknowledges an interpreter's participation in what is being studied. The interpretation of the human world assumes that, within it, the human is an issue to itself, and that every interpretation of the world is the interpretation of the webs of meanings humans have spun themselves. Hence the importance of local perspectives in Area

Studies: without knowing what people from an area make of their world – or how they create their world, understood not as the mere physical environment, but as a web of meanings – there is no understanding of the social and political world we attempt to study. From this point of view, the progressive disappearance of language-based academic programmes and the decline in foreign language skills in Anglo-American academia in the last two or three decades poses a greater threat to Area Studies, and to our knowledge and understanding of the wider world, than the withdrawal of governmental and non-governmental funding. In his contribution to this volume, Mark R. Beissinger rejects the oft-repeated comparison between social science disciplines, as supposedly theoretically and methodologically superior, and Area Studies as inferior: social science work and Area Studies knowledge are complementary and reinforcing. Being research fields rather than academic disciplines, Area Studies do not strive to develop or adopt one distinct Area Studies method. Such methodological exclusiveness and purity has been abandoned in all humanities and social sciences in any event; they have for a long time acknowledged the value and fruitfulness of various, competing and sometimes contradictory methods in their own work. The relationship between disciplines and Area Studies is better understood as overlap, complementarity and pervasion, rather than outright competition and mutual exclusion.

If one distinct research method is neither desirable nor possible, should not one distinct object within each Area Studies fields be assumed? This is easier said than done: areas are hardly physical phenomena, existing naturally by themselves. They are intellectual constructs, with shifting borders, drawn at different times with different aims in mind. However, this does not mean that areas are absolutely arbitrary or fictitious: they are based on historical, political, linguistic, cultural and religious legacies, real or perceived, and often supported by the self-perception of those who inhabit them. What exactly could or should be the object of study within such constructions largely depends on the legacy we choose to focus on, or on the research problems that guide our interest. This also means that scholars – not only the imperial gaze or local identification – can propose new areas whenever social, economic, cultural or political processes create the conditions for them.⁹

The contributors to the present volume address some of these issues and put forward conceptual, methodological and institutional solutions for problems discussed within Area Studies – and outside them – over the past few decades. The first chapter brings a detailed overview of the debate on the need for Area Studies research, and of the transformations they have undergone as a response not only to explicit criticism, but also to the wider changes in scholarship during this period. The following two chapters focus on understanding the concept of area, which is central to Area Studies, and ask how it can be understood, what makes an area a viable analytical category, and which consequences follow from this understanding in Area Studies methodology. The relationship between academic disciplines and Area Studies is the topic of the next two chapters: what the place of area-specific knowledge in social sciences is, and what Area Studies can learn from Comparative Literature. The last chapter presents the methodological aspects of a specific Area Studies research project based on the idea of mobility, interaction and interdependences, and serves as a *coda* to the preceding discussions.

In her chapter, Susan Hodgett revisits the myth of the post-Cold War crisis of Area Studies in greater detail. Instead of becoming irrelevant and disappearing, she maintains that Area Studies underwent a rich period of transformation and reshaping, and even forging closer alliances with various academic disciplines. The criticism directed at Area Studies in the early 1990s did not fall on deaf ears, and much of it has been taken on board. Hodgett points to the most important nodal points in this debate, citing examples of criticism and explaining how Area Studies evolved in response to it. Area Studies were said to be descriptive, parochial and oblivious to global forces; they were an exponent of hegemonic cultures; they maintained artificial historical boundaries and replicated colonial cartography; they lacked rigour and shied away from broader generalizations. In addition to this, the proponents of rational choice theory questioned the need for language-based study and deep cultural knowledge. The self-examination of Area Studies resulted in a challenge: social sciences do not have a monopoly on theory, methodological rigour and scientific approach; regions or areas are grounded in long-standing historical processes and remain valuable analytical categories. Moreover, inter-regional and cross-regional approaches can supply insights and knowledge that cannot be obtained in any other way, and the local perspective – to which Area Studies are responsive thanks to their language-based approach and reliance on deep cultural knowledge – represents an invaluable contribution to understanding the issues under study. In the second decade of the twenty-first century, Hodgett maintains, it is obvious not only that Area Studies can make a great contribution to academic knowledge about the world, but also that they can help improve disciplinary research methods.

This response to criticism directed at Area Studies, Hodgett points out, was at least in part enabled by the background drama that has taken place in the last three decades and concerned the traditional division of reality into regions entrusted to academic disciplines. Its outcome, however, is that we are less certain today that the traditional disciplinary divisions are necessary and that the boundaries between disciplines must be rigid and impermeable. Also, most of us agree that there is more than one way of evaluating various research methods. At the end of the second decade of the twenty-first century, we are ready to tolerate greater diversity in epistemology, knowledge sources and claims: the easing of rigid disciplinary divisions has also resulted in methodological approaches travelling from one discipline to another, being adapted for different purposes, modified and often improved in the process, and, as a consequence, shared between humanities, social sciences and Area Studies. In this context, Area Studies can raise their claim to being a theory-developing activity as much as the individual disciplines. Hodgett reiterates that the value of the local perspective – knowing how those we seek to understand interpret themselves and their world – has not been diminished, but that it remains the most urgent task of Area Studies. In order to understand a place better, a researcher must know 'how it feels to be there'.

Jan Kubik and Wendy Bracewell address the question of Area Studies' objects and ask how the existence of an area should be understood. Starting from the perspective of contextual holism and focusing on Central Europe, in his chapter Kubik proposes understanding areas as *situations*. Areas exist as discursive constructions, but they are no less real because of this. Whether the existence of an area such as Central Europe is confirmed, contested or rejected, the question is not whether Central Europe *is there*, but what happens when some actors construe their situation as living in Central Europe and compete with other actors who deny its existence or tell them that they actually live in *Mitteleuropa*, or East Europe, or New Europe, or *Intermarium* – that is, that they should construe their situation altogether differently. Here, building networks, both internal networks of cooperation and external networks of partnership, dominance or dependence, should be understood as the central activity that guides actors.

Kubik's contextual holism rests on four postulates. With regard to the first of them – *relationism* – Central Europe is placed between areas that are discursively more solidly articulated and less questionable: Russia on one side and Western Europe on the other. The actors who construe their situation as 'Central Europe' do not see themselves as part of either, but as being 'in between'. Being in between can further be understood as a source of strength, but also as a danger: the area in between can be, as Central Europe has been, claimed by both sides. Thus, this situation is marked by a sense of endangerment, lack of distinct identity and inconsequentiality. Seen through the paradigm of modernity, this situation is marked by underdevelopment, semi-periphery or periphery. These are the images that guide actors in their construction of networks of cooperation, or when responding to the actions of external actors. Kubik emphasizes the importance of identifying the communities of discourse that produce such images and situate an area in a broader picture.

The second postulate of contextual holism is *historicism*. The construction of an area is also based on the construction of historical legacies, real or perceived: material, cultural and institutional legacies are summoned to help people construct their own situation – their area. A legacy can also be an event inscribed in collective memory. Legacies are, Kubik maintains, unstable and shifting, constantly reinvented, claimed and reinterpreted, and can often be contradictory. Such is, for example, the construction of Central Europe by those who live in it and construe it as a part of the democratic West, yet distinct from it, culturally superior and more Western than the West. A more recent example of a claimed legacy in Central Europe is the 'two totalitarianisms' legacy as a definition of this situation. In light of recent political developments in Poland and Hungary, prompted by the refugee crisis, one wonders if we are witnessing the construction of yet another historical legacy that may be recalled to define Central Europe as a situation: namely, whiteness-*cum*-Christianity.

While these two postulates help bring together places into an area, Kubik's third postulate – *significance of scale* – introduces discord, difference and rift. Areal imagination is not homogeneous, but fractured, regional and contradictory. Even when all actors perceive their situation as the same, their interpretations of it can be conflicting. The fourth postulate – *informality* – proposes that informal practices be seen as areal, not just national or regional phenomena. The definition of an area can also be based on a specific combination of formal and informal imaginings of this area, and how they are constructed in discourses of self-identity. Starting from the contested area of Central Europe, Kubik shows that areas need not be constructed by imperialist scholars: Central Europe is a native concept, created, interpreted and reinterpreted by those who believe themselves to be within it. Deep cultural and language-based knowledge reveals how natives construct, conceptualize and understand their own area. An area, as an object of Area Studies research, is revealed when we approach it through a wide range of situations in which it is deployed as a venue of self-understanding.

Wendy Bracewell reconsiders Area Studies from a similar geographical perspective: Eastern Europe, which may or may not include Central Europe. In her chapter, Bracewell traces the genealogy of this concept and demonstrates its inherent instability: the borders and divisions that have formed Eastern Europe have been fluid and frequently shifting. The point is, claims Bracewell, not to conclude that Eastern Europe is thus an invalid analytical category, but to see who is defining it, where and when, and for what purpose. She demonstrates that various definitions of this area, in various historical periods and political constellations, have always depended on who was making the argument and with what purpose in mind, and, more importantly, that these arguments rarely arose from observable commonalities: they were almost always based on the logic of alterity. Bracewell also warns against simplistic reductions of Area Studies to 'the colonial paradigm' and recommends a more nuanced approach; like all other academics, Area Studies scholars are as likely to adopt official policies as to reject and oppose them. Accusing Area Studies of parochialism should be viewed with an equal measure of scepticism, she claims; Area Studies scholars not only test disciplinary methods and approaches against the peculiarities of specific contexts, but also produce knowledge that is at the same time contextual and simultaneously represents a contribution to wider projects of knowledge.

However, Bracewell's main emphasis is on the place that areas occupied in the successive transformations of research approaches in the recent past. In the constantly shifting epistemic environment, areas as categories of analysis became redundant in comparative research and in the 'spatial turn', but, to those who study transnational entanglements and cultural transfers, areas have become useful again. It is important to note that rejected and discarded categories rarely return in their previous forms: rather, they re-enter research approaches modified and adapted, and continue to display the scars received in battle. Thus, Bracewell points out that areas as categories of analysis do not return as bounded entities, but as shifting spaces of encounter. As the crisis in the 1990s sharpened Area Studies practitioners' awareness of the processes of framing areas, this knowledge became an important part of the critical Area Studies. Bracewell advocates Area Studies 'with and without borders': instead of debating areas' ontological status, we can accept them as heuristic devices, as spatial frameworks that generate questions, and within which these questions can be explored. The question is, Bracewell maintains, not if areas exist as such, but what they are useful for. 'Without borders' means understanding borders as interfaces as well as boundaries. Preserving the boundary between knowledge about an area and an academic discipline prevents dissolving one into another and maintains different perspectives, which can often be productive. The 'with and without borders' approach does not mean denying the political dimension of Area Studies, but being aware of the multiplicity of political perspectives involved; there is always more than one power at work in producing knowledge about an area, and those who give an account of the struggle between different powers, places, authorities and perspectives for imposing their own take on an area are already doing Area Studies, whether they admit it or not. Bracewell also advocates bringing into contact the perspectives and structures of different Area Studies in the form of cross-area studies, and closer connections with other space-based academic research fields, which may have different understandings of space. Borders can be preserved as heuristic devices, accompanied by historical awareness of their instability and of the multiple power-structures that constantly redraw them, yet made more permeable to allow fruitful traffic between Area Studies themselves and other academic research fields.

Two chapters in this collection discuss Area Studies from the perspectives shaped by the disciplines contributing to them. Mark R. Beissinger takes the social science perspective and points to the difference between present-day Area Studies and those shaped by the Cold War era. Beissinger distinguishes between three different models of Area Studies, which operate simultaneously but serve different purposes. The traditional area-driven model of Area Studies was meant to serve as a common ground in which various academic disciplines would interact and, hopefully, come together in a spirit of interdisciplinarity. Its purpose was to offer rounded knowledge of cultures and spaces: to get to know a culture from the perspectives of all academic disciplines involved in this project. The obvious shortcoming of this model is the fact that the disciplines rarely interacted as expected, and the interdisciplinary aim was never achieved. The discipline-driven model has a different purpose: instead of deepening knowledge of a particular place, it offers specific disciplines an opportunity to further their own theoretical issues. Social sciences always assume knowledge of context, and discipline-driven Area Studies give them space in which to unpack it and thus hold theory accountable to reality. Instead of being an opponent and competitor, Area Studies play, in fact, an important role in producing disciplinary knowledge, claims Beissinger. The third model is problem-driven Area Studies. It is created whenever addressing a particular problem requires cross-disciplinary inquiry and a larger geographical realm. It is based on the knowledge derived from particular disciplines and the existing body of knowledge about areas, but cannot be reduced to either. Beissinger sees all three models as interdependent.

Beissinger also discusses the institutional aspect of Area Studies, and with good reason: theoretical and methodological discussions aside, this is what the Area Studies crisis comes down to after all is said and done. If universities and research institutes do not hire scholars who define themselves as area specialists, who will do Area Studies in the future? If the number of area specialists in social science departments declines, it is reflected in the curricula offered to students and in publications that are produced, and knowledge about areas rapidly disappears from our intellectual horizon. This knowledge is still important for governments and policy-making. One of its purposes is also to challenge culturally based assumptions and bias. Living and working in an ever-closer globalized world requires knowledge of different cultures and understanding their different perspectives. The disappearance of area knowledge results in narrow-minded, parochial and culturally biased administrators, policy-makers, businesspeople and citizens in general. As a way out of this downward spiral, in which diminishing numbers of academic specialists for an area quickly result in no specialists at all – for it is not clear where they will come from if we refuse to replenish the pool of expertise at our universities – Beissinger offers the solution devised by his home university, Princeton, which offers social science departments an opportunity to open posts to be filled by scholars with expertise in both a discipline and an area, half of the post being financed by the university programme aimed at preserving Area Studies expertise. Beissinger concludes with a plea for preserving all three models of Area Studies: while the traditional area-driven model is still necessary for training students and providing area-trained journalists, businesspeople and administrators, the discipline-driven model is vital for the health of the social sciences. The third model, problem-driven Area Studies, fosters cross-disciplinary exchange and broadens academic expertise, but its success depends on the vitality and success of the previous two.

Zoran Milutinović approaches the issue of the future of Area Studies from the humanities perspective, but with a different aim: instead of asking what Area Studies can give to the disciplines, he asks what Area Studies can learn from the discipline of Comparative Literature. Similarly to Area Studies, Comparative Literature has also been reproached for lacking a clearly defined object and its own method. Comparative Literature as a discipline is always in crisis, yet perpetually reconstituting its object and reinventing its methods. In one of the books that periodically declare the death of Comparative Literature and put forward proposals for its resurrection, G. C. Spivak proposed forming an amalgam of Area Studies and Comparative Literature. This would give Area Studies a broader, worldly perspective, and Comparative Literature would be able to leave behind its focus on texts and begin dealing with real issues. Spivak's starting point is the exact opposite of Beissinger's: while the latter sees Area Studies as social sciences' poor relative, who needs defence and support, from Spivak's perspective Area Studies is an established academic field, which could take Comparative Literature under its wing and offer it some respectability. Comparative Literature can offer Area Studies its own disciplinary insights: Area Studies should include studying literature not merely as a component of an area, but as a great repository of background cultural understandings, which are sedimented in it without ever being conceptualized. If a cultural world is a totality of significance that all inhabitants of this world share, interpreting a world is possible only through interpreting the background understandings this world's language creates. Milutinović sums up the methodological criticism of Area Studies' shortcomings as two related ideas: a quest for essences and an obsession with purity. The charge that Area Studies failed to fully integrate the disciplines and offer a total presentation of areas is based on the assumptions that areas have essences, that logic, coherence and integration are proper to reality, and that the failure to create a unique interdisciplinary method prevented Area Studies from uncovering these areal essences. If, however, we admit that contingencies, different temporalities, discontinuities, contradictions, breaks and reversals are more proper to reality than coherence and integration, then the quest for essences is misguided, and multidisciplinarity appears to be a more suitable approach to areas. The obsession with areal purity is equally misleading, as it can only be postulated, but never confirmed: creolization has always been the rule, rather than an exception, in all cultures and societies. Methodological and disciplinary purity should be seen as a thing of the past: most disciplines have abandoned them and are happy working with impure methods. Comparative Literature can help Area Studies by offering itself as an example of a discipline that is always in crisis, in tension with its component disciplines and without a readily available object or method. Following many decades of periodically declaring its own death, Comparative Literature found its place among other fields of knowledge by becoming a testing ground for methodological and theoretical innovation. With each theoretical turn, the object of Comparative Literature changed. It appeared that there was not one object, waiting to be uncovered by it, but rather, the object(s) came into being as a result of questions asked. Thus, Comparative Literature became not a sum of knowledge stored in its component disciplines – the studies of national literatures – but a generator of questions that could not be asked in any of them. Similarly, Area Studies should generate questions that no single discipline can ask. Their proper object will keep appearing as a result, not as a starting point. In order to do this, Area Studies should become metaphorical rather than metonymical. The former abandons the pretence of offering total, integrated knowledge and full comprehension, and substitutes it with intensity of insight. Area Studies should not become a sum total of areal knowledges, but a meta-discipline which inspires disciplinary efforts, a field of theoretical innovation and experimentation in which new questions are asked, conceptual vocabularies proposed and new perspectives tested. This would mean – as it means for Comparative Literature – being in a permanent crisis, constantly seeking subversion of themselves, always looking for a proper object and being in a perpetual state of methodological uncertainty.

Claus Bech Hansen presents a case study that draws on the findings from the interdisciplinary research network Crossroads Asia, which between 2011 and 2016 joined several German universities in an effort to chart the future of Area Studies in an increasingly interdependent world. Hansen's contribution to the present volume shows that similar concerns and issues are being discussed in other academic settings as well. The focus of the Crossroads Asia research network was on interdependences, interactions and mobility, which help de-emphasize the borders between traditionally constructed areas and the alleged impenetrability and self-sufficiency ascribed to them. Similarly to Kubik's emphasis on networks, Hansen argues for Norbert Elias's figurational sociology, in which networks play a crucial role, as a useful Area Studies method. Elias was interested in networks of human beings, interdependent in ever-evolving networks of interactions, and thus stressed social processes rather than permanent states. Hansen also reminds the reader of the recent methodological and theoretical developments that emphasized approaches focused on mobility, interconnectivity and networks, and thus loosened both disciplinary and spatial borders. From the perspective of Elias's figurational sociology, space creates a situation in which agents produce and reproduce structures, and act within them. From this point of view, space – such as an area – becomes an arena of interaction of differently positioned actors. Hansen recommends processual engagement with mobility through mobile methods, which help us see the processual, evolving nature of figurations as they travel across the borders. Interdependences, interactions and mobility, the world set in motion by the forces of globalization, certainly present a great challenge for critical Area Studies.

Hansen's emphasis on mobility underlines a feature present in all preceding chapters in this volume: all contributors see Area Studies as a highly mobile and dynamic field, forging interactions and interdependences with other fields of knowledge, transforming their own assumptions, received orthodoxies and theories, and rebuilding conceptual frameworks. What we offer is a snapshot of their present state, and a series of propositions for the direction their scope, methods and aims should take. Area Studies have been in motion for several decades despite unfavourable external circumstances. We hope that this motion will not be arrested.

Notes

1   For informative summaries of criticism of Area Studies and some replies to it, see David Szanton, 'Introduction', in D. Szanton (ed.), *The Politics of Knowledge. Area Studies and the Disciplines* (Berkeley, Los Angeles and London, 2004); A. Mirsepassi, A. Basu and F. Weaver, 'Introduction: Knowledge, Power and Culture', in A. Mirsepassi, A. Basu and F. Weaver (eds), *Localizing Knowledge in A Globalizing World. Recasting the Area Studies Debate* (Syracuse, NY, 2003); Jon Gross and Terence Wesley-Smith, 'Introduction: Remaking Area Studies', in J. Gross and T. Wesley-Smith (eds), *Remaking Area Studies* (Honolulu, 2010).

2   The classical formulation of this argument is in Bruce Cumings, 'Boundary Displacement: Area Studies and International Studies During and After the Cold War', *Bulletin of Concerned Asian Scholars*, 29.1 (1997): 6–26.

3   Dipesh Chakrabarty, *Provincializing Europe. Postcolonial Thought and Historical Difference* (Princeton, NJ, 2007), p. xii.
4   Timothy Mitchell, 'Deterritorialization and the Crisis of Social Science', in Mirsepassi, Basu and Weaver (eds), *Localizing Knowledge in A Globalizing World*.
5   I. W. Roberts and Roger Bartlett, *History of the School of Slavonic and East European Studies 1916–2005* (London, 2009).
6   Ibid., p. 10.
7   Mirsepassi, Basu and Weaver, 'Introduction: Knowledge, Power and Culture', p. 4.
8   Szanton, 'Introduction', p. 23.
9   James D. Sidaway discusses the creation of new areas in 'Geography, Globalization, and the Problematic of Area Studies', *Annals of the Association of American Geographers*, 103.4 (2013): 984–1002.

Bibliography

Chakrabarty, Dipesh, *Provincializing Europe. Postcolonial Thought and Historical Difference* (Princeton, NJ, 2007).
Cumings, Bruce, 'Boundary Displacement: Area Studies and International Studies During and After the Cold War', *Bulletin of Concerned Asian Scholars*, 29.1 (1997): 6–26.
Gross, Jon, and Terence Wesley-Smith, 'Introduction: Remaking Area Studies', in J. Gross and T. Wesley-Smith (eds), *Remaking Area Studies* (Honolulu, 2010).
Mirsepassi, A., A. Basu and F. Weaver, 'Introduction: Knowledge, Power and Culture', in A. Mirsepassi, A. Basu and F. Weaver (eds), *Localizing Knowledge in a Globalizing World. Recasting the Area Studies Debate* (Syracuse, NY, 2003).
Roberts, I. W., and Roger Bartlett, *History of the School of Slavonic and East European Studies 1916–2005* (London, 2009).
Sidaway, James D., 'Geography, Globalization, and the Problematic of Area Studies', *Annals of the Association of American Geographers*, 103.4 (2013): 984–1002.
Szanton, David, 'Introduction', in D. Szanton (ed.), *The Politics of Knowledge. Area Studies and the Disciplines* (Berkeley, Los Angeles and London, 2004).

2

Twenty-first-century Area Studies: Blurring genres, evolutionary thought and the production of theory

Susan Hodgett

Over the last twenty years the author has been perplexed by the oft-posited collapse of my adopted discipline of Area Studies, as proclaimed by its numerous critics. And, as a social scientist, the author has remained profoundly aware of the deep self-examination undertaken by many Area Studies scholars subject to this extended barrage of intellectual excoriation. The argument offered in this chapter gives some account of this experience concerning the repeated denigrations of Area Studies as well as the individual reflexive contributions proffered by scholars in response, arguing that collectively this amounts to a recent shift in the discipline, in its commonplace direction, and its current academic credibility. Area Studies has long been portrayed as a discipline undergoing fundamental challenge, existential crisis and inevitable decline.[1] This chapter challenges that perception, suggesting alternatively that such a view is out of date and, in the millennium's second decade, ill informed. Rather than descending into obscurity, Area Studies is undergoing a period of rich intellectual curiosity, a boundary-crossing productivity, while playing an acknowledged role in informing and supporting other disciplines, including, for example, International Relations and Comparative Politics.[2]

This work was generously supported by the Arts and Humanities Research Council (grant number AH/N006712/1).

Realizing that we are witnessing a significant, if tentative, academic resurgence in the realm of Area Studies, this chapter marks this evolution as we move towards the end of the second decade of the new millennium. The chapter surveys some of the more conventional criticisms of Area Studies at the end of the twentieth century. It offers too, in rebuttal, an initial insight into how the subject has evolved since the 1990s and speculates a little on how those changes may progress in future. The chapter opens with a definition of what it is to be an Area Studies scholar as defined in the last decade of the twentieth century, moving on to explore the oft-reputed crisis it has endured.

On doing Area Studies at century's end

A year before the millennium Richard Lambert argued that '[a]n area specialist [is] someone who devotes all or a substantial portion of his or her professional career to the study of another country or region of the world'.[3] Suggesting that Area Studies is what area specialists do, he posited that Area Studies specialists 'tend to be with a broad region of the world, for narrower and narrower geographic specialization, moving from world region to country to section of the country'.[4] Furthermore, in Lambert's view, Area Studies post-Second World War seemed concerned mostly with the need to understand countries that the United States did not know.[5] The means to this evaluation was the establishment of Area Studies programmes supported by private foundations delivered by 600 American university programmes. His knowledge of the organization of early Area Studies allowed Lambert to recognize that scholars within such programmes were taken up with the demands of market-orientated economics, in contemplating differences from mainstream disciplinary foci, debating applied versus pure research and anticipating the growth of the new technologies. His argument suggests moreover that the hardening of attitudes concerning disciplinary boundaries got caught up in the foundations of American positivism, when disciplinary histories became set, so that 'the heart of Area Studies l[ay] in just four disciplines: language and literature, history, political science and anthropology'.[6] This development, Lambert argued, led directly to the decline of Area Studies and what he dubbed the *ologizing* of the subject, which included high specialization, language competency and the consequent building of barriers between Area Studies and the traditional social sciences. Subsequently, Lambert postulated that 'distinct tribes of scholars focus[ed] on the major world areas' and that 'most of the interaction ... [was] with the tribe and not ... the people outside'.[7] So, his argument develops, Area Studies became trans-disciplinary, with scholars' interests drawn from many disciplines, but individual research remaining concentrated within traditional disciplinary boundaries.[8] Thereby, Area Studies itself became regarded as a soft social science, one 'loosely related to public or private policymaking.'[9]

The 'crisis' of Area Studies

Some nine years later, Vincente Raphael[10] outlined how Area Studies suffered severe criticism of its ideological approaches from the traditional academic disciplines.[11] Rehearsing these arguments, he noted that 'area studies ... is now routinely described as a state of "crisis" besieged by calls to reinvent the institutional infrastructure and intellectual agendas for understanding different regions of the world at century's end'.[12] Such trenchant criticisms of Area Studies were commonplace at the turn of the century. The censure included labelling Area Studies as the product of post-Cold War security interests. Styled as merely descriptive, Area Studies was considered parochial and oblivious to global forces, therefore irrelevant, still believing that the building blocks of power remained with nation states. Further criticism of the deficiencies of Area Studies included that it gave too much importance to hegemonic cultures, while at the same time privileging written texts over oral and elite over non-elite cultures.[13] The rehearsal of such arguments had been commonplace, as Jung[14] tells us, since the 1999 controversy over Area Studies delineated by Tessler et al.[15] regarding strategies for understanding complex Middle Eastern politics. Furthermore, and gravely, Area Studies was accused of maintaining artificial historical boundaries and at the same time reflecting a mixture of colonial cartography and European ideas of civilization.[16] Such sustained and multifaceted onslaughts proved deeply damaging.

Gregory White has written of the depth of the challenge to the subject area, pointing out that assaults on Area Studies were undertaken by several social science disciplines questioning its relevance in the post-Cold War world, particularly during an era of fiscal austerity. Such attacks were vitriolic. Jung[17] recounts how the public benefit of Area Studies was questioned, along with its use to the state and its grasp of real world issues. Allied to this was the profound and essential question, 'is there still a need for specific regional expertise in an increasingly globalized world?'[18] In his 2014 article Jung regales us with a vivid account of an annual meeting of the Middle Eastern Studies Association in November 2001, wherein a 'full-fledged polemic attack against the "very sick discipline" of Middle Eastern Studies was undertaken', and followed up in the American press and publishing media.[19] Finally, he recounts the damning indictment of Middle Eastern Studies as a 'culture of irrelevance' accused of political bias and the implementation of faulty paradigms.[20]

Worse still came a fundamental accusation by social scientists that Area Studies broadly was 'preoccupied with the description of cultural details and historical specificities at the expense of comparative and generalizing research'.[21] Area Studies stood accused of failing to embrace theoretical research of appropriate scientific standard. Profoundly, per White, it was the generally accepted view that Area Studies overall proved 'less rigorous … eschews the building of scientific knowledge and the crafting of broader generalizations for mere description and worse, storytelling'.[22]

This was reinforced by the concurrent arrival of Rational Choice Theory in Political Science, which 'help[ed] us understand humans as self-interested, short-term maximizers',[23] challenged notions of embedded fieldwork in communities or regions, criticized the focus on language or deep cultural understandings, and was seen by some to have undone Area Studies. Later, as Ostrom (1990) tells us, moves towards expanded second-generation rational choice theories and behaviourism[24] continued to confront traditional approaches undertaken in regional or place-based study. Furthermore, such challenges were accompanied by postmodern claims that Area Studies itself was the embodiment of Western ambition to maintain control of the less developed world, aimed at achieving an unethical symbiosis and capitalist exploitation of the rest of the world through expanded global development. This corresponded with a general drift, in Europe at least, towards the acknowledgement of the concept of obscurantism[25] – as older sciences were increasingly challenged by modern forms of critical thought. The arrival of newer and more quantitatively focused ways of thinking about what works in research, in government or, indeed, in practice threw up ever more common questions to the academy over its older, regionally focused, embedded ways of working.

Self-examination in Area Studies

Such a welter of prolonged public challenges led to deep reflection by Area Studies academics on fundamental questions concerning the nature of their personal scholarship. Katherine Graham outlines the usual experience: 'The claim that one is pursuing, say, South American or East Asian studies rather than economic or urban geography consigns one to the periphery of the discipline, while simultaneously invoking the authority, authenticity, and mystery of "the field".'[26] The exclusion felt by scholars building research focused on people and place was reflected in personal success (or its lack) within the disciplines, and within schools, as Area Studies departments were merged, or closed, across the minority world around the millennium.[27] The difficult experience of hard to negotiate careers within Area Studies in the new century precipitated careful and personal scrutiny of professional futures. And, as significant as the angst about career progression, came the accompanying anguish over the shape of Area Studies in the twenty-first century. This journey of re-examination and renewal was not, however, unique. At the same time, other cognate disciplines were undergoing enormous challenge and change. For example, Geography, described in the 1970s as an 'introverted discipline',[28] moved from Geology and History to the mainstream social sciences, taking on board all necessary and associated physical and mental emendations. And, as Johnston describes, geographers negotiated a tricky path through both their intellectual milieu and their wider institutional settings to make an effective comeback in both domains. Others have struggled to record and outline these profound twentieth-century changes within the academy. Russell,[29] for example, noted that with the rise of the disciplines the inevitable outcome was not (as one might have hoped) communication to make complex understanding simpler; rather, it became knowledge 'to advance the activities of specialized communities'.[30] And such complex social organization of knowledge had severe implications. Russell articulates these consequences as producing a system wherein the disciplines became so diverse and independent that they 'require[d] no common language or even values or methods within the university in order to pursue those missions'.[31] Indeed, he goes as far as to maintain that the conventions, assumptions and methodologies of the various disciplines today 'are characterized more by their differences than their similarities',[32] ensuring that, in the end, the academy became beset by small and different, uncomprehending worlds. The evident disadvantage of such dysfunctional arrangements necessitated prescient change.

Self-examination is plain to see in the literature of the time. Questions proliferated, and within Area Studies they multiplied. Introspection included – what is the correct classification of area to study (does 'Asia' really exist?)? Can Asia, indeed any region, have a newer vision of its self-subject to the intensification of flows (capital, labour and transnational networks)? Moreover (and regarding Said, 1978), do older classifications including conceptions like 'the Orient' still have relevance today?[33]

Animated and detailed conversations sprang up in inter/national scholarly networks, considering whether 'Orientalism' was in truth a cultural infection of colonialism,[34] while pondering at the same time how states in postmodernity relate to transnational corporations. The rate and depth of self-analysis within Area Studies proved foundational, persistent and fundamental. Conversations commonplace within the academy during this time included contemplating the scale and size of appropriate study, the choice of methods to be used, reconceptualizing innovative spatial categories and reconsidering appropriate scales of analysis. Increasingly taking place was the process of *mixing up* traditional paradigmatic approaches. A cursory glance at the breadth of Area Studies literature over this period demonstrates that the interdisciplinary, the comparative and the multi-cultural arrived simultaneously, along with contingent challenges about where to study, how to study and with whom. Indeed, contemplation of similar challenges for today's researchers continues unabated. A report funded by Research Councils UK recently described interdisciplinary research as that which had 'cross disciplinary outcomes',[35] with multidisciplinary research dubbed as 'research that brings disciplines together'[36] and comparative research likely to include some combination of both. At century's turn, Area Studies underwent a substantial and profound self-examination concerning methods and approaches, which to this day bears plentiful fruit.[37]

Evolutionary thought within Area Studies – working together

Others have written of this process of re-evaluation undertaken at the beginning of this century.[38] Dirlik represents the millennial theoretical turns evident with the rise of Cultural Studies, Postcolonial Studies and Globalization Studies impacting upon the academy.[39] The interplay of complexity, events and a growing awareness of power (and its capacity to work against the powerless) was becoming ever more significant as Area Studies specialists began to contemplate the correct ways in which to undertake their research. Scholars contemporaneously considered the role of Civilization Studies, Islamic Studies, Indigenous Studies, Diasporic Studies and Confucian approaches to see what could be learned or adopted. Profound ways of understanding aligned with growing multifaceted processes as academics struggled to reconceptualize what Wang called the 'global imaginary'[40] and Hozic dubbed notions of borderlands and bloodlands.[41] By 2005, Sharma described the half-decade evolution of '[t]he peculiarly American study of the "non-western" world – going under the rubric of interdisciplinary "area studies" [as] in crisis'.[42] Commenting that its Cold War origins and policy-driven focus (having survived from the 1960s until the 1980s) is in trouble, her article described Area Studies as a product of the colonial powers (Europe, Japan and the United States). Simultaneously, Sharma argued, a profound struggle was under way to win the hearts and minds of the peoples of the former communist bloc as capitalism morphed into ever more complex forms.[43]

While the 'crisis' in Area Studies was perceived by some as dragging on and on, self-examination and self-criticism evolved within the academy as Area Studies scholars sought to contemplate their futures within the discipline constantly under attack.[44] Scholars in substantial numbers reconsidered their investment in Area Studies in the longer term. Some took clear aim. Heryanto argued that Area Studies had no strong disciplinary rigour or theoretical innovation, and thus no legitimacy to stand on a par with existing disciplines.[45] Hozic questioned whether Area Studies could really stand up to the objectifying gaze of American social science.[46] Graham and Kantor[47] challenged the notion that Area Studies was a 'soft' social science as it undertook reviewing its work with indigenous social sciences (including religious traditions). Academics, including Heryanto, contemplated the use of locally based Area Studies within chosen regions, South-east Asia, for example, after the 1990s; while Chen[48] radically suggested that Area Studies itself was method and Rausch[49] explored theory building *as* local contribution. Throughout the Area Studies community, and across the globe, experts pursued a growing and essential reflexivity in their research, their remits, their methodologies and their positions vis-à-vis the older and well-entrenched social sciences and humanities. More importantly, they contemplated the impact of their work upon the people and the countries or regions that they studied.

By 2007 confidence had grown sufficiently for Graham and Kantor to overtly challenge the accepted wisdom that social science represented theory, mathematics, rigorous methods, falsifiability/replicability and scientific approaches, while Area Studies limped along behind, badged as descriptive, cultural, historical or contextual.[50] Disabusing the idea that 'the best social analysis comes from a single cognitive approach, one that incorporates mathematics, quantitative methods, and replicability',[51] they argued rather that '[t]he best social analysis should incorporate several different cognitive styles of which the method relying on mathematics, quantitative methods and reproducibility is only one'.[52] Even the rancorous battle between political scientists and Area Studies specialists was mellowing somewhat, with those in Comparative Politics recognizing the benefit of engaging with area-specific approaches.[53] While some continued pointing up the ferocious struggles between Political Science's large-scale quantitative studies and deductive modelling versus Area Studies' regional-specific studies, others deliberately looked elsewhere. By the end of the first decade of the new century, Ahram[54] made a call thus: 'insights from area studies cannot be ignored by those aspiring to general theory, but at the same time, area studies itself must adopt a new approach to qualitative and mixed methods in order to assert its role in general theory development'.

His discernments were important. In an article likely to prove significant, Ahram acknowledges the benefits of appreciating the importance of the other – firstly by reconsidering definitions of the significance of region as an analytical category (grounded in historical processes rather than simple geographical givens). Secondly, he framed an appeal to colleagues on both sides of the divide to appreciate the other. What was important for the health of both disciplines, he intuited, were the insights of regional Area Studies to political scientists, and a newer, broader use of qualitative and mixed methods to encourage theory development for Area Studies scholars. This common-sense appeal to mutual benefit includes the offer of an opportunity for Area Studies to engage with what Basedau and Köllner[55] called 'a truly comparative area studies by adding inter-regional and cross regional comparison to the traditional repertoire of single, intra-regional studies'. This development proves necessary, the argument goes, as the current large-n studies fail to adequately account for regional variation.[56] Playing around with boundaries for both sets of practitioners leads Ahram to conclude that an '[e]xplicit emphasis on contextual boundaries generates important observable implications that can further hone theoretical arguments'.[57] Ahram's marking of the appeal to work together, combined with the clear possibility of profitable collaboration going forward, might hopefully inscribe the beginning of the end of the unproductive and prolonged character assassination of Area Studies.

By 2013, views on *doing* Area Studies had matured further. Claims were routinely made by Area Studies specialists demanding recognition of their work; co-production with local people and distribution of knowledge through local engagement were becoming the norm in terms of expected research progress. Methods had evolved to the extent that examining local practice, and how local networks were included in our plans, marked a significantly improved intellectual collaboration with indigenous peoples and communities. Acceptable practice for Area Studies by the century's second decade became '[k]nowledge production and dissemination about themselves, within and beyond formal academic institutions, within and beyond [the region]'.[58] Inclusion of priorities, thoughts, feelings and meanings of the local was increasingly viewed as commonplace rather than exceptional or gold standard. Graham and Kantor's work marked the arrival of sophisticated multiple research approaches, for

> insisting on a rigid division between 'soft' methods of area studies specialists and the 'hard' methods of social scientists [proved] simplistic. Social scientists, whether using quantitative methods or ones yielding replicable results, can make great contributions to the

understanding of society and politics ... Area studies specialists can also make such contributions, and – in addition – they can sometimes advance our understanding of quantitative methods themselves. The area studies approach can lead to a deep intellectual understanding of how people think ... Both ... need to be more appreciative of the intellectual contributions the other may make.[59]

Travelling theory

Some forty years ago, Edward Said suggested that theory undergoes changes in its 'representation and institutionalization' as it undertakes its journey from an earlier 'point of origin' to its later place of arrival.[60] Furthermore, he noted that 'theory in one historical period of national culture becomes altogether different from another period or situation'.[61] The recognition, therefore, that theory evolves and changes in both time and place proves useful in this argument. This chapter has contemplated changes undertaken as Area Studies has undergone a substantial re-examination of its role within the academy and within the societies that it studies. Moreover, such changes of role, remit and research methodologies have marked a growing, even radical, discourse on the usefulness, productivity and advantage of an international academy riven by deep, divisive and entrenched intellectual boundaries (created to protect well-established disciplines and, some might argue, reputable academic careers) rather than to better serve the interests of people or societies studied by addressing difficult, persistent, global problems unconstrained by semantics.

Interestingly, the role of the academy and the disciplines themselves had, some half a century earlier, come under detailed scrutiny in England. Then, a profound and explosive debate had transfixed the academy and the public, concerning the blurring of genres, or its lack, well beyond Area Studies. Within this sometimes-censuring public conversation was an examination of how best to educate the country (including future and professional researchers) especially within and between the natural and the human sciences. Fifty-seven years later, in 2016, Robert Whelan writing in the *Telegraph* noted the dramatic impact of C. P. Snow's 'Two Cultures and the Scientific Revolution' lecture (1959) and the sizzling redoubt three years later by F. R. Leavis at Cambridge University as returning to the fore in the new millennium. Back in the 1950s, according to Whelan, Snow had argued that a 'dangerously wide gap … had opened up between scientists and "literary intellectuals" within the United Kingdom'.[62] Britain at that time, he proffered, was engaging in decadence and false confidence, while the pernicious class system disparaged the modern and emerging science base and the new technologies. Leavis's castigating riposte lambasted Snow personally and professionally, raging at the tendency of the time to mediocracy within intellectual life. And, as Whelan observes,

> [s]uch was the intensity of debate that it might be supposed that these were age-old themes: but in fact, the idea of separating academic disciplines into groups known as science and humanities was no older than the 19th century. The term 'scientist' was only coined in 1833, and it was not until 1882 that … Matthew Arnold, discussed – under the title of 'Literature and Science' – whether or not a classical education was still relevant in an age of great scientific and technical advance.[63]

Today, the nature of public and higher education in the United Kingdom remains a matter of debate and contestation.[64] Beyond this lies the residue of arrangements for acceptable research conduct within the academy and the persistence of acknowledged, and sometimes unchallenged, divisions in disciplines, cultures and methods. Notwithstanding, academics around the world have begun once again to reflect on what has (or has not) changed since the infamous Cambridge spat nearly five decades earlier. Careful thought has gone into what we have learned in the intervening years. Building on the exchange between Snow and Leavis, Jerome Kagan, in his magnificent book *The Three Cultures* in the series on *Revisiting CP Snow*, ruminates upon the development of methods of research and (mis)understandings between the natural sciences, the humanities and the social sciences post-millennium.[65]

Close to sixty years after the initial debate, he proclaims the need for a 'passionate plea to scientists, humanists and artists to break out of the cocoons of premises that separate them'.[66] Having surveyed all three elements of the modern academy, Kagan petitions scholars today 'working in all domains of inquiry who have something to contribute to a deeper understanding of the human condition'[67] and, citing J. D. Barrow, argues '[t]here is no formula that can deliver all truth, all harmony, all simplicity. No theory of Everything can ever provide total insight.'[68]

Struggling with similar, and seemingly perpetual, intellectual challenges, Paul Feyerabend argued that ideas and entrenched traditions must not be allowed to have sole rights to the manipulation of knowledge, for 'No theory ever agrees with all the facts in its domain, yet it is not always the theory that is to blame.'[69] He goes on: '[f]acts are constituted by older ideologies, and a clash between facts and theories may be proof of progress'.[70]

In *Against Method*, Feyerabend argues that all methodologies contain their limits.[71] And he posits, in relation to method, that rationality and intellect acknowledge 'there is only one principle that can be defended under all circumstances and in all stages of human development. It is the principle: [of] anything goes.'[72] This, or some version of this approach, is the crux of the argument presented in this chapter. And, to paraphrase Feyerabend, it is still true that when we engage in social research (and not scientific absolutism) we discover that the shape and style of concepts are always ambiguous and inevitably constructed.[73]

Other eminent scholars have grappled with overcoming the challenge of the 'multitude of warring sects' within the academy.[74] Many have laboured with the motives, intentions and interpretation of texts and their makers. Some have gone as far as to conclude that 'using the methods of the natural sciences in the human sciences is [no more than] comically improper'.[75] There has also been the growing but urgent introspection concerning the very purpose of the modern university laid bare by Inglis 'to sustain the conversation of the culture, to keep in circulation in a nation's bloodstream certain moral lymphocytes whether transmitting human or natural science, thereby to make them tell in everyday life'.⁷⁶ Within the current maelstrom of scholarly introspection wrapped up in the ever-expanding, some might say, malevolence of the new technologies, changes in practice of the very enterprise of research have been unavoidable. Indeed, personal accounts of the experience of the undertaking of work in place, over a career, prove captivating. We read, with rather grim fascination, of the changing academic practice through enforced norms dressed up through managerial practice and bureaucracy, which has, step by step, overwhelmed the effectiveness of the modern academy.⁷⁷ We take note of Duffield's sound warnings that the digital collapse of distance in our twenty-first-century work will inevitably be accompanied by a dangerous terrestrial pulling apart.⁷⁸

Nonetheless, and positively, other appeals to a broader diversity of subject and specialist are coming to the fore as the new century matures. And, as Acharya has demanded of colleagues in International Relations, we must struggle to 'celebrate the differences among[st] … different theoretical, epistemological, and methodological approaches. But in so doing, [we] should … strive for greater respect for diversity in our knowledge sources and claims, historical experiences, and beliefs and approaches about world order'.⁷⁹ Moreover, by seeking out such diversity, those of us in Area Studies (like International Relations) 'will become [more] … vibrant, innovative, and inclusive … reflect[ing] the voices, experiences, interests, and identities of all of humankind'.⁸⁰

In its twenty-first-century incarnation, Area Studies has gone back to the future, returning to the earlier ideas of classical studies including culture in its fullest sense as literature, art, religion, philosophy, politics, architecture and mathematics. From this perspective, pursuing Area Studies offers enormous benefits, allowing scholars to eschew the traditional pre-set, deadening, disciplinary boundaries by addressing the everyday and messy complexities of the lives of places and peoples.⁸¹

Despite the commonplace criticisms of Area Studies referred to earlier in this chapter, this more diverse work encourages positive innovation in both theory and method. Peter Jackson, in reviewing the importance of Area Studies to the understanding of modern Asia, noted the critique of what he called the 'classical form of area studies based on the notion of culture-language areas'.[82] While observing that the death of Area Studies 'would leave students of Asian societies in a theoretically and politically fraught situation',[83] Jackson convincingly makes the argument for the necessity of Area Studies, claiming that what was necessary was a full-blown post-structuralist Area Studies to assuage the impact of cultural homogenization (in Asia). In this way, he offers a serious challenge to the economic determinism of Western post-structuralist theory based on the belief that cross-cultural analysis and post-structuralism itself can benefit from the methodological cross-fertilization within the broader and wider Area Studies rubric. So, Jackson argues, the Euro-American theoretical hegemony may be resisted and perhaps overturned for the benefit of broader populations and cultures.[84]

In the oft-tarnished glow of the new millennium, and with increasing recognition of globalization in every aspect of our everyday lives, it is unsurprising that peoples in every corner of the world seek to shape their own future.[85] That this may be achieved through influencing the nature of research undertaken by academics in their regions and communities should be unremarkable. Neither is it astounding that communities should try to actively shape that research or treat with suspicion those who resist local knowledge and significant contributions to what academics seek to understand in depth.

Blurring genres

So, it seems that a new genre-blurring epoch is upon us. A plethora of scholars have made innovative and important contributions, which together prove significant for the discipline of Area Studies. Gillian Hart has shown how historical ethnography can assist us with relational comparison,[86] Arjun Appadurai[87] has focused on the importance of circulatory processes, while Clifford[88] presents the case for ethnography to escape the local and Burawoy[89] envisages a global ethnography taking account of broader external forces. Importantly, and marking a significant departure, Marcus has argued for a polyvocal and multi-sited ethnography that is both policy related and theoretically informed,[90] while Gibson-Graham suggests Area Studies itself is 'a rich resource for the *theorization*, observation and enactment of economic difference' (emphasis added). Horschelmann and Stenning have advocated a Cosmopolitan Area Studies that 'seeks to provincialize universal western knowledge claims and ... become[s] more inclusive of, as well as relevant to, the concerns of people in the majority world'.[91] They have also made essential distinctions, presenting the importance of polyvocality with a critical edge, while practising deep reflection 'on the intimacy that engagement with the lives of others over sustained periods of times affords'.[92] Seeing the world from this altered perspective allows the development of place in a more complete context, while recognizing and acknowledging the new historicist and interpretivist directions available in a broader academic understanding.[93]

Some within the academy have already appreciated the significance of such developments. Kubik has marked the changes already in place, noting that 'today's political science often rewards the work by generalists-cum-area-specialists who are fluent in the most recent theorizing and have ... mastered ... cutting edge methodological tools ... because they possess a thorough empirical knowledge of their "areas"'.[94] His work on Eastern Europe demonstrates the point that Area Studies expects scholars to consider relationalism (to include structure and agency), historicism (the study of history in politics), constructivism (considering meaning, interpretation, processes and culture), formal–informal hybrids (structures and networks) as well as localism (including the micro in social and political processes). Through his theory of contextual holism Kubik articulates the dramatic but current success of dialogue with the contextualists.

One such example can be seen in the work of Kay and Oldfield, who have demonstrated that multidisciplinary Area Studies can provide a stimulating context to advance our understanding of the role that emotions play within the research process itself.[95] Having suggested that the nature of such studies draws people together, allowing the passions, anxieties and emotions of the researcher (and the researched) to be acknowledged within fieldwork, their work reveals how the researcher's history, characteristics and emotions matter in the nature of their subjective research. They take apart the actual experience of undertaking such work in Russia by generously giving of themselves.[96] Among their considerations are the lived experiences and emotional subjectivities of researcher and researched, bolstered by the central necessity of making time for critical reflection as part of the total research process.[97] Such personal insight, combined with a good dollop of professional bravery, demonstrates that post-millennium Area Studies scholars have considered the import of their studies, and also the significance of their chosen methods and the consequence of the research outcomes to others. Acknowledging the early foresight of some of our number, Vincente Rafael, at the turn of the century, made the case that

> [i]t is precisely the accidental nature of area studies, or more precisely the accidental ways by which their practitioners stumble into studying specific areas, that makes them worthwhile as sites for encountering *regions of otherness* the disciplines tend to discount. In this sense we can think of the putative weakness of area studies ... as their actual strength ... What ... we have in common is the fact that we not only study 'otherness' but often find ourselves through our travels and our readings in foreign languages to be an 'other'.[98] (italics added)

Isabell Schierenbeck, in contemplating the other, has also recommended that Area Studies must today examine different approaches to the 'local turn', making the most of our context-based methods through innovative research designs and interdisciplinary research involving locals.[99] By finding others, as well as ourselves, we know now that the development of an Area Studies methodology *must* involve institutions, actors and their goals. Such contextualized knowledge, Schierenbeck proffers, involves examining the local, including institutions and agency. The advantage of such work is, of course, its ability to question the common local/global binary, while creating new methods through inter-epistemological research in context. Simultaneously, too, we will refine and rethink older methodological approaches and analytical tools in our search to obtain deeper knowledge on local actors and their available agency. Such primary concerns have led others, including Somer, to speculate whether Area Studies, and in this case Turkish Studies, are, at this point in history, theory-consuming or theory-producing. After careful weighing up, Somer concludes: 'theory-developing critical case studies may present the most promising way Turkish Studies can utilize to simultaneously become more theoretically relevant and achieve a better understanding of Turkish society and politics'.[100]

Somer's local but insightful consideration of what Area Studies means in place (and to people – including, of course, scholars) offers a modern recognition that theory and practice needs must go hand in hand. Such collaboration proves necessary to address the deep complexities that trouble our societies as they struggle with challenges crossing borders, cultures, times and ethnicities. Most recently, it seems that ideas on theory production have expanded; and Area Studies itself has been able to assist with new vistas on old problems, combining comparative elements across countries and peoples. Atlas,[101] for example, strives to achieve a three-part conceptual framework (consisting of the Turnerian discourse, the Lipset Thesis and Borderlands Studies) in examining the history of the United States–Canada North American frontier while utilizing a range of scholarly literature, and to apply that knowledge in comparative analysis of national policies towards Indians and First Nations in the post-Civil War and post-Confederation period on the Great Plains and the Prairies.[102] Other scholars, including the author, have crossed disciplinary boundaries seeking an explanation of thinking and feeling of those studied in place but ranged across continents, while seeking a deeper emphasis on meaning or agency.[103] The development of prolonged interest in these boundary-crossing forays in the United Kingdom, and beyond, has been evident in the establishment of the Blurring Genres Research Network, supported by the United Kingdom Arts and Humanities Research Council, seeking to bridge established disciplinary boundaries between Area Studies,

Political Science, History, Anthropology, Philosophy and Drama, and including the work of policy-makers.[104] Interest in participating in such innovative scholarship has been international, including both speakers and attendees of this seminar series.

Area Studies in the twenty-first century is back to the future. Our work today has important public benefit. Academics and the academy are increasingly demonstrating this truth through research and impact. Our work is not done but rather, beginning anew. In 1978 Edward Said remarked in *Orientalism* that the Orient was 'almost a European invention now ... disappearing'. Its time was over and 'it seemed irrelevant that Orientals themselves had something at stake in the process'.[105] For Said, in the 1970s, the Orient was the place of Europe's many colonies and 'the source of its civilizations and languages, its cultural contestant, and one of its deepest and most recurring images of the other'.[106] Presciently, in the introduction to his seminal work, he refers to Orientalism and Area Studies interchangeably, with an Orientalist (and an Area Studies scholar) 'being one who teaches, writes about, or researches the Orient ... whether the person is an anthropologist, sociologist, historian, or philologist – either in its specific or its general aspects'.[107] And, moreover, invoking Foucault's concept of discourse, he comments: 'without examining Orientalism as a discourse one cannot possibly understand the enormously systematic discipline by which European culture was able to manage – and even produce – the Orient politically, sociologically, militarily, ideologically, scientifically, and imaginatively during the post-Enlightenment period'.[108] It is this notion of *discourse* that nearly forty years later remains imperative. Said's insight proves as important today as it was in the 1970s. Area Studies continues to be crucial to deep and satisfactory understanding of place and people in addressing difficult, modern and persistent problems. At best, it involves a frank conversation with power, intellect, policy, culture, morals, about 'we' and 'they' and why we *still* do not fully understand each other. And it addresses matters of the local, including structures and institutions, as well as the inevitable evolution of societal norms.

Conclusion

At the turn of the century, in his inimitable fashion, Clifford Geertz tried to reckon up his life and its 'piled up' learning. He observed that 'the study of other people's cultures ... involves discovering who they think they are, what they think they are doing, and to what end they think they are doing it'.[109] To achieve this, Geertz noted the need to 'gain a working familiarity with the frames of meaning within which ... [people] enact their lives ... learning how, as a being from elsewhere with a world of one's own, to live with them'.[110] *Living with those we seek to understand* is surely the most urgent undertaking of Area Studies. It remains as necessary today as it was at the end of the Second World War when it was established to engage in deep examination of place and people. Today, three notable additions must be added to the achievements of modern Area Studies. First is the full involvement of local people in the creation of our research, enabling us to get *under the skin of those we seek to know* and to *better understand place*. Second is the realization that how *people feel* in undertaking such work impacts upon the being and doing of that work and our capability to excel at the work which we undertake, and the consideration of its reception. Thirdly, a new generation of scholars are emerging, deeply instilled with profound intellectual inquisitiveness, who are willing to risk careerist censure to find out what it feels like to *be there*. And, as Mairead NicCrath and Emma Hill have perceptively pointed out in an excellent article on this topic, *being there* is sometimes all that we can reasonably hope to achieve.[111]

In the twenty-first century, Area Studies scholars have renewed their belief in the fundamental power of their research. They have regained their confidence in the inductive weight of their studies of peoples and place. In this process, Jung (2014) has recorded how they have necessarily questioned social scientists' claims that they failed to create theory-driven research being overly preoccupied with culture, history and description.[112] Significantly, too, Jung notes that in the end all scholars, including social scientists, must, like Weber, acknowledge that 'each of us knows that what he has accomplished will be antiquated in ten, twenty, fifty years … the very meaning of science is to engage in a chain of scientific progress that will completely outdate one's own achievements within the course of time'.[113]

This chapter has charted the resurrection of Area Studies in the early twenty-first century, explored the self-examination of Area Studies scholars in the doing, and presented an account of a renewed and reinvigorated discourse, a theory-borne discipline, in the first eighteen years of this century. It has argued that this revitalized *conversational scholarship*, taken as a whole, positively *blurs the genres* between the traditional disciplinary boundaries in the social and human sciences. And it acknowledges that our understanding becomes ever more complex and insightful as Area Studies scholars have proposed, disposed, discussed, redefined and renegotiated this important intellectual and theoretical shift. As Duffield has concluded from his experience as both researcher and practitioner in the field, much is today at stake to 'control a world that is no longer understood'.[114] In outlining our unending and, some might say, foolish drive to capture and objectify, Duffield argues that we must once again strive to 'regain … what has been taken and made distant'.[115] In such imperative, indeed dangerous, circumstances the need for a modernized, contextual and multi/interdisciplinary Area Studies proves more urgent for a restored humanity and subjectivity in our everyday work.

The reach and fundamental importance of today's Area Studies is clear. Recently, Acharya appealed to International Relations specialists to explore regional worlds, in their full diversity and interconnectedness, to engage with their subjects and to use methods requiring deep and substantive integration of both disciplinary and Area Studies knowledge.[116]

Abrahamsen, too, in considering the future of the study of Africa, noted that bringing the continent into the study of International Relations cannot just be a case of 'add Africa and stir',[117] as the 'continent does not enter the discipline as a neutral object of study'.[118] Moreover, she argues, the case for the necessary negotiation on epistemological and methodological challenges *between the disciplines* and of 'making it possible to study Africa simultaneously as a place *in* the world and *of* the world' (italics added) proves crucial. Such ability is necessary in the final analysis for the capture of the continent's politics and societies as both unique and global.

Today, Area Studies scholars share with International Relations specialists (and other academic colleagues) the belief that the academy needs the profound motivation to examine ideas and norms and their circulation between *all* levels of a shrinking globe, both local and global. Despite all the odds, and in a new century, we continue discussing the significance of area to our lived world, in our everyday stories and lives, in our commonplace studies. And, increasingly, in what some have claimed a post-truth world,[119] the need for an ever-deeper *knowledge* and *experience* of *place* and *peoples* achieved through informed and scholarly discourse simply will not go away.

The author wishes to thank Professors Tony Chafer, Patrick James and Fred Inglis for their generous contributions of suggestions for improvements to this chapter.

Notes

1. Miriam Sharma, 'Beyond the Boundaries of Asia Pacific Area Studies', *Futures*, 37 (2005): 989–1003.
2. Ariel Ahram, 'The Theory and Method of Comparative Area Studies', *Qualitative Research*, 11.1 (2011): 69–90, and Rita Abrahamsen, 'Africa and International Relations: Assembling Africa, Studying the World', *African Affairs* (2016) Advance Access 8 December, 1–15.
3. Richard Lambert, 'Blurring the Disciplinary Boundaries: Area Studies in the United States', *American Behavioral Scientist*, 33.6 (July 1990): 712–732.
4. Ibid.
5. Ibid., p. 714.
6. Ibid., p. 727.
7. Ibid., p. 722.

8   Ibid., p. 728.
9   Ibid., p. 732.
10 Vincente Rafael, 'Regionalism, Area Studies and the Accidents of Agency', *American Historical Review*, 104.4 (October 1999): 1208–1220.
11 Dietrich Jung ('The Ottoman–German Jihad: Lessons for the Contemporary Area Studies Controversy', *British Journal of Middle Eastern Studies*, 41.3 (2014): 248) has outlined multifarious criticism of Middle Eastern Studies in detail in footnotes in his articles referenced in this paper. Herein he cites several sources of political and scholarly attacks on Area Studies.
12 Rafael, 'Regionalism, Area Studies', p. 1210.
13 Sharma, 'Beyond the Boundaries', p. 991.
14 Jung, 'The Ottoman–German Jihad'.
15 Mark Tessler et al., 'Introduction: The Area Studies Controversy', in Mark Tessler, Jodi Nachtwey and Anne Banda (eds), *Area Studies and Social Science: Strategies for Understanding Middle East Politics* (Bloomington, IN, 1999).
16 Ibid., p. 992.
17 Jung, 'The Ottoman–German Jihad', p. 248.
18 Ibid.
19 Ibid.
20 Ibid.
21 Ibid.
22 Gregory White et al., Book reviews, *The Journal of North African Studies*, 5.1 (2000): 165.
23 Elinor Ostrom, 'A Behavioral Approach to the Rational Choice Theory of Collective Action: Presidential Address', *The American Political Science Review*, 92.1 (1998): 1–22.
24 See outline of development of behaviourism offered by https://plato.stanford.edu/entries/behaviorism/ (accessed 29 October 2016).
25 *[mass noun]* The practice of deliberately preventing the facts or full details of something from becoming known: English Oxford Living Dictionaries, https://en.oxforddictionaries.com/definition/obscurantism (accessed 15 December 2016).
26 Katherine Gibson-Graham, 'Area Studies after Post Structuralism', *Environment and Planning*, 36 (2004): 405.

27 John Canning, 'Teaching on Less Commonly Taught Area Studies', *Centre for Languages, Linguistics and Area Studies* (2003), available at https://www.llas.ac.uk/events/archive/588.html (accessed 21 May 2018).
28 Ron Johnston, 'Sixty Years of Change in Human Geography', School of Geographical Sciences, University of Bristol, Paper prepared for the History of Postwar Social Science Seminars, London School of Economics, 25 April 2006.
29 David Russell, *Writing in the Academic Disciplines: A Curricular History* (Illinois, 2002), p. 23.
30 Ibid.
31 Ibid.
32 Ibid.
33 Sharma, 'Beyond the Boundaries', p. 992; Jung, 'The Ottoman–German Jihad'.
34 Sharma, 'Beyond the Boundaries', p. 993.
35 Jonathan Adams, Tamar Loach and Martin Szomszor, *Interdisciplinary Research: Methodologies for Identification and Assessment. Do We Know What We Are Measuring?* (London, 2016), p. 2.
36 Ibid.
37 Sierk Horn, 'Interdisciplinary Engagement as an Acculturation Process: The Case of Japanese Studies', *Social Science Japan Journal*, 16.2 (2013): 251–277; Fabian Schafer, 'The Re-articulation of Cultural Studies in Japan and Its Consequences for Japanese Studies', *International Journal of Cultural Studies*, 12.1 (2009): 23–41; Samah Selim, 'Nation and Translation in the Middle East', *The Translator*, 15.1 (2009): 1–13.
38 Paul Feyerabend, *Against Method* (London, 1993).
39 Arif Durlik, Asia Pacific Studies for the New Millennium, address presented to Conference on Remaking Asia Pacific Studies, University of Hawaii, 2–5 December 2002; Feyerabend, *Against Method*.
40 Ban Wang, 'The Cold War, Imperial Aesthetics, and Area Studies', *Social Text*, 10.3 (2002): 45–65.
41 Aida Hozic, 'Eastern European Studies: A Question and Some Ambivalence', *Eastern European Politics & Societies and Cultures*, 29.2 (2015): 433–439.
42 Sharma, 'Beyond the Boundaries', p. 989.
43 Ibid., p. 990.

44 Anthony Rausch, 'Creating Tsugaru Studies: The Paradox of Area Studies at the Local Level', *Journal of International and Area Studies*, 16.2 (2009): 35–51.
45 Anson Heryanto, 'The Intimacies of Cultural Studies and Area Studies: The Case of Southeast Asia', *International Journal of Cultural Studies*, 16 (2013): 309.
46 Hozic, 'Eastern European Studies', p. 437.
47 Loren Graham and Jean Michel Kantor, '"Soft" Area Studies Versus "Hard" Social Science: A False Opposition', *Slavic Studies*, 66.1 (2007): 1–19.
48 Kuan-hsing Chen, *Asia as Method* (Durham, 2010).
49 Rausch, 'Creating Tsugaru Studies'.
50 Graham and Kantor, '"Soft" Area Studies', p. 1.
51 Ibid.
52 Ibid.
53 Stephan Hanson, 'The Contribution of Area Studies', *Qualitative & Mixed Method Research*, 6.2 (2008): 35–43; Peter Katzenstein, 'Area Studies and Regional Studies in the United States', *Political Science and Politics*, 34.4 (2001): 789–791.
54 Ahram, 'Theory and Method', p. 70.
55 Matius Basedau and Patrick Köllner, 'Area Studies, Comparative Area Studies and the Study of Politics: Context, Substance, and Methodological Challenges', *Zeitschrift für Vergleichende Politikwissenschaft*, 1.1–20 (2007), cited in Ahram, 'Theory and Method', p. 70.
56 Ibid.
57 Ahram, 'Theory and Method', p. 82.
58 Heryanto, 'The Intimacies of Cultural Studies', p. 313.
59 Graham and Kantor, '"Soft" Area Studies', pp. 18–19.
60 Richard Clark, *Travelling Philosophy*, available at https://www.cavehill.uwi.edu/fhe/histphil/chips/archives/2006/docs/clarke.aspx (accessed 6 October 2016).
61 Ibid., p. 226.
62 Robert Whelan, 'Fifty Years On, CP Snow's "Two Cultures" Are United in Desperation', *Telegraph*, 4 October 2016, available at http://www.telegraph.co.uk/technology/5273453/Fifty-years-on-CP-Snows-Two-Cultures-are-united-in-desperation.html (accessed 4 October 2016).

63 Ibid.
64 Fred Inglis, Review of 'What are Universities for?' by Stefan Collini, *Times Higher Education* (2012), available at https://www.timeshighereducation.com/books/what-are-universities-for/418997.article (accessed 30 October 2016).
65 Jerome Kagan, *The Three Cultures: Natural Sciences, Social Sciences and the Humanities in the 21st Century* (Cambridge, 2009), p. 251.
66 Ibid., p. 266.
67 Ibid., p. 275.
68 Ibid.
69 Feyerabend, *Against Method*, p. 5.
70 Ibid., p. 11.
71 Ibid., p. 23.
72 Ibid., pp. 18–19.
73 Ibid., p. 208.
74 Hirsch quoted in Quentin Skinner, 'Motives, Intentions and the Interpretations of Texts', *New Literary History*, 3.2 (1972): 394.
75 Fred Inglis quoted in R. A. W. Rhodes, 'Thinking On: A Career in Public Administration', *Public Administration*, 89.1 (2011): 202.
76 Inglis, Review of 'What are Universities for?'
77 One fascinating account of research undertaken over a career raising many red flags of sources for current and future concern is available in Mark Duffield's account ('From Immersion to Simulation: Remote Methodologies and the Decline of Area Studies', *Review of African Political Economy*, 41:suppl. 1 (2014): 75–94).
78 Ibid., p. 90.
79 Amitav Acharya, 'Global International Relations (IR) and Regional Worlds: A New Agenda for International Studies', *International Studies Quarterly*, 58 (2014): 656.
80 Ibid., p. 657.
81 Graham and Kantor, '"Soft" Area Studies', p. 3.
82 Peter Jackson, 'Space, Theory and Hegemony: The Dual Crises of Asian Area Studies and Cultural Studies', *Sojourn*, 18.1 (2003): 1.
83 Ibid.
84 Peter Jackson, 'Mapping Poststructuralism's Borders: The Case for Poststructuralist Area Studies', *Sojourn*, 18.1 (2003): 42.

85 Anthony Giddens, *Globalization*, Reith Lecture One, BBC (1999), available at http://news.bbc.co.uk/hi/english/static/events/reith_99/week1/week1.htm (accessed 27 October 2016) and Manuel Castells, *The Power of Identity* (Chichester, 2010).
86 Gillian Hart, 'Denaturalizing Dispossession: Critical Ethnography in the Age of Resurgent Imperialism', *Antipode*, 38.5 (2006): 978–1004.
87 Arjun Appadurai, *Modernity at Large: Cultural Dimensions of Globalization* (Minneapolis, 1995).
88 James J. Clifford, 'Notes on Travel and Theory', *Return to Inscriptions*, 5 (2010): 1–7.
89 Michael Burawoy, 'Manufacturing the Global', *Ethnography*, 2 (2001): 147–159.
90 George Marcus, 'Contemporary Problems of Ethnography in the Modern World System', in J. Clifford and George Marcus (eds), *Writing Culture. The Poetics and Politics of Ethnography* (Berkeley, CA, 1986).
91 Kathrine Horschelmann and Alison Stenning, 'Ethnographies of Postsocialist Change', *Progress in Human Geography*, 32.3 (2008): 339–361.
92 Ibid., p. 355.
93 Mark Bevir, *The Logic of the History of Ideas* (Cambridge, 1999).
94 Jan Kubik, 'Between Contextualization and Comparison: A Thorny Relationship Between East European Studies and Disciplinary "Mainstreams"', *East European Politics & Societies and Cultures*, 29.2 (2015): 353.
95 Rebecca Kay and Jonathan Oldfield, 'Emotional Engagements with the Field: A View from Area Studies', *Europe Asia Studies*, 63.7 (2011): 1275.
96 Ibid., p. 1277.
97 Ibid., p. 1286.
98 Rafael, 'Regionalism, Area Studies', p. 1215.
99 Isabel Schierenbeck, 'Beyond the Local Turn Divide: Lessons Learnt, Relearnt and Unlearnt', *Third World Quarterly*, 36.5 (2015): 1023–1032.
100 Murat Somer, 'Theory-consuming or Theory-producing? Studying Turkey as a Theory-developing Critical Case', *Turkish Studies*, 15.4 (2014): 585.

101 Pierre Atlas, 'Constructing and Enforcing the "Medicine Line": A Comparative Analysis of Indian Policy on the North American Frontier', *American Review of Canadian Studies*, 46.3 (2016): 320–348.
102 Atlas examines historiography begun by Frederick Jackson Turner's 'Frontier Thesis', formulated in a paper 'The Significance of the Frontier in American History', delivered to the American Historical Association in 1893 in Chicago, which has shaped America for historians, popular culture and American politics. He combines this with ideas from the American political sociologist Seymour Martin Lipset, in work beginning in the 1960s, who posits that the differences between the United States and Canada were forged at the two countries' points of origin. Also, he includes the importance of modern Borderlands Studies on sameness, not difference between Canada and the USA.
103 Susan Hodgett and Marguerite Cassin, 'Feelingful Development; Redefining Policy Through Interpretation', *British Journal of Canadian Studies*, 25.2 (2012): 267–286, and Susan Hodgett and David Clark, 'Capabilities, Well-being and Multiculturalism: A New Framework for Guiding Policy', *International Journal of Canadian Studies*, 44.2 (2011): 163–184.
104 Blurring Genres Research Network is an AHRC initiative involving Susan Hodgett (Ulster University), R. A. W. Rhodes (Southampton University), Mark Bevir (University of East Anglia), Manchester University, SOAS and UK Civil Service Learning; see https://www.ulster.ac.uk/faculties/arts-humanities-and-social-sciences/schools/applied-social-policy-sciences/research/blurring-genres (accessed 1 July 2019).
105 Edward Said, *Orientalism* (London, 1978), p. 9.
106 Ibid.
107 Ibid., p. 10.
108 Ibid., p. 20.
109 Clifford Geertz, *Available Light* (Princeton, 2000), p. 16.
110 Ibid.
111 Mairead Nic Craith and Emma Hill, 'Re-locating the Ethnographic Field from "Being *There*" to "*Being* There"', *Anthropological Journal of European Cultures*, 24.1 (2015): 42–62.
112 Jung, 'The Ottoman–German Jihad', p. 248.
113 Ibid., p. 264.

114 Duffield, 'From Immersion to Simulation', p. 90.
115 Ibid.
116 Acharya, 'Global International Relations'.
117 Abrahamsen, 'Africa and International Relations', p. 1.
118 Ibid.
119 Oxford Dictionaries Word of the Year 2016 is '*post-truth* – an adjective defined as "relating to or denoting circumstances in which objective facts are less influential in shaping public opinion than appeals to emotion and personal belief"'; see https://en.oxforddictionaries.com/word-of-the-year/word-of-the-year-2016 (accessed 1 July 2019).

Bibliography

Abrahamsen, Rita, 'Africa and International Relations: Assembling Africa, Studying the World', *African Affairs*, Advance Access 8 December (2016), 1–15.

Acharya, Amitav, 'Global International Relations (IR) and Regional Worlds: A New Agenda for International Studies', *International Studies Quarterly*, 58 (2014): 647–659.

Adams, Jonathan, Tamar Loach and Martin Szomszor, *Interdisciplinary Research: Methodologies for Identification and Assessment. Do We Know What We Are Measuring?* (London, 2016).

Ahram, Ariel, 'The Theory and Method of Comparative Area Studies', *Qualitative Research*, 11.1 (2011): 69–90.

Appadurai, Arjun, *Modernity at Large: Cultural Dimensions of Globalization* (Minneapolis, 1995).

Atlas, Pierre, 'Constructing and Enforcing the "Medicine Line": A Comparative Analysis of Indian Policy on the North American Frontier', *American Review of Canadian Studies*, 46.3 (2016), 320–348.

Basedau, Mathius, and Patrick Köllner, 'Area Studies, Comparative Area Studies and the Study of Politics: Context, Substance, and Methodological Challenges', *Zeitschrift für Vergleichende Politikwissenschaft*, 1.1–20 (2007): 105–124.

Bevir, Mark, *The Logic of the History of Ideas* (Cambridge, 1999).

Burawoy, Michael, 'Manufacturing the Global', *Ethnography*, 2 (2001): 147–159.

Canning, John, 'Teaching on Less Commonly Taught Area Studies', *Centre for Languages, Linguistics and Area Studies*, 14 March 2003, available at https://www.llas.ac.uk/events/archive/588.html (accessed 21 May 2018).

Castells, Manuel, *The Power of Identity* (Chichester, 2010).

Chen, Kuan-hsing, *Asia as Method* (Durham, 2010).

Clark, Richard, *Travelling Philosophy*, available at https://www.cavehill.uwi.edu/fhe/histphil/chips/archives/2006/docs/clarke.aspx (accessed 6 October 2016).

Clifford, James, J., 'Notes on Travel and Theory', *Return to Inscriptions*, 5 (2010): 1–7.

Duffield, Mark, 'From Immersion to Simulation: Remote Methodologies and the Decline of Area Studies', *Review of African Political Economy*, 41:suppl. 1 (2014): 75–94.

Durlik, Arif, Asia Pacific Studies for the New Millennium, address presented to Conference on Remaking Asia Pacific Studies, University of Hawaii, 2–5 December 2002.

Feyerabend, Paul, *Against Method* (London, 1993).

Foucault, Michel, *Discipline and Punish: The Birth of the Prison* (New York, 1995).

Geertz, Clifford, *Available Light* (Princeton, 2000).

Gibson-Graham, Katherine, 'Area Studies after Post Structuralism', *Environment and Planning A*, 36 (2004): 405–419.

Giddens, Anthony, *Globalization*, Reith Lecture One, BBC (1999), available at http://news.bbc.co.uk/hi/english/static/events/reith_99/week1/week1.htm (accessed 27 October 2016).

Graham, Loren, and Jean Michel Kantor, '"Soft" Area Studies Versus "Hard" Social Science: A False Opposition', *Slavic Studies*, 66.1 (2007): 1–19.

Hanson, Stephan, 'The Contribution of Area Studies', *Qualitative & Mixed Method Research*, 6.2 (2008): 35–43.

Hart, Gillian, 'Denaturalizing Dispossession: Critical Ethnography in the Age of Resurgent Imperialism', *Antipode*, 38.5 (2006): 978–1004.

Heryanto, Anson, 'The Intimacies of Cultural Studies and Area Studies: The Case of Southeast Asia', *International Journal of Cultural Studies*, 16 (2013): 303–316.

Hodgett, Susan, and Marguerite Cassin, 'Feelingful Development; Redefining Policy Through Interpretation', *British Journal of Canadian Studies*, 25.2 (2012): 267–286.

Hodgett, Susan, and David Clark, 'Capabilities, Well-being and Multiculturalism: A New Framework for Guiding Policy', *International Journal of Canadian Studies*, 44.2 (2011): 163–184.

Horn, Sierk, 'Interdisciplinary Engagement as an Acculturation Process: The Case of Japanese Studies', *Social Science Japan Journal*, 16.2 (2013): 251–277.

Horschelmann, Kathrine, and Alison Stenning, 'Ethnographies of Postsocialist Change', *Progress in Human Geography*, 32.3 (2008): 339–361.

Hozic, Aida, 'Eastern European Studies: A Question and Some Ambivalence', *Eastern European Politics & Societies and Cultures*, 29.2 (2015): 433–439.

Inglis, Fred, Review of 'What are Universities for?' by Stefan Collini, *Times Higher Education* (2012), available at https://www.timeshighereducation.com/books/what-are-universities-for/418997.article (accessed 30 October 2016).

Jackson, Peter, 'Space, Theory and Hegemony: The Dual Crises of Asian Area Studies and Cultural Studies', *Sojourn*, 18.1 (2003): 1–41.

Jackson, Peter, 'Mapping Poststructuralism's Borders: The Case for Poststructuralist Area Studies', *Sojourn*, 18.1 (2003): 42–88.

Johnston, Ron, 'Sixty Years of Change in Human Geography', School of Geographical Sciences, University of Bristol, Paper prepared for the History of Postwar Social Science Seminars, London School of Economics, 25 April 2006.

Jung, Dietrich, 'The Ottoman–German Jihad: Lessons for the Contemporary Area Studies Controversy', *British Journal of Middle Eastern Studies*, 41.3 (2014): 247–265.

Kagan, Jerome, *The Three Cultures: Natural Sciences, Social Sciences and the Humanities in the 21st Century* (Cambridge, 2009).

Katzenstein, Peter, 'Area Studies and Regional Studies in the United States', *Political Science and Politics*, 34.4 (2001): 789–791.

Kay, Rebecca, and Jonathan Oldfield, 'Emotional Engagements with the Field: A View from Area Studies', *Europe Asia Studies*, 63.7 (2011): 1275–1293.

Kubik, Jan, 'Between Contextualization and Comparison: A Thorny Relationship Between East European Studies and Disciplinary "Mainstreams"', *East European Politics & Societies and Cultures*, 29.2 (2015): 352–365.

Lambert, Richard, 'Blurring the Disciplinary Boundaries: Area Studies in the United States', *American Behavioral Scientist*, 33.6 (1990): 712–732.

Marcus, George, 'Contemporary Problems of Ethnography in the Modern World System', in J. Clifford and George Marcus (eds), *Writing Culture. The Poetics and Politics of Ethnography* (Berkeley, CA, 1986).

Nic Craith, Mairead, and Emma Hill, 'Re-locating the Ethnographic Field from "being *there*" to "*being* there"', *Anthropological Journal of European Cultures*, 24.1 (2015): 42–62.

Ostrom, Elinor, 'A Behavioral Approach to the Rational Choice Theory of Collective Action: Presidential Address', *The American Political Science Review*, 92.1 (1998): 1–22.

Ostrom, Elinor, *Governing the Commons: The Evolution of Institutions for Collective Action* (New York, 1990).

Rafael, Vincente, 'Regionalism, Area Studies and the Accidents of Agency', *American Historical Review*, 104.4 (October 1999): 1208–1220.

Rausch, Anthony, 'Creating Tsugaru Studies: The Paradox of Area Studies at the Local Level', *Journal of International and Area Studies*, 16.2 (2009): 35–51.

Rhodes, R. A. W., 'Thinking On: A Career in Public Administration', *Public Administration*, 89.1 (2011): 196–212.

Russell, David, *Writing in the Academic Disciplines: A Curricular History* (Illinois, 2002).

Said, Edward, *Orientalism* (London, 1978).

Schafer, Fabian, 'The Re-articulation of Cultural Studies in Japan and Its Consequences for Japanese Studies', *International Journal of Cultural Studies*, 12.1 (2009): 23–41.

Schierenbeck, Isabell, 'Beyond the Local Turn Divide: Lessons Learnt, Relearnt and Unlearnt', *Third World Quarterly*, 36.5 (2015): 1023–1032.

Selim, Samah, 'Nation and Translation in the Middle East', *The Translator*, 15.1 (2009): 1–13.

Sharma, Miriam, 'Beyond the Boundaries of Asia Pacific Area Studies', *Futures*, 37 (2005): 989–1003.

Skinner, Quentin, 'Motives, Intentions and the Interpretations of Texts', *New Literary History*, 3.2 (1972): 393–408.

Somer, Murat, 'Theory-consuming or Theory-producing? Studying Turkey as a Theory-developing Critical Case', *Turkish Studies*, 15.4 (2014): 571–588.

Tessler, Mark, et al., 'Introduction: The Area Studies Controversy', in Mark Tessler, Jodi Nachtwey and Anne Banda (eds), *Area Studies and Social Science: Strategies for Understanding Middle East Politics* (Bloomington, IN, 1999).

Wang, Ban, 'The Cold War, Imperial Aesthetics, and Area Studies', *Social Text*, 10.3 (2002): 45–65.
Whelan, Robert, 'Fifty Years On, CP Snow's "Two Cultures" Are United in Desperation', *Telegraph*, 4 October 2016, available at http://www.telegraph.co.uk/technology/5273453/Fifty-years-on-CP-Snows-Two-Cultures-are-united-in-desperation.html (accessed 4 October 2016).
White, Gregory, et al., Book reviews, *The Journal of North African Studies*, 5.1 (2000): 165–179.

3

How to think about 'area' in Area Studies?

Jan Kubik

Contextual holism to the rescue

Building on my earlier essay where I argued that the best work on post-communism has shown at least some features of what I called *contextual holism*, I am beginning to develop here a novel approach to Area Studies. Most people reflecting on this topic concentrate their efforts on the word 'studies' and usually attempt to define the approach's specific methodology (for example, interdisciplinarity), reconstruct its intellectual genealogy and identify its political and ideological entanglements. My investigation is driven by unhappiness with what appear to be imprecise and unexamined uses of the term 'area'. If the area approach means the rejection of universalism and a postulate of studying problems in the context of relevant cultures and histories, based on the fluent knowledge of pertinent languages, it is not clear why this approach is called 'Area' Studies and not, say, 'cultural', 'local' or 'contextual' studies. In short, why call it 'area'?

Contextual holism, an approach I started defining several years ago while working on post-communist transformations in Eastern and Central Europe, is based on five principles or research directives: (1) constructivism, (2) relationism ('weak' structuralism), (3) historicism, (4) attention to scale and (5) focus on informality (formal–informal hybrids).

Constructivism postulates that the manner in which people conceptualize, model or envision the world around them matters for what they do (how they act). The ontology of constructivism is anti-naturalist (the social world is different from the natural world); thus, the methodology consistent with this position requires interpretation (for example, of the meaning people attach to the actions of others). Scholars who agree with an (anti-naturalist) assumption that the *signifying process* through which people build models of the world has political relevance proceed to study how such models are constructed, transmitted, maintained and received, and how this whole machinery of cultural construction influences, and is influenced by, political and economic processes. The so-called Thomas Theorem is the most succinct articulation of the basic premise of constructivism: 'If men define situations as real, they are real in their consequences.'[1] The concept of situation will be central in my examination of an area, in this case Central Europe, 'from the native point of view'. It is one of the key concepts of symbolic interactionism,[2] a branch of Sociology that traces its roots to Thomas's work. It was also used by the eminent Polish art historian, Mieczysław Porębski, one of my teachers. In an extremely insightful essay, 'Polishness as a Situation', he offered the following definition: 'The situation called Polishness is conditioned by the existence of a spiritual community – partially territorially coherent, partially dispersed in a diaspora – that coalesces around specific historically conditioned symbols. This spiritual community defines its continuance in terms of these symbols and derives from them the perpetuation of continuance and dignity.'[3] Porębski enumerates and briefly characterizes several symbols that help to establish and maintain Polishness: locations, books, images, sounds, tastes and colours. He also identifies the state of endangerment as a powerful and reoccurring factor influencing Polishness as a situation. In my analyses I will emphasize that there usually are several ways in which members of a given group define their situation. The situation, like almost every other element of culture, is a contested notion or image – as the 'natives' rarely, if ever, agree how to define it. This is certainly true when it comes to defining the situation through the lens of the concept of 'area'.

Relationism calls for an approach to the socio-political reality that tries to avoid the extremes of individualism and holism or, in a somewhat different formulation, agency and structure. Quite a few scholars have come to realize that this seemingly intractable duality cannot be sidestepped but must be unpacked and theorized – even if imperfectly – if we hope to improve our understanding of many important processes occurring in any region.[4] McFaul, for example, observes that, while 'actor-centric, cooperative approaches to democratization offer a useful starting point for explaining post communist regime transformations', they focus excessively on elites and their deals,[5] and downplay the role of popular mobilization that – as we know from the literature on social movements – must be analysed as a process in which agency and structural constraints influence each other. Relationism, as I see it, postulates therefore to study the interaction between structure and agency iteratively, and it emphasizes the significance of *networks*. Here, I am interested in networks an 'area' is constituted by and/or embedded in. It also postulates to pay careful attention to various *contexts*, as approaches excessively focused on agency (particularly more formalized ones) do not provide sufficient tools to account for the various contexts within which actors act.[6]

In an influential essay on democratic transitions, Schmitter and Karl argue that the significance of actors' agency varies, depending on the phase of the process. They see a heightened role of agency during the transition to a new system, but structural factors become more significant during consolidation. As they put it, during transition the role of 'courageous individuals' and contingency are dominant,[7] but a student of consolidation must shift attention to structural factors such as 'capitalist class conflicts, long-standing cultural and ethnic cleavages, persistent status conflicts and international antagonisms'. In brief, researchers must retool as they move from studying transition, which is underdetermined, to studying consolidation, which is overdetermined.[8] In the phase of transition (before the regime breakthrough), elite actors strategize and act in often highly unpredictable and rapidly changing situations. But during regime consolidation the role of elite's actions declines in relative importance. Now much depends on what non-elite actors do in the dramatically changed situations, how they respond to the new institutional environment 'engineered' by the elites in a top-down manner. In their actions, non-elite actors tend to be constrained by their socio-economic structural location and a reservoir of narratives drawn from their 'cultures of reference', which are often local. In such narratives elements of novelty are intertwined with the resurrected fragments of 'usable pasts' that often contain more or less stereotypical images of what 'our area' *really* is all about, what the historical legacies that shape its culture are, and how 'we', as that area's agents, are supposed to act.

In sum, relationism postulates to merge sensitivity to a historically established set of constraints, including dominant or rising in a given culture's narratives, with a contextualized study of agency (or the study of contextualized agency), particularly actors' efforts to build, protect or resist being included in various networks. Often, empirical lenses need to be focused on concrete, localized, national or area-bound communities of discourse where common definitions of the situation are formulated. The creation and maintenance of area networks is facilitated when such definitions include representations of the 'area' that actors then employ in their dealings with 'others', particularly those who are construed as being 'outsiders' to 'our' area.[9]

The third building block of contextual holism, *historicism* (or historicizing), is not uniform as there are at least *four separate ways to introduce history to the study of contemporary issues*. The first is to debate the relative causal significance of historical and contemporary factors in the explanation of today's phenomena. The second is related to establishing sufficiently deep causal chains in explaining studied processes.[10] The third revolves around the task of properly historicizing the studied phenomena and reconstructing the actors' cultural worlds from within they were acting, without imputing to them motivations and concerns that did not exist at the time of action. Fourth is to study the formation of legacies, whose cultural layer is not simply 'inherited' from the past, but is constructed by the actors acting in the present.[11]

The study of historical memory and its role in post-communist political battles is a good example of this type of historicizing approach. For example, there is an emerging body of work on Central Europe as a distinct memory area.

The fourth principle of contextual holism, *attention to scale*, alerts us to the fact that the manner in which a given political, economic or cultural process unfolds depends on its location in the whole system. The rhythms and mechanisms of change at the national level can be quite different from their counterparts occurring at the local, regional or area levels. State socialism was perhaps the most powerful standardizing and homogenizing machine in history, yet regional differences and local specificities did not disappear completely. Actually, some carefully monitored cultivation of subnational traditions was officially tolerated and not infrequently financed by the party-state. After the fall of state socialism, regionalism and localism exploded as cultural phenomena and the renaissance of subnational politics, often spurred by the devolution of power and decentralizing administrative reforms, commenced. These processes and their consequences need to be carefully studied, as the official, 'national' discourses on belonging or not to a specific area may be quite different from the discourses proposed by regional or local actors, who may, for example, see their region as a meaningful part of some area like Central Europe, while downplaying the strength of their region's embeddedness in a nation state. This illustrates well one of the key points of this chapter: an image of an area, such as Central Europe, appears in specific discourses propounded by concrete actors and influences their thoughts and actions to various degrees and with consequences that very much depend on specific cultural and political contexts within which such discourses are propagated.

According to the fifth and final premise of contextual holism, in each part of the world much action transpires at the interstices between official structures and informal networks. This means that in order to understand what is going on we need to investigate the context-specific *mix (hybrid) of formal and informal mechanisms*, as is convincingly argued by Guha-Khasnobis, Kanbur and Ostrom.[12] To illustrate the necessity of studying such mixes, it is enough to reflect for a moment on the nature of state socialism. It would not have survived as long as it did had it not been for extensive informal economic networks propped up by massive informal (unofficial) cultures. Such networks often developed into complex social worlds that made surviving communism possible. Informality provided a crutch that sustained the state socialist economy, but – paradoxically – it also contributed to the system's demise by nourishing anti-regime movements.[13] At least in the pioneering countries, such as Poland and Hungary, post-communism emerged not out of the *totalitarian* barren land of suppressed society, but rather from a beehive of activity in a *post-totalitarian* system, where people organized in semi-official and unofficial sectors of the economy, clandestine political spaces and/or private networks. Not surprisingly, the legacy of *informality* is extensive and deeply rooted in many areas of life. For some observers, this 'unwanted' and 'damaging' legacy of state socialism is a burden that slows down post-communist societies in their efforts of becoming 'normal';[14] but for others it is, rather, a blessing in disguise as it helps people navigate the uncertain post-communist reality. It seems to be both.

Two points regarding informality are central to my argument for the usefulness of contextual holism in understanding the significance of area, in this case Central Europe. First, it is important to see informality not as an unwelcome legacy of the communist system or an undesired by-product of the new capitalist/democratic system, but rather as an inescapable, albeit functional, component of the *transitory process*. Very often people need to resort to informal mechanisms to survive or advance in life, and that includes developing ways of imagining the social world around them that are often substantially different from the official views. The way people construe 'their' area, a unit bigger than the national state, is the case in point. For example, the authorities may be promoting an idea that the best strategic option for the country is to emphasize its belonging to 'Central Europe', while many/most of the people will rather see themselves as part of 'Europe'. Second, people's informal vision of the 'proper' area may be to a large degree a continuation of the way this area was imagined in informal discourses of the previous periods, in this case not only the communist times but also earlier eras. The point is to examine the legacies of informal, unofficial social imaginings, not just the official ones.

The spirit of contextual holism is to be found in many corners of today's social sciences. After several years of ascendancy, at least some adherents of methodological and theoretical universalism, of either the statistical or the game theoretical variety, are beginning to accept the necessity of a dialogue with the 'contextualists'. They seem to be realizing that, in order to have an impact on the world of policy-making, advice needs to be tailored to specific conditions that are shaped by (specific) history, embedded in (specific) social situations and framed by (specific) cultures, at least sometimes articulated and practised at the level of the area. Many area experts, who share at least some premises of contextual holism, are at the same time interested in making general contributions to global or at least inter-regional bodies of knowledge, for example by engaging in comparative projects with scholars studying other areas.[15] The task is not easy, as the logic of contextualizing pushes a researcher towards the detail, while the logic of comparison calls for at least some measure of abstraction, but it is exactly this tension that provides intellectual energy for the practitioners of Area Studies.

In Table 1 I provide a summary of the argument developed in the rest of the chapter. Following the methodological directives derived from contextual holism, I will examine various ways in which area can be conceptualized, imagined, visualized and employed in practice to direct people's actions. The analysis begins in the third column – Culture. Here I define various ways of imaging the area situation. In column four I am trying to identify the ideas and images that have powerful political consequences, as they influence the strategic thinking of influential political actors. The fifth column contains my attempts to find the concepts of the area that play roles in economic analyses. But before I proceed with my examination, the key concept of this chapter – the area as the situation – is introduced and briefly analysed.

Table 1 Principles of Contextual Holism and Central Europe as an Area

Principle	Principle as tool of 'capturing' the area situation	Culture/constructivism	Politics	Economy
Relationism	Defining the area situation via (the images of) internal and external networks	Existential in-betweenness: does Central Europe exist?	Strategic in-betweenness: between 'The West' and Russia Remedies: Intermarium Visegrád Four	Centre-semi-periphery-periphery dynamics Low-innovativeness, 'second-class' economies
Historicism	Legacies as tools of defining the area situation	'Auschwitz' versus 'Gulag' – legacies of two totalitarianisms	Legacies of totalitarian/post-totalitarian institutions	Legacies of command economy: Homo Sovieticus
Historicism	Critical junctures that impact the area situation	Memory wars over game-changing events (commemorating the fall of communism)	Imposition of the Soviet-style state socialism	'Shock therapy' (differential impact of neoliberalism)
Scale	Subnational perspectives on the area situation	Glocal identification (specific regional imaginings of the area)	Region-area nexus as a rival of nation state	Regions as economic actors collaborating with areas
Focus on formal/informal hybrids	Hybridity typical for the area situation	Cultures of informality	(Mild case of) nomenklatura capitalism	Corruption/informality

Throughout the chapter I employ a mix of what anthropologists call the 'emic' and 'etic' approaches. The former instructs the researcher to look at the world through the eyes of the people s/he studies, 'from the native's point of view' in Clifford Geertz's memorable phrase. The basic question is whether the cultural construct of an 'area' plays a role in cultural worlds from within which people think about and act in the world. The etic approach relies on the researcher's own concepts, in order to find the 'objective' determinants of emic concepts, images and discourses. Since every 'area' is a cultural construct that has a specific genealogy, structure and meaning, such an investigation is hard to conduct *in abstracto*; it must begin with studying the ways a specific area is imagined, often in competing discourses proposed by individuals, groups and organizations whose discursive work is influenced by the factors that remain outside of their control, for example the geo-political location. My example is the area variably referred to as 'Central Europe', 'Mitteleuropa' or 'Intermarium', and a handful of other terms. I will examine the way the area has been imagined and named by various actors, mostly in the period that followed the fall of communism in 1989. Since both spatial and temporal contexts matter in such an examination, my application of contextual holism includes some thoughts on post-communist transformations. I will not attempt to review the massive literature in several disciplines and languages; I will merely discuss several examples, mostly drawn from Polish sources, needed to illustrate my contention that contextual holism is a useful tool for a systematic and critical examination of *Area* Studies.

Area as the situation

In what sense is 'area' the situation? What are the factors determining or at least influencing the manner in which people define their situation as having something to do with an area, not just locality, a nation state or the 'globe'? In order to answer these questions I will use the tools of contextual holism. The directive of constructivism dictates that

I privilege the emic approach, so the investigation begins with the images and concepts constituting an area that vie for dominance in native culture(s). I will provide some examples of how both the 'natives' themselves and/or others construe the cultural parameters of the natives' collective existence in terms of an area, by attributing to it certain cultural traits and providing specific interpretations of economic and political realities that impact the functioning of the area.[16] Discourses actors propose are heavily influenced by historically established ways of thinking as well as institutional and material realities that encourage or discourage people to construe their situation in terms of an area. Moreover, actors not only discursively construct the world around them, but they also act in order to establish or maintain institutions. For the sake of brevity, I will group these historical, material, institutional and action-oriented factors into political and economic categories and examine them with the help of the four remaining epistemological directives of contextual holism. This method helps not only to organize the analysis, but also to detect some attributes of an 'area' – in this case Central Europe – that may not be otherwise noticed.

'Central Europe' serves well as a model for such an exercise, for there exists massive literature on this concept/image, its cultural attributes, its geographical referents and its potential as a discursive template for building networks. One strand in this literature touches upon a key issue of Area Studies: the inherently unstable nature of the very concept or image of the area. For example, much intellectual energy has been spent on trying to answer the question of whether Central Europe actually exists, and I suspect there have been similar discussions about other areas.[17] But this question is ill posed. An area is first of all a discursive construction that is developed and used intensely by some actors, moderately by others and totally neglected by yet another group. Some actors are 'natives'; some others are more or less influential 'outsiders'. There are periods when a given understanding of an area becomes salient in cultural and political debates, yet at other times its role is negligible or absent. Thus, in accordance with the Thomas Theorem, the task is not to determine 'objectively' if a given area exists, but to study what happens when some actors construe their situation in terms of a specific definition of 'their' area and compete, socially and politically, with other actors who may be using another concept or not using any conception of the area at all. Moreover, the terms of such debates change, as identities are fluid, because 'others' may be modifying their definitions of 'us', often with powerful social and political consequences.[18] As the Hungarian writer Péter Esterházy noted, after 1989 he was treated first as an 'East European', then a 'Central European', then a 'New European' and finally a 'Non-core European'.[19]

According to Polish historian Antoni Podraza,[20] the concept of Central Europe was first used systematically at the beginning of the twentieth century, though early references are to be found in the writings of Friedrich List, an influential historical economist who wrote foundational texts not only on economic nationalism, but also on the Central European economic area.[21] Discussed by historians, social scientists, essayists and writers, the concept indicates the existence of a culturally distinct entity endowed with specific traits to be found neither in the 'West' nor in the 'East'.[22] There are, of course, various, sometimes conflicting, conceptualizations and imaginings of Central Europe and its attributes, but one thing is certain: attempts to articulate this area's distinctiveness have never gone out of fashion.[23]

There is one conception of this area's identity, once influential, that did lose its lustre: Mitteleuropa. The centre of gravity of the whole area signified by this concept was the powerful culture of the German-speaking world. The conception has several versions, two being most important: predominantly imperialistic 'Prussian' and multi-cultural 'Habsburg'.[24] But the main gist of the idea seems to have always been imperial, certainly as propagated by the most influential proponents of this specific conceptualization of the area: Partsch and Naumann.[25] The rise of Nazism, the Second World War and the Holocaust totally destroyed the usability of this construction; the rise of the Iron Curtain made its revival impossible for a long while. After 1989 and the German reunification, a few authors began contemplating the idea's revival, but it does not seem to have caught up.[26]

To summarize, the concept of Central Europe has played an important role in historical debates for quite some time. It has also functioned as a meaningful tool for cultural and political entrepreneurs building *internal networks* and mobilizing publics for political and economic initiatives. This latter role has come to the fore of important debates in and about the region when the image/concept of Central Europe was turned into an instrument helping to establish and cultivate dissident networks.[27] This particular usage was brought to the attention of Western intellectual audiences in the mid-1980s, mostly thanks to two influential essays published in *The New York Review of Books* by Milan Kundera and Timothy Garton Ash.[28]

Relationism and networks

From a constructivist perspective, relationism postulates looking for various ways in which people imagine and then conduct their collective existence as *networked*, both internally and externally. An area is thus seen as a situation that facilitates building *internal* networks of cooperation, but also locks its inhabitants, at least potentially, in larger *external* networks of partnership, dominance or dependence. When a given area is seen as solidly articulated and central in a given network it is predisposed to be dominant; when it is construed as unstable and peripheral it often ends up being dependent. To analyse the situation of Central Europe in terms of *networks* I rely on three conceptual tools: existential in-betweenness, strategic in-betweenness and the centre-semi-periphery-periphery triad.

The kind of in-betweenness that for the lack of a better term I call existential has several versions, but all of them suggest an area caught between two other areas that are more powerful politically and more self-confidently articulated, 'the East' and 'the West', or Russia and Western Europe. The concept indicates that the collective existence of the area inhabitants is pervaded by the sense of indeterminacy and endangerment. Situated neither in the West nor in the East, the area is defined positively as having its own, unique cultural substance or negatively as not being a part of the other two areas. In-betweenness is related to the situation of cultural inchoateness that sometimes is seen as a source of creative and original insights into the mysteries of the human condition (Gombrowicz, Musil, Kafka, Broch, Hašek), but often is construed as debilitating weakness and a source of the inferiority complex. The more crisply articulated cultures, including Russian culture, are looked at with envy and fear, but also with contempt or hatred. Even the area's 'high' culture, once the source of its claim to continental dominance or at least parity with 'high' cultures of other areas, has proven to be an unreliable defence against the reoccurring existential doubt. Kundera, in arguably the most influential essay on this conundrum, first reminds us of the extraordinary eruption of cultural creativity in Central Europe at the beginning of the twentieth century, but then observes that by the mid-1980s the area ended up in a situation best described as a tragedy. Unexpectedly, he sees its main root not in the damage inflicted by the Soviet domination, but in the Western incomprehension of a place where 'true' cultural values, including the cultivation of literary excellence or philosophical debate – gradually forgotten in the West – were still so important that they even nourished anti-Soviet revolts.[29]

An area whose situation is defined, in both self-images and external categorizations, in terms of in-betweenness and proneness to existential trembling can be easily presented as a legitimate target of conquest in the discourses of political entrepreneurs representing more self-confident areas. When in-betweenness is not just a topic of cultural and literary musings, but enters the geo-political thinking of various foes of the area, the sense of endangerment becomes one of the key elements of the definition of the situation. For people who see themselves as Central Europeans this is a well-known condition. How can it be ameliorated? The place to begin is to capture the essence of geo-political imagining that construes this area as unstable or inconsequential. The in-betweenness of Central European situation is a part-and-parcel of geo-political thinking about Eurasia I call *symmetrical bilateralism*. Eurasia is conceptualized here as a space caught in the long-term, titanic conflict between two grand civilizations, Russian and 'Western'. In this view Central Europe does not have its own area identity; it is merely a battleground. Not intentionally, one wants to believe, its people are de facto treated as expendable pieces on the chessboard of a grand geo-political game. Moreover, the two sides of the struggle are seen as essentially very similar, each with its well-defined, equally legitimate and easily comparable interests. Central Europe disappears in this type of thinking; its in-betweenness becomes inconsequentiality. The discursive grip of symmetrical bilateralism on geo-political imaginary can be broken by developing its alter ego: *asymmetrical multilateralism*. Asymmetry means assuming that the Western and Russian cultural and political systems are sufficiently different from each other to invalidate a claim that the political decision-making processes are carried out in both systems according to similar rules of the game. Very few scholars in today's comparative politics doubt the existence of such asymmetry.[30] To begin with, the West has a complex, composite political system with the preponderance of democratic mechanisms, while Russia's system is increasingly authoritarian. The articulation of interests and identities, including those involved in the geo-political thinking about Central Europe (particularly if the Baltic states are included in this concept), is therefore quite different in both systems. Tolstrup carefully analyses this asymmetry and sees Russia as playing the role of a 'black knight' in democratization of the region.[31] He scrutinizes the situation in 'Near Abroad' of Russia, particularly in Belarus, Moldova and Ukraine, but, given Russia's recent actions to destabilize the situation in Central Europe, the term is applicable here as well.

While the existence of a basic symmetry between the West and Russia when it comes to defining geo-political interests can be debated, the postulate of multilateralism introduces a radically different political optics than the idea of bilateralism. From a multilateral perspective, interests and identities articulated in the area are seen as sovereign and legitimate, and therefore its representatives in international fora must be treated as partners equal to the 'East' and 'West'. But in order to be able to demand that the area is seen as a legitimate player in a multilateral view of the world, the area's elites need to articulate and realize a uniting vision of commonality of interests and identities that is strong enough to sustain a strategic network of area actors. Do such visions exist? In addition to the idea of Central Europe, cultivated predominantly in artistic and literary circles but also by the younger generation of scholars and practitioners of international relations,[32] there is a construct of 'Intermarium', associated with various efforts to signal a distinct geo-political stance and develop a viable strategy for defending area interests, without the German domination inevitably associated with Mitteleuropa as the organizing concept.[33]

Intermarium refers to the area between the Black and Baltic Seas. The actual shape of the area differs in various conceptualizations, but it always incorporates the lands usually designated as Central Europe (Poland, Czechia, Slovakia and Hungary). The concept, particularly popular among the authors representing the right side of the political spectrum, is based on a sharp distinction between the two 'others' of the Central European area.[34] As Chodakiewicz, the author of a massive treatise on Intermarium, writes: 'The most crucial task is to define "East" and "West." There are moral, ideological, cultural, geographical and geo-political definitions. For us "the West" consists of the sphere of freedom; "the East" denotes the opposite.'[35] Chodakiewicz notes the tension in the Intermarium's situation, caught between the indeterminacy of its in-betweenness and the status of the easternmost outpost of the Western civilization, but he considers it primarily as

> an eclectic and autonomous outpost of the West. Yet, neither completely of the West, nor of the East, the area retains the characteristics of both. At times, it serves as a Western rampart; at other times as a thoroughfare; and also as a launching pad for aggression both ways; but always as a meeting place for all and sundry. This is where the West and the East meet, interact, complement each other, and, occasionally, clash. This experience makes the Intermarium a sui generis phenomenon.[36]

Chodakiewicz's main goal is to instruct American policy-makers that the area defined as Intermarium is definitely not a part of any Russian geo-political conception, for example a portion of the Russian-dominated

Eurasia.³⁷ It is instead 'an area of coexistence, convergence, and clash of many cultures, [that] has historically been a staunch defender of Western Civilization despite long spells of alien domination'.³⁸ Its identity has been long in development, but it is essentially linked to Western Civilization, with which it shares 'the pluralistic heritage of Greek ethics, Roman law, and Christian religion stemming from Judaism'.³⁹ It is also an area built on the legacies of the multi-cultural and multi-ethnic Polish-Lithuanian Commonwealth that were particularly strongly present in the geo-political thinking of Józef Piłsudski, one of the architects of independent Poland after 1918 and the most dominant political figure on the country's inter-war political scene.

The Visegrád Group (Visegrád Four, or V4) is an alliance that was built around ideas similar to Intermarium, albeit on a smaller scale. Founded at a meeting in Visegrád on 15 February 1991, the alliance of the Czech Republic, Hungary, Poland and Slovakia has had a troubled history, particularly in the 2010s when the electoral victory of right-wing populists in Hungary and Poland started generating tension with the two other partners. Nonetheless, the Group's existence is clearly an expression of thinking among many people in these four countries that they can and do see their situation as defined by belonging to a specific area that they need to cultivate and defend.

In the approaches that emphasize economic rather than political or cultural trajectories of Europe (and the world), Eastern Europe is often construed as an area characterized by historically established backwardness. The issue is controversial and hotly debated,⁴⁰ but the image of backwardness has retained its powerful pull on many minds. Immanuel Wallerstein proposed the most influential analysis of its origins and consequences based on a simple tripartite model of centre, semi-periphery and periphery. The concept of semi-periphery is often applied to Central Europe, while, roughly speaking, Eastern Europe is seen as a periphery of the 'West'.

Building partially on the work of Polish historians, particularly Adam Małowist, Wallerstein offered a theory of the developmental dynamic whereby the rise of centres is accompanied by the emergence of semi-peripheries and peripheries in what he called the modern world-system. While looking at Europe, he theorized that in the process culminating in the sixteenth century, the developmental trajectory of Central Europe, encompassing in his work East Elbia, Poland, Bohemia, Silesia, Hungary and Lithuania,[41] veered off from the common European pattern, as the area experienced the 'manorial reaction' and eventually its main economic engine, agriculture, came to be dominated by a set of labour relations known as 'second serfdom'.[42] As this system took root, the divergence of the Eastern and Western parts of the continent intensified and, eventually, the West emerged as the system's economic (and political) centre, while the various sub-regions of the 'East' began sliding to the status of its semi- or full peripheries. The idea of the peripheral or semi-peripheral status of Central Europe, as well as its causes and consequences, has since been extensively debated in many works on the region. It is the subject of an influential volume edited by Daniel Chirot, where Peter Gunst, for example, carefully reconstructs the pattern of agricultural relations that sets Central Europe (in his work called East Central Europe) apart from both Western and Eastern Europe.[43]

Recently, several younger scholars in the area, perhaps most prominently Tomasz Zarycki, produced nuanced studies that rely extensively on the categories of centre, semi-periphery and periphery. Zarycki writes almost exclusively about Poland – one of the volumes he edited is simply titled *Poland as a Periphery* – but he clearly sees this country as representative of the broader Central European situation.[44] And going beyond Wallerstein, he examines not only economic but also political and cultural dimensions of (semi-)peripherality. What is particularly interesting in these studies are attempts to determine whether the area situation of the places like Poland or Central Europe is better captured as periphery or semi-periphery. Or, what kind of periphery a given area is. So, for example, Poland can be construed as an internal periphery vis-à-vis the Western centre, while Russia is an external periphery. For the actors in the area, such classificatory exercises have very serious political consequences. As Zarycki observes, in several areas of the world there are projects designed to solidify their images as semi-peripheries, as such a taxonomic location makes it easier to realize the ultimate goal of emerging as an alternative centre. He notes such a desire in the area, associated for example with the concept of Intermarium, although he sees it as less ambitious and crisp than a similar attempt organized by the BRICS countries. Partially, the reason for this limited success may be related to the fact that Intermarium seems to be attractive for only one side of the political spectrum. It is, in Zarycki's view, 'articulated with increasing frequency by conservative political forces, thus Eurosceptic, particularly clearly in Poland and Hungary'.[45]

Finally, Zarycki employs effectively Stein Rokkan and Derek Urwin's distinction between interface and external peripheries.[46] Interface peripheries are peripheral vis-à-vis two centres. It is thus an idea similar to my concept of in-betweenness and, as such, together with the concept of semi-periphery, it is a robust conceptual tool for analysing the area situation, certainly when applied to Central Europe. The concept of in-betweenness connotes a potentially creative ambiguity that may help produce exceptional works of art and literature and thus assert distinct identity. The concept of interface periphery signals a different potentiality: under certain circumstances such a situation may be economically beneficial as both centres compete to show that they are 'good' masters. It is the situation of the Benelux countries or Switzerland. But as I observed earlier, briefly reviewing Tolstrup's work, when the competing centres have different interests in the peripheral area the effects may be detrimental rather than beneficial. Such is the situation of Central Europe, where Russia, relatively weak economically, is seen by many people as projecting its political power via various destabilizing actions, while the West is usually seen as offering economic assistance (via the European Union) and strategic stability (via NATO).

Historicism

As noted earlier, I assume that there are four specific methodological directives associated with the principle of historicism. Each helps to illuminate a different dimension of the construction of an area image or concept. First, the consideration of the relative weight of 'historical' and 'contemporary' factors in the explanation of 'today's' salience and features of areas such as Central Europe may help to explain the depth of the concept's attractiveness. Second, there is a related issue of determining the length of causal chains in explaining the persistence of a specific image or concept of the area.[47] This is related to the study of legitimizing claims of having 'old' or even 'ancient' historical roots.[48] Third, it is helpful to properly historicize the studied phenomena and reconstruct the actors' cultural worlds, from within which a given image of the area has emerged. That helps to observe the evolution in the structure and meaning of the image or concept. Fourth, while studying the formation of legacies, it is worthwhile to begin with a distinction between material, institutional and cultural legacies, and emphasize that the last are not simply inherited from the past, but constructed by the actors acting in the present.

It seems that 'Central Europe' belongs to those concepts that are constantly reinvented by various individual and collective actors, ranging from literary scholars to experts on foreign relations and politicians. Its contemporary elaborations are multiple; it is an image or concept that is very much 'alive'. It does not have a long history, as its first appearance is dated to the mid-nineteenth century, but the process of formation of specific economic, political and cultural features, usually attributed to the area, has been much longer.

The manner in which a discursive construct, for example a specific concept or vision of an area, is articulated and implemented, and how effectively it mobilizes people, is partially determined by the understandings of the world characteristic of a historical period in which it is all happening. In the introductory part of the chapter I summarized Schmitter and Karl's argument that, during the regime consolidation phase, the elites that initiated the process may have less control than during transition. A few years ago experts started arguing that the Central European liberal-democratic elites, often having dissident pedigree, presided over political consolidation that brought those countries into the ranks of 'regular' democracies. Given the recent rise of right-wing populist governments, particularly in Hungary and Poland, this argument has been challenged. Among the causes of what is seen by most observers as a serious turbulence in democratic consolidation, if not backsliding, is the idea that previous, predominantly liberal, elites botched the earlier stages of consolidation. As a result, the tenuous elite consensus of the early years of consolidation is gone, the elite is intensely fragmented, and there is a mobilization of new civil society actors who challenge many conceptualizations previously taken for granted in the dominant liberal political culture. The meaning of 'Central Europe' is hotly contested again, as new and often non-elite actors propose its reconceptualization. Under communism and during the early years of transition and consolidation, the concept served to separate the area from the 'East' and create a cultural bridge to the 'West'. In the 2010s, in some new discourses – usually coming from the right – it has been used to separate the area from the 'West', assert its political sovereignty and underscore its cultural superiority as a carrier of 'unspoiled' European values. As I pointed out earlier, Chodakiewicz envisions a similar role for 'Intermarium', a concept that suggests a way of looking at the area that is both culturally distinct and politically sovereign.[49] There are also proposals for reconceptualizing or reimaging Intermarium by explicitly contrasting it with the political imaginary suggested by the concept of Central Europe.[50]

According to the *Merriam-Webster Dictionary*, a legacy is 'something transmitted by or received from an ancestor or predecessor or from the past'. As I argued in my earlier work, in order to grasp the essence of cultural legacies we need to focus not on 'received from' but rather, on 'transmitted'. Whereas material legacies – and, to a large extent, institutional legacies as well – exist independently of the will and designs of most actors, cultural legacies must be transmitted, and cultural scenarios embedded in them must be enacted by at least some of them. In short, cultural legacies are 'real' only insomuch as they inform (cause) actors' behaviour.

Material legacies have been often used to mark the boundaries of Central Europe. Many authors point out the existence of a specific architectural style, for example of the train stations, and the particular ambiance of urban spaces.[51] While material legacies have a layer – their materiality – that exists independently of the interpretive work of cultural entrepreneurs, cultural legacies are fully constructed. Their constructed or invented nature is apparent when we think about the emergence or invention of a historical memory (a form of cultural legacy) that had been earlier poorly articulated or non-existent.[52] One such legacy, quite central to the articulation of the specific Central European experience of the Second World War, is the construction that compares or even equates the suffering inflicted by the Nazis with that caused by the Soviets. Many intellectuals and politicians from the area argue that only this part of Europe suffered from both totalitarianisms and this fact needs to be properly reflected in the emerging, common historical memory of the whole continent. While this idea is often rejected in the West, it is rather uncontroversial in Central Europe and the Baltic countries. Droit, for example, discusses the complexities of formulating common European memory under the heading of 'the Holocaust and the Gulag in opposition'.[53]

Scholars engaged in an intense debate on the nature and consequences of the totalitarian system's legacies grapple also with the question of to what degree these legacies set apart the post-communist area from other areas of the world. And some writers make distinctions between the subtypes of post-communist legacies and see the Central European experience as sufficiently different from, say, the experience of the Soviet Union or Yugoslavia.[54] That sense of an atleast partially different way in which communism was practised in Central Europe is invoked to define the specificity of Central Europe, both by natives and by external observers.

Finally, there is the concept of Homo Sovieticus (HS), a model of the human being ostensibly common to the whole post-communist area, and thus attributed also to Central Europe. This is a vision of the human being unable to function in democracy and a market economy due to the ill-formed habits developed under communism. The study of HS brings to the front the problem of regions (sub-areas), as the experience of communism was not uniform and people's coping strategies varied, depending on the opportunities created by a specific version of state socialism. I have not conducted a study designed to detect a Central European sub-type of HS, but strongly suspect that such a generalized cultural syndrome might have never existed. In my own study of two regions of Poland I demonstrated that the general Polish pattern of HS is largely a fiction, as the differences in the situations of various subnational regions were often quite pronounced. I suspect that the variety of coping strategies with the deficiencies of state socialism, embedded in and encouraged by specific regional cultures, was so extensive that looking for a Central European model of Homo Sovieticus is futile.[55]

For historicism an area is constructed not only as a legacy of processes or series of events, but also of critical junctures or singular tipping points. These concepts seem to be particularly effective in the study of area as the situation. Do 'the natives' of an area share historical memories of specific events? What are the candidates for such events in the area of Central Europe? The Soviet takeover? The fall of communism? In a study Michael Bernhard and I designed and carried out with a group of colleagues, we investigated the manner in which the fall of communism was commemorated on the twentieth anniversary of the event.[56] The Central European states of Slovakia, the Czech Republic, Poland and Hungary were the cases in the study. No common Central European pattern emerged. Actually, one of the surprising conclusions of our work was the existence of several patterns. Poland and Hungary, two countries that extricated themselves from communism via negotiations and in many ways had been initially the 'leaders' of post-communist transformations, ended up with what we called fractured memory regimes when it came to the collective remembering of the fall of communism. Slovakia also had a fractured memory regime, but here the main source of fracturing was ethnicization of politics. In the Czech Republic we identified the only pillarized memory regime in the whole studied group. Its main feature is relative tolerance for the coexistence of different memory regimes.

The legacy of the Soviet conquest at the end of the Second World War, understood as a tipping point, is quite central for shaping the political imaginary of Central Europe, particularly Poland, the area's largest country. By contrast to other parts of Europe conquered by the Soviets, in this part of the continent the intensity of armed resistance to the Soviet takeover was relatively high and its memory constitutes one of the cornerstones of the area's specificity.

When it comes to the post-1989 economic trajectory, the introduction of the neoliberal economic reforms constitutes a truly momentous tipping point. While not all countries emerging from state socialism opted for their most radical version, dubbed 'shock therapy', the Central European quartet did. As a result, the (economic) situation of Central Europe has been characterized in terms that set this area apart from other post-communist areas. For example, in an influential study Bohle and Greskovits classify the economic system in the Visegrád countries (as noted above, one popular conceptualization of the area under study) as embedded neoliberalism. Its dominant feature is 'a permanent search for compromises *between* market transformations and social cohesion in more inclusive but not always efficient systems of democratic government'.[57]

Scale

Does a given concept of the area, cultivated in elite discourses, penetrate other layers of culture? Do, for example, regional cultures articulate with the dominant area concept, such as 'Central Europe'? In my own fieldwork in Cieszyn Silesia, a region whose culture is strongly influenced by Protestantism, I never heard people relating their regional situation to the area situation defined in terms of Central Europe, although they were often quite articulate and knowledgeable about the broader historical and geo-political context impacting their region. The broader concept that I heard several times was 'the Habsburg legacy', best exemplified by a man who once told me: 'From here it is closer to Vienna than Warsaw.' There is a literature on the phenomenon that can be best described as 'unevenness' of the state. Borderlands often have ambiguous identities and their inhabitants may not be as attached to nation states as their co-nationals living in more central regions of the country. It is there where people tend to construe their situations as complex, multivalent and sometimes related to a transnational conception of an area, rather than a nation state. Such non-national imagining of collective identity often becomes an object of political battles, as the adherents of such identities draw the ire of nationalist politicians and intellectuals for whom the national identity trumps all other attachments. Border areas are also places where people think about their 'economic location' as a part of networks that do not need to be national, but transnationally defined, sometimes with the help of an area concept.

Informal/formal hybrids

'The literature on informality is grounded in geographical, socio-cultural and political-economic areas', writes Ledeneva, and the massive *Global Encyclopaedia of Informality* she just published with a team of collaborators concludes that, even if patterns of informality cluster spatially, they do so in a manner that does not necessarily correspond to the map of nation states.[58] Nor does it seem to correspond neatly to the division of the world into areas such as, for example, Central, Western or Eastern Europe. While there is an extensive literature on the exceptional role informal practices, usually referred to as 'corruption', played under state socialism and have continued to play after 1989 in post-communist societies, it does not make a distinction between, say Central and Eastern Europe. Several authors have written about the cultures of corruption, but they also do not see a specific Central European pattern of informality.[59] The literature on nomenklatura capitalism and oligarchy does suggest, however, that in Central Europe, presumably due to some of its historically shaped cultural features and the nature of the transitory process, in which the counter-elites hailing from dissident movements managed to contribute to the establishment of a relatively well-functioning system of checks and balances, these phenomena are not as detrimental as in Eastern Europe, particularly Russia.[60]

Conclusions

Using the directives of contextual holism (constructivism, relationism, historicism, attention to scale and focus on formal–informal hybrids) I proposed a novel way of looking at Area Studies. Instead of organizing my analysis around the theoretical and methodological issues prompted by the word 'studies', my departure point was 'area'. I reconstructed several conceptions various actors, both 'natives' and outsiders, have used to define a part of the European continent in terms of the concept/image of Central Europe and several related concepts. To what degree my results are applicable to other areas needs to be determined. Only careful studies of the natives' own imaginings of their situations in terms of an 'area' can provide an answer. But the lessons of this study should be helpful in examining the grip other area concepts/images have on the social and political imagination of people living in other parts of the world.

Let me summarize the directives that can be applied in the studies of other areas. The directive of relationism calls for reconstructing the role the 'area' or 'area situation' plays as a guiding image or concept in actors' efforts to construct networks of cooperation or to respond to being 'networked' by other, often more powerful, external actors. First, the situation of an area should be analysed in terms of its existential and geo-political status in a broader system of areas (in between, peripheral or central) and its consequences. Second, the economic dimension of the area situation can be fruitfully analysed with the help of the

Wallersteinian centre-semi-periphery-periphery triad, the centrepiece of his world system (global) theory. Consistently with the philosophy of constructivism, the primary task is to identify the communities of discourse that produce such diagnoses, determine their relative power in domestic and international political fields and, finally, try to assess the social, political, cultural and economic implications of formulating and disseminating specific concepts and images of a given area situation.

The postulate of historicism directs the researcher's attention to the impact the legacies of both processes and critical junctures may have on people's proclivity to construe their situation in terms of an area. Among the questions that may be usefully asked are: what are specific material, institutional and cultural legacies through which people cultivate their self-definitions in terms of an area situation? What are the events that are central in collective memory that sustain the image of collective existence as in some important sense related to the area situation?

While considering the significance of scale, one is prompted to examine imaginings and/or concepts of the area that emerge in sub-national, regional cultures. The definition of the situation of a given nation state in terms of an area that is proposed, say, by the central government may not be shared by the elites of various regions whose cultures may have distinct trajectories that are not easily reducible to the overarching 'national' narrative typically propounded by the central government. A question one may want to ask is: what tensions do exist between the imaginings of the area by central and local elites of a given nation state?

Finally, there is a set of issues that arise if the researcher does not only study official, formal forms of cultural production, but also looks for informal (sub)cultures and specific patterns in which the two mesh in formal–informal hybrids. The distinction is particularly important in non-democratic situations, where official visions of the governments may be quite distinct from the visions circulating at various levels of informal cultural production in the society. The questions that come to the fore here include: what are the area-specific combinations of formal and informal imaginings of the area? How are they constructed in influential discourses of self-identity?

There are three main lessons from my exercise. First and most important is that 'areas' and 'Area Studies' have certainly not been invented exclusively by Western scholars and policy-makers, who – we are often told – created this approach *ab nihilo* to build a detailed knowledge of the world and who, at least in some cases, have been driven by instrumental considerations of the Cold War. Quite the contrary; 'Central Europe', 'Mitteleuropa', 'Intermarium' and other related concepts or images have turned out to be powerful discursive building blocks of the 'native' social and political imaginary in this part of Europe. The second main lesson is that, in order to define and practise Area Studies, while taking the concept/image of 'area' seriously, the researcher must develop deep, multi- and often interdisciplinary knowledge of the relevant part of the world, built on the understandings of the 'natives' and their conceptualizations of their situation. Third, in order to reconstruct the manner in which the concept is employed, it is advisable to examine the widest possible range of situations, to determine when and how the concept or image of area is employed. I suggest that the tools derived from the approach I called contextual holism can be very useful to systematize such an investigation.

Notes

1. William I. Thomas and Dorothy Swaine Thomas, *The Child in America: Behavior Problems and Programs* (New York, 1928), p. 572. For a thorough discussion of the Theorem's origins and proper attribution, see Robert Merton, 'The Thomas Theorem and "The Matthew Effect"', *Social Forces*, 74.2 (1995): 379–424.
2. Robert E. Park and Ernest Burgess, in a treatise regarded as the foundational work of symbolic interactionism, write: 'common participation in common activities implies a common "definition of the situation". In fact, every single act, and eventually all moral life, is dependent upon the definition of the situation. A definition of the situation precedes and limits any possible action, and a redefinition of

the situation changes the character of the action.' *Introduction to the Science of Sociology* (Chicago, 1921), p. 764.
3   Mieczysław Porębski, 'Polskość jako sytuacja', *Znak*, 11–12 (1987): 390–391.
4   This task is, of course, at the centre of many major theoretical works. The most influential is, arguably, Anthony Giddens' theory of structuration. Efforts to overcome the structure–agency dichotomy are also vigorous in various versions of new institutionalism. See James Mahoney and Kathleen Thelen (eds), *Explaining Institutional Change: Ambiguity, Agency, and Power* (Cambridge, 2009).
5   Michael McFaul, 'The Missing Variable: The "International System" as the Link Between Third and Fourth Wave Models of Democratization', in Valerie Bunce, Michael McFaul and Kathleen Stoner-Weiss (eds), *Democracy and Authoritarianism in the Postcommunist World* (Cambridge, 2010), p. 9.
6   'It is the doctrine that transactions, interactions, social ties, and conversations constitute the central stuff of social life.' See Charles Tilly and Robert E. Goodin, 'It Depends', in R. E. Goodin and C. Tilly (eds), *The Oxford Handbook of Contextual Political Analysis* (Oxford, 2006), p. 11. This chapter provides a useful explication of the 'relational' ontological position and contrasts it to other ontologies of the social. See also F. Bönker, K. Müller and A. Pickel, 'Cross-disciplinary Approaches to Postcommunist Transformation: Context and Agenda', in F. Bönker, K. Müller and A. Pickel (eds), *Postcommunist Transformation and the Social Sciences* (Lanham, 2002), p. 24.
7   Schmitter and Karl, 'The Conceptual Travels', pp. 175–176.
8   Ibid., p. 176.
9   Additionally, the concept of agency needs to be carefully reconsidered because people's ability to affect the world varies and depends on the whole set of factors. As Mahmood argues, 'if the ability to effect change in the world and in oneself is historically and culturally specific (both in terms of what constitutes "change" and the means by which it is effected), then the meaning and sense of agency cannot be fixed in advance, but must emerge through an analysis of the particular concepts that enable specific modes of being, responsibility, and effectivity'. Saba Mahmood, *Politics of Piety. The Islamic Revival and the Feminist Subject* (Princeton, 2005), pp. 14–15.

10 Grzegorz Ekiert and Stephen E. Hanson (eds), *Capitalism and Democracy in Central and Eastern Europe. Assessing the Legacy of Communist Rule* (Cambridge, 2003).
11 I wrote on the construction of legacies in Jan Kubik, 'Cultural Legacies of State Socialism: History-making and Cultural-political Entrepreneurship in Postcommunist Poland and Russia', in Ekiert and Hanson (eds), *Capitalism and Democracy*, pp. 317–351.
12 Basudeb Guha-Khasnobis, Ravi Kanbur and Elinor Ostrom, *Linking the Formal and Informal Economy. Concepts and Policies* (Oxford, 2006).
13 Natalia Letki and Geoffrey Evans, 'Endogenizing Social Trust: Democratization in East-Central Europe', *British Journal of Political Science*, 35 (2004): 518.
14 William L. Miller, Åse B. Grødeland and Tatyana Y. Koshechkina, *A Culture of Corruption. Coping with Government in Post-communist Europe* (Budapest, 2001).
15 For a nuanced analysis of how such contributions are made and what ethical and political issues are involved, see Michael Kennedy, *Globalizing Knowledge. Intellectuals, Universities, and Publics in Transformation* (Stanford, 2014).
16 Identities are always constructed via a complex interplay of 'self-identification and the identification and categorization of oneself by others'. Rogers Brubaker and Frederic Cooper, 'Beyond Identity', *Theory & Society*, 29.1 (2000): 15.
17 See, for example, Jeremy Eades, 'The Development of Asia Pacific Studies: A Case Study of Internationalization in Japanese Higher Education', in T. Wesley-Smith and J. Goss (eds), *Remaking Area Studies. Teaching and Learning Across Asia and the Pacific* (Honolulu, 2010).
18 Western academics often treat 'areas' as concepts exclusively or predominantly created and used in the discourses of Western academic and policy-making establishments. The role of 'native' constructions is ignored or marginalized. See, for example, Ian Klinke, 'Area Studies, Geography and the Study of Europe's East', *The Geographical Journal*, 181.4 (2015): 423–426.
19 Péter Esterházy, 'How Big Is the European Dwarf?', in D. Levy, M. Pensky and J. Torpey (eds), *Old Europe, New Europe, Core Europe. Transatlantic Relations After the Iraq War* (London, 2005), s. 74.
20 See Antoni Podraza, 'Europa Środkowa jako region historyczny', 2004, available at http://jazon.hist.uj.edu.pl/zjazd/materialy/podraza.

pdf (accessed 5 February 2018). Podraza relies here on Jacques Droz's *L'Europe Centrale. Evolution historique de l'idee de Mitteleuropa* (Paris, 1960). For an English version of this essay, see Antoni Podraza, 'Central Europe as a Historical Region' in Jerzy Kłoczowski (ed.), *Central Europe Between East and West* (Lublin, 2005).

21 On List, see Roman Szporluk, *Communism and Nationalism. Karl Marx Versus Friedrich List* (Oxford, 1988). Buchowski and Kołbon also emphasize the significance of Liszt's ideas and date the beginning of their influence to 1841. See Michał Buchowski and Izabela Kołbon, 'Od "Mitteleuropy" do Europy Środkowej. Zarys dziejówidei', *Sprawy Narodowościowe. Seria nowa*, 19 (2001): 15.

22 I am sidestepping a discussion among historians on whether the concept of 'East Central Europe' is more adequate. It tends to be privileged by Polish historians, while their Hungarian and Czech colleagues tend to stick to 'Central Europe'. Among the historians writing in English, Joseph Rothschild's magisterial work is entitled *East Central Europe Between the World Wars* (Seattle and London, 1974). Johnson, by contrast, writes about Central Europe. See Lonnie R. Johnson, *Central Europe: Enemies, Neighbors, Friends* (Oxford, 1996).

23 Marta Cobel-Tokarska and Marcin Dębicki, *Słowo i terytorium. Eseje o Europie Środkowej* (Warszawa, 2017).

24 'The notion of *Mitteleuropa* carries diverse connotations, many far from positive. It should be noted that the *Mitteleuropa* fondly recalled by Habsburg-era nostalgics stands in clear oppositions to the Prussian understanding of *Mitteleuropa*. The Habsburg multi-national vision is a negation of the Prussian state-centric ideal first promoted by Friedrich Naumann and others, and later adopted by Nazi geopoliticians.' Luiza Bialasiewicz, 'Back to *Galicia Felix*?', in C. Hann and P. R. Magocsi (eds), *Galicia. A Multicultured Land* (Toronto, 2005), p. 178.

25 Josef F. M. Partsch, *Mitteleuropa. Die Länder und Völker von den Westalpen und dem Balkan bis an den Kanal und das Kurische Haff* (Gotha, 1904); Friedrich Naumann, *Mitteleuropa* (Berlin, 1916).

26 Anna Sosnowska offers an interesting set of comments on 'Mitteleuropa Versus Central Europe'. Available at https://www.aspenreview.com/article/2017/mitteleuropa-versus-central-europe/ (accessed 3 January 2018).

27 See Weronika Parfianowicz-Vertun, *Europa Środkowa w tekstach i działaniach. Polskie i czeskie dyskusje* (Warszawa, 2016). Bialasiewicz observes: 'During the Cold War, the geographical imagination of Mitteleuropa enabled Polish, Czech, and Hungarian dissidents and literary dreamers to leap outside of the closed spaces of the bi-polar divide and place themselves in the West.' Bialasiewicz, 'Back to *Galicia Felix?*', p. 163.

28 Milan Kundera, 'The Tragedy of Central Europe', *The New York Review of Books*, 26 April 1984, and Timothy Garton Ash, 'Does Central Europe Exist?', *The New York Review of Books*, 9 October 1986. Todorova emphasizes the role of the area authors, Jenő Szűcs, Czesław Miłosz and Milan Kundera. See Maria Todorova, *Imagining the Balkans* (New York, 1997), p. 141.

29 Kundera, 'The Tragedy of Central Europe'.

30 See, for example, Henry Hale, *Patronal Politics. Eurasian Regime Dynamics in Comparative Perspective* (New York, 2015).

31 'Russia's goals in the region seem to be incompatible with those of the West, and this means that the possible positive influence that, for example, the EU, NATO, or the US, can exert in the area is actively counterbalanced and maybe even "crowded out" by the negative influence of Russia.' Jakob Tolstrup, 'Studying a Negative External Actor: Russia's Management of Stability and Instability in the "Near Abroad"', *Democratization*, 16.5 (2009): 940. See also Jacob Tolstrup, *Russia vs the EU: The Competition for Influence in Post-Soviet States* (Boulder, CO, 2013).

32 Zlatko Šabic and Petr Drulak (eds), *Regional and International Relations of Central Europe* (Basingstoke, 2012).

33 Buchowski and Kołbon, 'Od "Mitteleuropy"', p. 21.

34 It was an organizing concept for several groups of dissidents in the 1980s in Poland. See, for example, Buchowski and Kołbon, 'Od "Mitteleuropy"', p. 22.

35 Marek Jan Chodakiewicz, *Intermarium: The Land Between the Black and Baltic Seas* (New Brunswick, NJ, 2012). A thorough, critical review of this book was written by David Katz and published in *Israel Journal of Foreign Affairs*, 7.2 (2013). Accessed at http://defendinghistory.com/wp-content/uploads/2013/03/Dovid-Katz-review-of-Intermarium-in-Israel-Journal-of-Foreign-Affairs-7-2-2013.pdf (accessed 27 June 2019). In the Polish

language, it received a book-length treatment from another prominent figure of the right, Leszek Moczulski.
36 Chodakiewicz, *Intermarium*, p. 16.
37 https://geopoliticalfutures.com/intermarium-three-seas/ (accessed 27 June 2019).
38 Chodakiewicz, *Intermarium*, p. 16.
39 Ibid., p. 19.
40 Anna Sosnowska, *Zrozumieć zacofanie. Spory historyków o Europę Wschodnią (1947–1994)* (Warsaw, 2004). See also 'Why Is Eastern Europe Backward', *Aspen Review*, 4 (2013), available at https://www.aspenreview.com/article/2017/why-is-eastern-europe-backward/ (accessed 3 February 2018).
41 Immanuel Wallerstein, *The Modern World-system. Capitalist Agriculture and the Origins of the European World-economy in the Sixteenth Century* (New York, 1974), p. 94.
42 Wallerstein, *The Modern World-system*, p. 95.
43 Peter Gunst, 'Agrarian Systems of Central and Eastern Europe', in D. Chirot (ed.), *The Origin of Backwardness in Eastern Europe* (Berkeley, 1989).
44 See, in particular, Tomasz Zarycki, 'Polska jako peryferie stykowe', in T. Zarycki (ed.), *Polska jako peryferie* (Warszawa, 2016).
45 Ibid., p. 106.
46 Stein E. Rokkan and Derek W. Urwin, *Economy, Territory, Identity: Politics of West European Peripheries* (London, 1983).
47 Grzegorz Ekiert and Stephen E. Hanson (eds), *Capitalism and Democracy in Central and Eastern Europe. Assessing the Legacy of Communist Rule* (Cambridge, 2003).
48 Arjun Appadurai, 'Past as a Scarce Resource', *Man*, New Series 16.2 (June 2001): 201–219.
49 Such ideas have broader circulation, also outside the area. Friedman, for example, writes: 'The governments in Poland and Hungary are anathema to the multilateral, collectivistic framework of the EU, and Brussels has criticized them accordingly. But neither Warsaw nor Budapest has given in to EU demands. The Intermarium therefore is more than a military alliance.' See George Friedman, 'Reality Check. From the Intermarium to the Three Seas', 7 July 2017, available at

https://geopoliticalfutures.com/intermarium-three-seas/ (accessed 3 January 2018). Anna Sosnowska offers an interesting set of comments on 'Mitteleuropa Versus Central Europe', available at https://www.aspenreview.com/article/2017/mitteleuropa-versus-central-europe/(accessed 3 January 2018).

50 See, for example, Sosnowska on 'Mitteleuropa Versus Central Europe'.
51 'Much of Central Europe possesses a similar cultural landscape and may be regarded as one cultural area. Common cultural links are visible if one looks at the architecture of cities which were once part of the Austro-Hungarian Empire. Whether it is Brno in Moravia, Bratislava, Vienna, Budapest, Kraków, Lviv, Ljubljana, or peripheral Chernivtsi in Ukraine, one may find the same type of theatre architecture, similar city halls and railway stations from about 1900.' See Monika Murzyn, 'Heritage Transformation in Central and Eastern Europe', in P. Howard and B. Graham (eds), *The Ashgate Research Companion to Heritage and Identity* (Aldershot, 2008), p. 317.
52 The phenomena covered by the concept of cultural legacies share many features with the concept of historical memory.
53 Emmanuel Droit, 'The Gulag and the Holocaust in Opposition: Official Memories and Memory Cultures in an Enlarged Europe', *Vingtième Siècle. Revue d'histoire*, 2.94 (2007): 101–120. See also Marek Kucia, 'The Europeanization of Holocaust Memory and Eastern Europe', *East European Politics and Societies*, 20.1 (2016): 97–119.
54 'the prospects for democratization and democratic deepening were significantly better in countries with favorable legacies (such as the relatively developed, ethnically homogenous countries of East Central Europe with their longer histories of statehood, democracy, and bureaucratic competence) than in many of the fledgling new states emerging from the former Soviet Union and Yugoslavia'. See Grigore Pop-Eleches, 'Historical Legacies and Post-Communist Regime Change', *The Journal of Politics*, 69.4 (2007): 909.
55 Myron Aronoff and Jan Kubik, *Anthropology and Political Science: A Convergent Approach* (Oxford, 2013). See in particular my chapter, 'Homo Sovieticus and Vernacular Knowledge'.
56 Michael Bernhard and Jan Kubik (eds), *Twenty Years After Communism: The Politics of Memory and Commemoration* (New York, 2014).

57 Dorothee Bohle and Bela Greskovits, *Capitalist Diversity on Europe's Periphery* (Ithaca, 2012), p. 3.
58 Alena Ledeneva with A. Bailey, S. Barron, C. Curro and E. Teague (eds), *The Global Encyclopaedia of Informality: Understanding Social and Cultural Complexity*, 1 (London, 2018), p. 21.
59 William L. Miller, Åse B. Grødeland and Tatyana Y. Koshechkina (eds), *A Culture of Corruption? Coping with Government in Post-communist Europe* (Budapest and New York, 2001).
60 Ion Marandici, 'Oligarchic State Capture: Wealthy Elites and State Autonomy in Communist and Post-communist Countries' (PhD dissertation, Rutgers University, 2017).

Bibliography

Appadurai, Arjun, 'Past as a Scarce Resource', *Man*, New Series 16.2 (June 2001): 201–219.

Aronoff, Myron, and Jan Kubik, *Anthropology and Political Science: A Convergent Approach* (Oxford, 2013).

Ash, Timothy Garton, 'Does Central Europe Exist?', *The New York Review of Books*, 9 October 1986.

Bernhard, Michael, and Jan Kubik (eds), *Twenty Years After Communism: The Politics of Memory and Commemoration* (New York, 2014).

Bialasiewicz, Luiza, 'Back to *Galicia Felix*?', in C. Hann and P. R. Magocsi (eds), *Galicia. A Multicultured Land* (Toronto, 2005).

Bohle, Dorothee, and Bela Greskovits, *Capitalist Diversity on Europe's Periphery* (Ithaca, 2012).

Bönker, F., K. Müller and A. Pickel, 'Cross-disciplinary Approaches to Postcommunist Transformation: Context and Agenda', in F. Bönker, K. Müller and A. Pickel (eds), *Postcommunist Transformation and the Social Sciences* (Lanham, 2002).

Brubaker, Rogers, and Frederic Cooper, 'Beyond Identity', *Theory & Society*, 29.1 (2000).

Buchowski, Michał, and Izabela Kołbon, 'Od "Mitteleuropy" do Europy Środkowej. Zarys dziejów idei', *Sprawy Narodowościowe. Seria nowa*, 19 (2001).

Chodakiewicz, Marek Jan, *Intermarium: The Land Between the Black and Baltic Seas* (New Brunswick, NJ, 2012).

Cobel-Tokarska, Marta, and Marcin Dębicki, *Słowo i terytorium. Eseje o Europie Środkowej* (Warszawa, 2017).

Droit, Emmanuel, 'The Gulag and the Holocaust in Opposition: Official Memories and Memory Cultures in an Enlarged Europe', *Vingtième Siècle. Revue d'histoire*, 2.94 (2007): 101–120.

Droz, Jacques, *L'Europe Centrale. Evolution historique de l'idee de Mitteleuropa* (Paris, 1960).

Eades, Jeremy, 'The Development of Asia Pacific Studies: A Case Study of Internationalization in Japanese Higher Education', in T. Wesley-Smith and J. Goss (eds), *Remaking Area Studies. Teaching and Learning Across Asia and the Pacific* (Honolulu, 2010).

Ekiert, Grzegorz, and Stephen E. Hanson (eds), *Capitalism and Democracy in Central and Eastern Europe. Assessing the Legacy of Communist Rule* (Cambridge, 2003).

Esterházy, Péter, 'How Big Is the European Dwarf?', in D. Levy, M. Pensky and J. Torpey (eds), *Old Europe, New Europe, Core Europe. Transatlantic Relations After the Iraq War* (London, 2005).

Friedman, George, 'Reality Check. From the Intermarium to the Three Seas', available at https://geopoliticalfutures.com/intermarium-three-seas/ (accessed 3 January 2018).

Guha-Khasnobis, Basudeb, Ravi Kanbur and Elinor Ostrom, *Linking the Formal and Informal Economy. Concepts and Policies* (Oxford, 2006).

Gunst, Peter, 'Agrarian Systems of Central and Eastern Europe', in D. Chirot (ed.), *The Origin of Backwardness in Eastern Europe* (Berkeley, 1989).

Hale, Henry, *Patronal Politics. Eurasian Regime Dynamics in Comparative Perspective* (New York, 2015).

Johnson, Lonnie R., *Central Europe Enemies, Neighbours, Friends* (Oxford, 1996).

Kennedy, Michael, *Globalizing Knowledge. Intellectuals, Universities, and Publics in Transformation* (Stanford, 2014).

Klinke, Ian, 'Area Studies, Geography and the Study of Europe's East', *The Geographical Journal*, 181.4 (2015): 423–426.

Kucia, Marek, 'The Europeanization of Holocaust Memory and Eastern Europe', *East European Politics and Societies*, 20.1 (2016): 97–119.

Kundera, Milan, 'The Tragedy of Central Europe', *The New York Review of Books*, 26 April 1984.

Ledeneva, Alena, with A. Bailey, S. Barron, C. Curro and E. Teague (eds), *The Global Encyclopaedia of Informality: Understanding Social and Cultural Complexity*, 1 (London, 2018).

Letki, Natalia, and Geoffrey Evans, 'Endogenizing Social Trust: Democratization in East-Central Europe', *British Journal of Political Science*, 35 (2004): 515–529.

Mahmood, Saba, *Politics of Piety. The Islamic Revival and the Feminist Subject* (Princeton, 2005).

Mahoney, James, and Kathleen Thelen (eds), *Explaining Institutional Change: Ambiguity, Agency, and Power* (Cambridge, 2009).

Marandici, Ion, 'Oligarchic State Capture: Wealthy Elites and State Autonomy in Communist and Post-communist Countries' (PhD dissertation, Rutgers University, 2017).

McFaul, Michael, 'The Missing Variable: The "International System" as the Link Between Third and Fourth Wave Models of Democratization', in Valerie Bunce, Michael McFaul and Kathleen Stoner-Weiss (eds), *Democracy and Authoritarianism in the Postcommunist World* (Cambridge, 2010).

Merton, Robert, 'The Thomas Theorem and "The Matthew Effect"', *Social Forces*, 74.2 (1995): 379–424.

Miller, William L., Åse B. Grødeland and Tatyana Y. Koshechkina (eds), *A Culture of Corruption? Coping with Government in Post-communist Europe* (Budapest and New York, 2001).

Murzyn, Monika, 'Heritage Transformation in Central and Eastern Europe', in P. Howard and B. Graham (eds), *The Ashgate Research Companion to Heritage and Identity* (Aldershot, 2008).

Naumann, Friedrich, *Mitteleuropa* (Berlin, 1916).

Parfianowicz-Vertun, Weronika, *Europa Środkowa w tekstach i działaniach. Polskie i czeskie dyskusje* (Warszawa, 2016).

Park, Robert E., and Ernest Burgess, *Introduction to the Science of Sociology* (Chicago, 1921).

Partsch, Josef F. M., *Mitteleuropa. Die Länder und Völker von den Westalpen und dem Balkan bis an den Kanal und das Kurische Haff* (Gotha, 1904).

Podraza, Antoni, 'Europa Środkowa jako region historyczny', available at http://jazon.hist.uj.edu.pl/zjazd/materialy/podraza.pdf (accessed 5 February 2018).

Podraza, Antoni, 'Central Europe as a Historical Region', in Jerzy Kłoczowski (ed.), *Central Europe Between East and West* (Lublin, 2005), pp. 30–45.

Pop-Eleches, Grigore, 'Historical Legacies and Post-communist Regime Change', *The Journal of Politics*, 69.4 (2007): 908–926.

Rokkan, Stein E., and Derek W. Urwin, *Economy, Territory, Identity: Politics of West European Peripheries* (London, 1983).

Rothschild, Joseph, *East Central Europe Between the World Wars* (Seattle and London, 1974).

Sosnowska, Anna, *Zrozumieć zacofanie. Spory historyków o Europę Wschodnią (1947–1994)* (Warsaw, 2004).

Sosnowska, Anna, 'Why Is Eastern Europe Backward', *Aspen Review*, 4 (2013), available at https://www.aspenreview.com/article/2017/why-is-eastern-europe-backward (accessed 27 June 2019).

Sosnowska, Anna, 'Mitteleuropa Versus Central Europe', available at https://www.aspenreview.com/article/2017/mitteleuropa-versus-central-europe (accessed 3 January 2018).

Szporluk, Roman, *Communism and Nationalism. Karl Marx Versus Friedrich List* (Oxford, 1988).

Šabic, Zlatko, and Petr Drulak (eds), *Regional and International Relations of Central Europe* (Basingstoke, 2012).

Thomas, William I., and Dorothy Swaine Thomas, *The Child in America: Behavior Problems and Programs* (New York, 1928).

Tilly, Charles, and Robert E. Goodin, 'It Depends', in R. E. Goodin and C. Tilly (eds), *The Oxford Handbook of Contextual Political Analysis* (Oxford, 2006).

Todorova, Maria, *Imagining the Balkans* (New York, 1997).

Tolstrup, Jakob, 'Studying a Negative External Actor: Russia's Management of Stability and Instability in the "Near Abroad"', *Democratization*, 16.5 (2009).

Tolstrup, Jakob, *Russia vs the EU: The Competition for Influence in Post-Soviet States* (Boulder, CO, 2013).

Wallerstein, Immanuel, *The Modern World-system. Capitalist Agriculture and the Origins of the European World-economy in the Sixteenth Century* (New York, 1974).

Zarycki, Tomasz, 'Polska jako peryferie stykowe', in T. Zarycki (ed.), *Polska jako peryferie* (Warszawa, 2016).

4

Eastern Europe, with and without borders

Wendy Bracewell

In the early years of the twenty-first century, the young Polish artist Jan Dziaczkowski (1983–2011) created a series of collages, inserting images of socialist-era architecture, monuments and everyday life into postcards of famous western European scenes. Grey tower blocks loom over Piccadilly Circus and march alongside the Leaning Tower of Pisa; a statue of Lenin dwarfs the building of Gropius's Dessau Bauhaus; Princess Diana glances up from work at an industrial loom; young women in headscarves, carrying rakes and brooms, stride purposefully through the Louvre or take notes, accompanied by a herd of cows, in front of a portico supported by caryatids.[1]

The series was entitled *Keine Grenze* or 'no border'. Its impact depends on the viewer recognizing the ways that these images do in fact encode the two sides of a border, that between Cold War Eastern Europe and the West: on the one side concrete monoliths, party leaders and women-as-workers, on the other side high culture, tourism and bustling commerce. Precisely how the collages erase this division is open to interpretation. Is the artist in fact reinstating ideological and aesthetic borders by juxtaposing socialist modernism with the canonical highpoints of Western civilization? Or are these scenes from an imagined post-Second World War past in which the Red Army did not halt at Berlin but continued as far as London, the fantasy of a twenty-first century in which all Europeans grapple equally with the legacy of communism? Perhaps they comment on the ways neither architectural styles nor political ideologies lend themselves to neat geographical divisions – after all, the concrete of the really-existing

Centrepoint building just beyond Piccadilly rhymes convincingly with the tower block glorifying the Communist Party of the Soviet Union that Dziaczkowski has inserted in the foreground. Or do these images summon up a contemporary, mobile world in which east European migrants now cross Europe's Cold War border to work or travel, but nonetheless carry their own historically formed identities with them? In the context of the EU's 2004 eastward enlargement, the images (and their German title) inevitably read as an ironic comment on politicians' claims to have erased Europe's Cold War divisions.

These ambiguities of interpretation hint at why Eastern Europe might be a fruitful starting point for reconsidering Area Studies.[2] What is the genealogy of Eastern Europe as a concept and as an object of academic research? What is the position of East European Studies in the twenty-first century, and how might its assumptions be revised and its borders re-mapped? Can a project of Eastern Europe both with and without borders contribute to the reinvention of Area Studies more broadly?

**

Dziaczkowski's collages depend heavily on the signifiers of the Cold War, but the concept of a bounded and recognizable Eastern Europe is both older than the post-Second World War geo-political order and less clearly defined than the territories formerly ruled by Europe's communist regimes. The area so designated has been historically contingent, its borders and divisions fluid and frequently shifting, according to different, sometimes contradictory, criteria. Eastern Europe is not equivalent to 'the eastern half of Europe' in geographical terms, not simply because of the resulting anomalies (e.g. 'East European' Prague lying to the west of Vienna and Stockholm), but also in view of the frequent exemptions or qualifications made on non-geographical grounds (Cold War Greece being the most striking example). It is often more revealing to examine who is defining Eastern Europe or competing labels, where and to what purpose, than it is to assess the validity of the criteria – historical, cultural, political or economic – used to delimit such areas.

The term Eastern Europe and its close cognates in other western European languages (*Osteuropa, L'Europe orientale*) only appeared in general use to designate a distinctive territory with shared characteristics in the early nineteenth century, though scattered references appear from the early eighteenth century, usually in the purely geographical sense of 'the eastern part of Europe'.[3] Through the eighteenth century, the more usual mental map of Europe was oriented North–South, with classical ethnography, climate theory and religious-political competition shaping long-standing polemics over the qualities to be attributed to each side of this division. It was the Enlightenment in France that radically revised this imaginative geography of Europe, though not by reorienting the map away from North–South through the invention of a single, coherent Eastern Europe, as so influentially argued by Larry Wolff.[4] (Critics have pointed out that the eighteenth-century sources used by Wolff fail to use the term 'Eastern Europe' and retain the designation 'Northern' for Russia and Poland, often grouping these states with Sweden and Denmark, and that to project the Cold War division of Europe back into the eighteenth century, where the sources instead speak of individual peoples or places rather than clearly defined areas, is anachronistic.)[5]

The achievement of the French *philosophes* was instead to theorize Europe as a whole in terms of a teleological vision of history built around concepts of progress and civilization that privileged particular forms of technological and cultural change as developed in the great urban centres of north-western Europe. They defined 'Europeanness' through confrontation with a variety of others, including internal ones. It was not only eastern Europeans, but also 'backward' southern Italians or Irish, 'degenerate' Greeks, 'savage' Icelanders, 'uncivilized' Swiss or Breton villagers or a 'barbaric' urban rabble who could serve as foils for the arbiters of an ideal Europeanness, though each specific not-quite-European might occupy a different place in the march of history, from savagery to (potential) perfectibility to decadence.[6] This effort to classify and rank degrees of Europeanness was further encouraged as early Enlightenment anthropology (or a universalist 'Science of

Man') developed towards a much more particularist ethnology, or the science of the different *varieties* of mankind, increasingly conceived in hierarchical and determinist terms. Thus, the intellectual origins of Europe's twentieth-century geo-cultural divisions can indeed be placed in the Enlightenment, as Wolff argues, but it is more helpful to see these eighteenth-century projections of self and other in terms of a self-congratulatory scale of centre–periphery difference, rather than geographically divided East–West or North–South. (It is tempting to see contemporary scholars who focus solely on 'Eastern Europe', or 'the Southern Question' or 'the Orient', in explanations of the evolution of the idea of Europe as suffering from that specific form of myopia caused by imagining areas as bounded, separate and distinct.)

Eastern Europe as an explicit label for a coherent entity has a more recent genealogy, though with significant variations according to context. It emerged in German usage in the early nineteenth century as a response to the waning of the Ottoman threat and the rise of a Russian one. Liberal fears of an increasingly powerful reactionary, legitimist and interventionist Russian monarchy helped to shift Russia out of its former imagined place in the North (now left to Scandinavia) and placed it firmly in an 'Asiatic' and 'despotic' East. *Osteuropa* in German usage long retained an emphasis on Russia and its western borderlands.[7] In French usage, in contrast, the idea of a distinctive European East spread in the mid-nineteenth century as a response to Panslav ideas: *L'Europe orientale* was the equivalent of 'Slavonic Europe' and helped widen the territory of Eastern Europe beyond Russia to the rest of the Slav world. Ezequiel Adamovsky has shown how this Eastern Europe was constructed as a 'space of absence', lacking elements thought fundamental to 'Western civilization' – effective restraints on the power of the sovereign, urbanization and a bourgeoisie, and an independent civil society – whether these were conceived as negative or sometimes positive attributes. Adamovsky gives the resulting discourses of East European difference the label of 'Euro-Orientalism', underlining the way the binary stereotypes of Europe versus the Orient were adapted to new divisions of space, and showing how they served to organize and regulate relations of power.⁸ English usage of the term 'Eastern Europe' became entrenched still later: appearing as general currency shortly after the First World War (largely in response to the new post-war political order and building on Halford Mackinder's influential characterization of 'East Europe' lying at the centre of the 'geographical pivot' of world power), and becoming increasingly common during and after the Second World War.⁹

The powerful stereotypes and prejudices of Euro-Orientalism meant that the term 'Eastern Europe' – from the nineteenth century onwards – was used primarily to denote others, only seldom as self-description. When it was used in the eastern half of the continent, it was generally employed to differentiate the observer's position from those societies and cultures perceived as more 'eastern', in a self-defensive process that has been described as 'nesting orientalism'.¹⁰ Similar processes were also reproduced *within* east European societies, as with 'class orientalism' directed towards social inferiors, 'internal orientalism' aimed at domestic peripheries, or 'self-orientalism', manifested as an internalized sense of backwardness and shame. However, such east European 'ideologies of Eastness' have not necessarily translated into the acceptance of an explicitly 'East European' selfhood.¹¹ More frequent assertions of a distinctive Central European self have also been shaped by self-defensive urges, with the difference that such definitions can be understood as establishing a distance vis-à-vis both East *and* West, on the one hand resisting the pejorative connotations of Easternness, and on the other defying relegation to a mere periphery of a more advanced West.¹² 'The Balkans', like Eastern Europe, was also initially defined from without as an ambiguous demi-Europe, as analysed by Maria Todorova.¹³ However, while these external definitions may have emphasized the degree of Balkan difference from a truly European core, local adaptations of the Balkan concept have also called attention to patterns of connection, interaction and convergence (the very opposite of western definitions of Balkanization as fragmentation, as Diana Mishkova has pointed out).¹⁴ The point to be underlined here is that these labels were not solely produced outside and projected onto the region, however defined, but were co-produced by local actors, through adaptation, reworking and sometimes re-projection.

After the First World War the establishment of the independent successor states reinforced a tripartite division of Europe into West, East and something in between. However, there was no consensus as to what this 'something' was. The appropriate terminology was hotly debated, particularly within the region: should it be understood in terms of *Mitteleuropa, Zwischeneuropa,* Slavic Europe, Central Europe (sometimes itself divided into West-Central and East-Central Europe), 'New' Europe or an Eastern Europe marking the boundary with an implicitly non-European Russia? Different interests and visions of the future underpinned the choice of terminology: was it a 'shatter zone', a buffer and bridge, or a sphere of German or Russian influence? Where did the boundaries lie, and were the criteria contemporary, political and contingent, or cultural, historical and 'natural'? And, if the latter, which of the numerous cross-cutting indicators overrode the others? The answers to these questions depended on who was making the argument, and to what ends: irreconcilable interests were not conducive to agreement on terminology.[15]

These multiple differentiations were temporarily resolved by a new polarization of Europe after the Second World War (one which also elevated the East/West division over other European fractures). The concept of a cohesive Eastern Europe, now including the Soviet Union, became entrenched in the capitalist West as a synonym for the European socialist republics, though the primarily ideological basis for the collective label was tinged with older Euro-Orientalist prejudices. The post-war shift in the imagined location of Greece, from the East to the West, underlines the primacy of ideology, however: geopolitics outweighed the cultural, economic and political factors that otherwise might have placed Greece in Eastern Europe. On the other hand, while representatives of the socialist states often spoke in geopolitical terms of 'the West' as the enemy of communism, they rarely identified themselves as 'Eastern Europe'. A different self-descriptive terminology – the socialist 'camp' or bloc – implied ideological choice and not cultural or geographical destiny. And, at least at first, this self-designation also laid claim to a revolutionary shift in the location of progress and modernity, even if this was eventually followed by retreat and retrenchment in the face of Soviet military intervention, Cold War competition over consumption as well as production, and political sclerosis. (This in turn fed the disillusioned and backward-looking revival of 'Central Europe' in opposition to a variously defined East – *and* an indifferent West – in certain parts of the region in the 1980s.)[16]

After 1989–1991 and the collapse of the socialist regimes, many in both East and West predicted the end of a distinctive Eastern Europe, perhaps best summed up by the opening line of a 1990 article by Hungarian-born Charles Gati in *Foreign Affairs*, subtitled 'The Morning After': 'Eastern Europe is now east-central Europe.'[17] But the earlier label hung on, though less often with a Russian component: the EU accession states were often complimented with the term 'the former Eastern Europe', as if they had somehow shifted their geographical location as well as changed their political and economic framework. However, when citizens of these countries exercised their right to travel and work across Europe, disapproving observers lumped them together and stigmatized them as 'East European', using the same label for corruption, xenophobia, aggressive nationalism or populism when these occurred in accession states (though these same phenomena were rarely 'un-European' when observed in western member countries). 'Post-socialism' or 'post-communism' offered a more neutral label, for both insiders and outsiders, as a term indicating the shared experience of state socialism and subsequent radical transformation processes. However, an analytical category built on shared legacies could also be applied as an implicit geographical designation, grouping together countries in the east of Europe while usually excluding such states as Mongolia, Vietnam or China. The competing solutions, in journalism, diplomacy and academic usage, indicated that the criteria of area could be sliced and diced in different ways.

This brief sketch of Eastern Europe and its variants highlights the contested nature of these area labels, projected, disputed, claimed or rejected, subdivided and renegotiated. The arguments have nearly always been underpinned by the logic of alterity rather than arising from observable commonalities, though shared economic, political or social factors, historical patterns or cultural traits have all been pressed into service in the process. The salient categories of difference have changed with new anxieties or alliances, contributing to the unstable and contingent – though scarcely arbitrary – nature of the definitions. These have developed within an overarching East/West framework, although those nations and places designated as East European have not necessarily accepted the denomination. Nonetheless, insider voices have also contributed to the East–West orientation of Europe, particularly through their own local 'ideologies of Eastness'. However, the underlying binary division could also produce much more complex configurations, as the arguments over Central Europe or an East–West political, economic or cultural 'gradient' indicate.[18]

But the salient point here is not the criteria or even the purposes of such definitions, revealing as they may be. It is that there was never a consensus. What 'area' meant could not be taken for granted as solid and self-evident in this part of Europe: it was always up for debate and challenge. And, in consequence, even while they passionately argued for their own definitions, proponents of these debates also produced some notable reflections on the criteria, purposes and implications of area concepts, whether in inter-war debates about the limits and divisions of European history, meditations in the 1980s on supra-national cultural collectivities or deconstructions of the symbolic geography of the region in the 1990s. From this perspective, Dziaczkowski's 'without borders' collages represent a provocation to the viewer, calling for reflection not just on the contradictions of EU integration but also on the ambiguities of Europe's East/West divisions. While unstable and fluid frontiers are by no means unique to Europe's eastern edge, its competing and interacting discourses of inclusion and exclusion, connection and difference make this a fruitful site for thinking through the purposes and possibilities of area concepts.

***

East European Area Studies – as institutionalized in university departments, research institutes and specialist journals – has been subjected to a now well-established critique, reflecting a wider reassessment of Area Studies in general. The narrative has focused on the conscription of western East European Studies to Cold War and post-1989 geo-politics and the ways in which the resulting knowledge has been compromised and rendered suspect. According to this critique, East European Studies was the product of the same geo-political gaze that produced Eastern Europe in the first place, being predicated on a political and intellectual distance between western experts and the objects of their knowledge. State interests demanded that this knowledge be useful and problem-solving (predictive or, after 1989–1991, prescriptive). Area Studies critics have seen state-controlled funding as the mechanism by which academic energies were harnessed to this purpose, with the ebb and flow of Euro-Atlantic strategic interest determining the establishment and fortunes of institutions devoted to East European Studies. Precisely how individual scholars were conscripted into this is usually less clearly articulated, though the implication is that it came down to ideological alignment, institutional coercion or individual conformism. Area and discipline are conceived as separate and opposing intellectual fields in this portrayal, with East Europeanists depicted as isolated from mainstream disciplinary methods, theories and problems, though the integration of multiple disciplinary approaches to the object of study is conceded a 'pragmatic holism' – though at the expense of oversimplifying a problematically undifferentiated Eastern Europe. In spite of the fact that versions of this narrative have circulated since at least the 1960s, the main stimulus for recent iterations was the sudden and radical collapse of the Cold War division of Europe after 1989–1991. This laid bare the limits of East European Studies' capacity to predict change and highlighted the pragmatic motives behind state funding, particularly as investment rapidly shifted to other areas of concern. Even as multidisciplinary East European Studies was reinvented in response to new crises, attracting new participants from other fields and under other labels – transitology, conflict (and post-conflict) studies or EU integration studies – the same criticisms continued, of a 'colonial paradigm' subservient to hegemonic state interests from one direction, and of a lack of disciplinary rigour from the other.[19]

Admittedly, the foregoing summary is something of a caricature, but the criticisms levelled at East European Studies often themselves caricature the practices held up to analysis. It is conventional to respond that things are much more complicated than that,[20] but in what follows the point is what the airbrushed complexities reveal about the character of East European Studies, broadly understood, and about the processes by which knowledge is produced. Looking at the details reveals not unthinking conscription to geo-political power but rather the entangled character of East European Studies, and the intellectual consequences of its unorthodox (though not undisciplined) constitution.

The extent to which western scholars of Eastern Europe have spoken on behalf of power is a matter of time, place and degree. The paradigmatic model for academic subservience to political demands is not Cold War East European Studies or even US Sovietology, but Nazi-era *Ostforschung*, conscripted to the subjection and exploitation of the territories and peoples to Germany's east, with the instrumentalization of academic research ensured both by targeted funding and by the willingness of the *Ostforscher* to 'work towards the Führer' in anticipating the commands of the state.[21] Elsewhere, state direction of western East European Studies has rarely been so all-encompassing, even if those in charge might have wished it so. This has been the case even under the highly centralized state-funding regime of UK Higher Education, where the School of Slavonic and East European Studies provides a good illustration of the academic power/knowledge relationship. Established in 1915 with the explicit intention of influencing Britain's war aims and post-war policy on behalf of the 'small nations' of Eastern Europe (and with direct financial support from their heads of state), its founders' hopes that SSEES would shape British diplomacy were curtailed by official suspicion of the researchers' bias (not least because most of the first generation of scholars were recruited from the region). After the

Second World War, in very different circumstances, not least the decision to rely on more conventional state educational funding, successive academic managers were happy to 'work towards the Foreign Office', not just in mission statements responding to UK strategic needs but on occasion through personnel decisions. Most controversially, in 1950 this meant not renewing the contract of a founder member of the British Communist Party hired to lecture on Soviet institutions, over public protests about academic freedom from members of staff and students.[22] But, as this suggests, top-down managerial and bottom-up academic views did not always completely coincide. Nor have strategic funding initiatives invariably had the intended results: subsidies for language training, for instance, may have been intended to nurture expertise for diplomatic or military needs, but what students actually did with their skills could vary widely (at least two Soviet spies, Kim Philby and Geoffrey Prime, had been students on University of London Russian courses). And, of course, academics have long been adept at responding to the language of funding calls to further their own research interests. Partly because of doubts about academic trustworthiness, the Foreign Office generally preferred to rely on its own research departments to underpin policy-making about the region. The same could be said about US government agencies, which as early as the late 1950s were relying on their own in-house experts, increasingly under the aegis of what David Engerman has labelled 'para-academic enterprises' existing at a distance from academic debates and scholarly norms (e.g. RAND, Washington think-tanks or university-based policy institutes such as the Hoover Institution at Stanford). However, the degree to which even this in-house knowledge achieved policy traction was also in practice subject to political manipulation and government infighting.[23]

The same lack of congruence between official prescript and academic practice can also be seen elsewhere. Even during the height of anti-communist McCarthyism the field accommodated a spectrum of political perspectives – something already apparent in the OSS Research and Analysis Branch, the wartime precursor to academic Area Studies in the United States.[24] Some scholars, particularly in policy-oriented subjects, benefited from a revolving door between the academy and government, though the career of someone like Zbigniew Brzezinski (Polish-born national security advisor to Jimmy Carter, and an opponent of Cyrus Vance's pursuit of détente, arguing for direct engagement with Eastern Europe as a means of countering Soviet power) highlights the sharp divisions in approach that could exist within government, as well as in the academic world. Equally, both US and European academics, inside and outside the circles of power, could and did voice criticism of official policy towards the region as misconceived, blinkered and ultimately counter-productive. (The critique of the university–state nexus tends to ignore these more critical perspectives, though they certainly aspired to change, if not set, official policy.) In general, the degree to which academic production directly served state interests could vary widely and was not always predictable.[25] However, geo-politics and state funding worked to create structures within which a wide range of disciplines – including literature and philology – could work to produce knowledge about Eastern Europe, not all of it with an immediately practical application.

These structures also accommodated a cosmopolitan mix of scholars. There was never a clear-cut division between western 'experts' and their objects of study in eastern Europe. SSEES was scarcely alone in recruiting specialists from the region. This was a necessity for the rapid development of post-Second World War area expertise in the United States, which had little pre-war tradition of scholarship focused on Eastern Europe.[26] And scholars from the region had a great, even a decisive, influence in many aspects of western East European Studies. This included some of its ideological leanings – Cold War anti-communism in western East European Studies was certainly reinforced by successive waves of émigré scholars (and, on a slightly different tack, one might also point to the large role played in western Soviet studies by émigrés from Russia's borderlands, with their own specific perspectives).[27] Anti-communism was by no means the rule, however, and reform-minded émigrés were also an important part of the story, particularly after 1956 in Hungary and 1968 in Czechoslovakia. Western scholars had their own entanglements with their regions of study, often going beyond scholarly interest. Richard Clogg, in his memoir of academic life in UK area studies in the 1970s–1980s, recalls totting up a list of staff at SSEES who were married to aliens: 'a disproportionately high number, beginning at the top'.[28] This was also more widely true (and may well have contributed to official suspicion of the ideological bona fides of area scholarship).

However, a more important consequence of such cross-cultural flows for our understanding of the way area knowledge was produced was the fact that academics travelling from East to West had a direct influence on the ways that East European Studies were pursued outside the region. One way in which this happened was that they carried with them their own scholarly traditions. These included highly developed disciplinary schools – Polish sociology, Hungarian approaches to economics and economic history, or Russian formalism and the Prague linguistic school. Émigré scholars (as well as those publishing in translation in the West) also contributed importantly to the critical use of Marxist theory in analysing economic and political change. But their perspectives could also operate at a micro level, for instance importing locally inflected concepts of the frame and the scale appropriate for specific questions. This was not necessarily limited to an insistence on a national framework, though 'nationalist' was an easy label with which to disparage émigré scholarship. In addressing issues that went beyond contemporary Warsaw Pact relationships, it is striking how productively many such scholars resisted the undifferentiated concept of 'the Soviet Bloc' characteristic of official Cold War perspectives, looking instead to other units of analysis: culturally determined regions, imperial legacies, or developmental patterns. Such approaches then had a profound influence on subsequent western scholarship. An example is that of Oscar Halecki's *Limits and Divisions of Europe* (New York and London, 1950), which emerged from inter-war Polish–Czech–German debates over the character and role of central Europe, but was influential in western historiography for its challenge to a simple East–West division of European history (and to a certain extent, the exclusion of Russia from that history).[29]

A different example of moving beyond the focus on the national hinges on the personal experience of émigré dislocation and the cosmopolitan ability to operate in multiple linguistic environments. For successive waves of scholars from eastern Europe (Georg Lukács, Roman Jacobson, René Wellek; or Tzevtan Todorov and Julia Kristeva), this 'productive insecurity' contributed to the development of modern literary theory, shaped by the effort to look beyond the national characteristics of literature – rendered irrelevant by their circumstances – and formulate abstract laws to grasp its workings.[30] A further layer of complexity could be added by following the strategic and scholarly appropriation, adaptation and rejection of concepts and approaches from West to East, or indeed in other directions. These might include important, though uneven, counter-flows of theoretical influences before 1989 (translations of, for instance, Levi-Strauss into Polish before 1970; Herbert Marcuse or Franz Fanon into Serbo-Croat in the 1960s and 1970s; Immanuel Wallerstein into Hungarian in the 1970s); strategic use of 'Western' concepts and paradigms by indigenous or returnee scholars after 1989–1991 for purposes of prestige or self-legitimation; and subsequent debates over hierarchies of knowledge and the relative value accorded to 'western theory' and 'local knowledge'.[31] In short, it is impossible to isolate western and east European contributions to knowledge about the region: in terms of both personnel and research perspectives, the two are inextricably entangled.

And, finally, the polarization between 'area' and 'discipline' in East European Studies has rarely been so absolute or so consistent as is claimed. Rather than being firmly defined by the logic of either/or, forcing scholars to choose between adherence to the conventions of a discipline or immersion in the particularities of a place and culture to the exclusion of wider theoretical concerns, East European Studies has primarily been characterized by both/and. Whether located in the humanities or the social sciences, academics working on east European subjects have necessarily tested the methods, presuppositions and assumptions of their disciplines against the sometimes intractable peculiarities of local and specific contexts in relation to a wider world. And they have made contributions, in turn, to problems and approaches in the disciplines, whether measuring economic growth in non-capitalist economies, comparing the trajectories of modernizing societies, examining conflicts and cleavages in a non-democratic system, or querying grand narratives from positions outside the mainstream. Debates around the poverty of disciplinary theory on the one hand, or the parochialism of an area focus on the other, are, paradoxically, testimony to a close area–discipline enmeshment in East European Studies: for the most part they have arisen *within* the field, and often signal other tensions – between academic and policy relevance, for instance, among political scientists concerned with the region in the 1960s and 1970s, or the asymmetrical relations between post-colonial and post-socialist studies.[32]

Cross-disciplinary fertilization and collaboration are often lauded as the greatest theoretical and methodological advantages of Area Studies. Yet interdisciplinarity is not necessarily inherent in Area Studies. In East European Studies, the way it has been practised has been historically contingent, and often asymmetrical in the disciplines involved rather than holistic. Thus, for instance, nineteenth- and twentieth-century scholars engaged in nation-building across eastern Europe were the pioneers of interdisciplinary Area Studies approaches, drawing simultaneously on Philology, Ethnography, History and Geography in a single project of (self-)knowledge. Elsewhere, the combinations could be quite different. In the UK Bernard Pares introduced interdisciplinary 'Slavonic Studies' at Liverpool University in 1907, inspired by a similar approach in Berlin and focusing on language and literature as the primary means of understanding the wider culture. This focus also underpinned the approach at SSEES, under Pares' influence: the core disciplines remained Philology, Literature and History (with a joint post with the LSE in Economics). It was only in the 1960s that new posts in the social sciences were finally added (many of them also held jointly with other institutions and only loosely integrated into the research context).[33] In the United States, the emphasis was instead on the social sciences from the beginning in the OSS's Research and Analysis Branch, which brought together academics from History, Economics, Political Science and Geography: the so-called 'chairborne division' of the war effort.[34] Post-war Area Studies of the region continued this emphasis, with the humanities disciplines far less closely entwined in US Cold War East European Studies (language teaching for pragmatic purposes was another matter).

But precisely how these disciplines have interacted has also been contingent. Holistic interdisciplinary projects have largely been promoted by external pressures and incentives. Large-scale projects and funding faded after the immediate wartime and post-war problem-oriented impetus; since the early 1990s they have revived with EU-funded projects focused on European integration and stability. However, East European Studies' methodological and theoretical interdisciplinarity has more typically been spontaneous, traced by what Marjorie Garber, the Harvard cultural critic, has called 'desire lines', borrowing an urban planning term for unauthorized pedestrian-created paths to characterize the traffic between disciplines.[35] The heaviest traffic in East European Studies has probably run between the different social sciences, but has also drawn in aspects of the humanities. Modernization theory, for instance, originally developed in Sociology, became a widely shared paradigm for East European Studies scholars pursuing problems dealing with economic change, the development of political institutions or the influence of literacy on cultural production. As the term 'paradigm' suggests, some such initially spontaneous connections have been cemented in place, becoming so normalized as to have lost their interdisciplinary connotations, and then challenged not because they troubled disciplinary norms but because of criticism from different directions, theoretical as well as empirical.

This process of cross-disciplinary path-beating has not been peculiar to East European Studies. Fields such as gender, nationalism, Holocaust studies or borderland studies have been created by criss-cross interdisciplinary desire lines that now scarcely raise an eyebrow. In spite of claims that interdisciplinarity as a method defines Area Studies in general, for East European Studies at least it would be more accurate to say that it is *multi*disciplinarity that has given the field its special character. To the extent that academics have worked within the institutional structures of East European Studies, whether in programmes, departments, journals or conferences, they have also rubbed up against the ideas, assumptions and approaches of colleagues working from different disciplinary perspectives on the same part of the world. (The same at least in theory. In practice, the differences between Balkanists and Russianists, say, can be at least as great as those between distinct disciplines.) Importantly, this close contact has been social as well as scholarly, promoting the sort of informal exchange that encourages cross-disciplinary intellectual communication. The advantage of multidisciplinary Area Studies is that it maximizes the potential for interdisciplinary serendipity by stoking the desire and shortening the lines connecting the disciplines. But the primary impetus remains the problem itself. Interdisciplinarity is not simply an abstract exercise or rule breaking for its own sake.

In conclusion, this sketch attempts to show the complex ways in which area, discipline, interdisciplinary connections, politics, legacies and the circulation of people and ideas have entwined and interacted in the field of East European Studies. The knowledge that has emerged from these encounters has been multifaceted: not solely contextual and particular but simultaneously contributing to wider projects of knowledge (not least challenging universalist aspirations). Still, although it is difficult to see this project as constituted along clear-cut borders – between them and us, area and discipline, humanities and social sciences, left and right, East and West – East European Studies has been haunted by such divisions and has returned to them repeatedly, not least in debates about the character and value of area-based knowledge. In this sense, Jan Dziaczkowski's collages, simultaneously eliding the borders between East and West and at the same time drawing the viewer's attention to them, stand as a nicely ironic metaphor – not so much for East European Studies as for this outline of its genealogy and recent history. But many of the possible versions of 'borderlessness' that can be read into those same collages – entangled histories, shared legacies, mobile cultures – are also transferable to the Area Studies project. East European Studies cannot easily be bracketed off from other fields of study, whether in disciplinary terms or in relation to Europe and the wider world.

***

The events of 1989–1991, the Yugoslav wars of the 1990s and EU eastwards expansion in the 2000s all contributed to a prolonged sense of crisis in western East European Studies. 'Eastern Europe' no longer appeared as a single, separate unit (if it ever had done), and both the purpose and the coherence of East European Studies were put in doubt. If 1989 marked a 'return to Europe', as the slogan had it, why should scholars insist on a backward-looking East European distinctiveness? What tied an EU-bound east-central Europe to the fractious Balkans? These questions were reflected in institutional form, in changes in the names of journals and professional associations and in departmental mergers, accelerated in some cases by shifting official funding regimes that de-emphasized eastern Europe in favour of other priorities.[36]

The same sense of crisis underpinned a lively debate over the very idea of a bounded, 'natural' Eastern Europe and its sub-units or alternatives. Beginning in the 1990s, a series of influential studies drew on the model of Edward Said's *Orientalism* to analyse the ways western actors (travellers, journalists and diplomats, as well as academics) had 'invented' or 'imagined' Eastern Europe, the Balkans or Russia as useful 'others', laying bare the self-interested motives that animated these projections.[37] These discussions had serious implications for the conceptualization and practice of East European Studies. It was not just that geo-political interests tainted the field by association, or that its referent evaporated under deconstruction. If Eastern Europe or the Balkans were simply epiphenomena, brought into being as a reflection of western interests and anxieties, then there was no reason to pay attention to anything outside or beyond the all-powerful West. Though phrased as a critique of western scholarship and a sympathetic defence of its objects, in practice this deconstructive trend had the effect of marginalizing the study of eastern Europe.[38]

This approach soon came under criticism from two directions. The first queried one-sided assumptions about the primacy of external, western agency in the construction of Europe's imaginative geographies. (This could scarcely be labelled Eurocentrism, but the thrust was the same; 'West-centrism'?) This prompted a productive line of research into east European contributions to the production of Europe's mental maps and the uses to which these actors put such concepts.[39] The other direction of critique centred on structural criteria for defining historical regions, particularly in terms of political, historical and cultural frameworks or clusters of characteristics. Here there were many different and often conflicting arguments, advancing particular traits or boundaries as determinative, from Huntington's clashing 'civilizations' to Bideleux and Jeffries' semi-peripheries, to choose only two post-1989 framings of Eastern Europe.[40] The tendency in these debates was to reaffirm the objective existence of the area (however defined) prior to subjecting it to analysis. The many possible overlapping and contradictory possibilities, however, continued to destabilize essentialist or 'scientific' approaches to defining the region.[41]

At the same time, various research topics across the disciplines were causing renewed reflection on Eastern Europe and related area configurations as categories of analysis. The diversity of outcomes in the processes of post-communist transition, as well as continuing differences between post-communist and non-communist societies, led political scientists, in particular, to examine the effects of historical legacies – but the legacies of *which* histories? This problem required analysts to consider different eras (pre-communist, communist era, post-communist), institutional structures (empires, nation states and the Soviet Bloc, but also ecclesiastical frameworks or legal systems), and social and economic patterns. No single area definition could encompass all these cross-cutting and overlapping histories. As Grigore Pop-Eleches has pointed out, Eastern Europe as a category might work as a framework for analysing the specific legacies of communist rule, but it is much less appropriate for a longer-term perspective, both because it arbitrarily bisects Europe's more gradual East–West and North–South economic and cultural gradients, and because of the radically different historical experiences of the countries grouped together within that category.[42] This discussion reflected a debate over scale and the selection of cases that emerged in other comparative projects as well. Arguments over inter-regional generalization versus regional specificity prompted one notable polemic over understanding democratization processes,[43] but similar issues of framing and the most appropriate units of analysis cropped up in many other fields of comparative research set in the region, from memory studies to the history of mass violence and genocide.[44] In these debates, Eastern Europe emerged as just one possible framework, not necessarily constructed on an arbitrary basis, but primarily useful for its heuristic potential.

While the spatial turn and comparative research tended to deconstruct Eastern Europe (or at least to draw attention to its constructed nature), a new interest in transnational entanglements and cultural transfers turned attention to Eastern Europe and its variants as meso-regions, units existing above and beyond the level of the nation state, but from this perspective constituted through connections and relationships rather than shared characteristics. Thus, for instance, Marcel Cornis-Pope and John Neubauer, the editors of a four-volume *History of the Literary Cultures of East-Central Europe*, defined its setting as a 'liminal and transitional space' in between various hegemonic powers and influences, and stretching from the Baltic to the Balkans. This then set the stage for a discussion of the literary cultures of the region not through separate national literatures but in terms of internal and external influences, transfers and interconnections, grasped through the interfaces or 'nodes' at which interactions took place.[45] A similarly ambitious project (also in four volumes), *Entangled Histories of the Balkans*, pursued the same project of transcending national(ist) histories by examining contacts, transfers and interactions within and beyond the regional framework.[46] In both these cases, the transnational approach has helped reinvent the object of area studies less as bounded entities and more as shifting and asymmetrical spaces of encounter.

But juxtaposing these two projects raises the question of why choose this or another wider or narrower area, East-Central Europe or the Balkans, particularly when the connections traced extend well beyond the regional framework? Doesn't the transnational meso-regional approach merely reconstruct and reinforce conventional definitions of areas? In fact, these projects, in large part because of their ambitious scope, underline the utility of multiple spatial frameworks, each appropriate to a specific period or problematic. The study of interactions and connections problematizes bounded, stand-alone approaches to nation states or meso-regions, but it also shows that the problem cannot be solved simply by shifting up a scale, placing it 'in context'. East-Central Europe appears as a zone of divergences and disjunctures, as well as encounters and transfers, while the history of the Balkans is entangled not just on an intra-regional level, but also in ways that make sense in both European and 'Near Eastern' contexts, as well as linking (or dissolving into) still other spaces of interaction, for example the oceanscapes of the Mediterranean, the Adriatic and the Black Sea.[47]

All in all, the sense of crisis in East European Studies beginning in the 1990s, together with wider intellectual trends, worked to produce a more critical awareness of what went into the framing and reproduction of a variety of spaces, including Eastern Europe, as an object of study and challenged static and bounded concepts of 'area'. In the meantime, however, institutional East European Studies is once again on the rise, fuelled by political developments (EU relations with its eastern neighbours, right-wing populism, the response to the refugee crisis, the challenge of 'illiberal democracies' and uncertainty in relation to Putin's Russia, including the war in Ukraine), security concerns (including the need for regional and linguistic expertise), the perceived utility of Area Studies expertise for practical application by business and policy users, employment opportunities and even the intellectual possibilities of interdisciplinary interaction. To an extent, East European Studies' funding is still determined by state interests: in the United States, federal funding for area research hinges on a demonstration of 'policy relevance', while in the UK, the funding mechanism covered by REF requires proof of 'impact' on non-academic audiences, though it is worth underlining that this covers all academic research, across the sciences and humanities, and not simply Area Studies. (Inevitably, evidence of influence on policy-makers – rather than poetry-readers – is the easiest to come by.)

So at present, the question is no longer how to 'normalize' East European Studies, or whether to dissolve it into its constituent disciplinary parts. Instead, the issues are the challenges and opportunities that these circumstances bring, and the staying power of the lessons learned in the recent period of self-reflection. Some lingering anxieties may be overblown: seeing East European Studies as subservient to 'strategic interest' overstates either academic naivety or cynicism, and denies individuals' agency and commitment. Academics, like others, grapple as best they can with real-world problems, and must take responsibility for their ethical and political choices. More problematic is something else that is inherent in Area Studies: the temptation to focus more on the *differences* that distinguish a region – let us say Eastern Europe – than on variation within the region, or even more, the common traits that it shares across regional borders. There is almost a professional reflex to put the emphasis on specificity and uniqueness, on 'East Europeanness'. This is not just because to do otherwise undermines the coherence of an area and thus the justification for its study. It also allows the area specialist to claim the privileged position of interpreter of a specific East European 'otherness' – and, in the process, reproduces that 'otherness', those ideologies of Eastness. Subject/object relations in East European Studies remain an ethical problem. At the same time, however, the entangled character of East European Studies discussed above – constituted neither as solely externally nor internally generated knowledge – usefully problematizes the location of subject and object: the boundaries between them, like the boundaries of Eastern Europe, are not easy to specify.

This brings us back to the possibility of an Area Studies project inspired by Dziaczkowski's collages: East European Studies with and without borders. What might it involve? East European Studies, as emphasized above, has employed a wide variety of units of analysis, scaling up and down: from neighbourhoods to cities to states to regions to the area, by whatever name. That said, all such spatial frameworks, while empirically ascertainable, in scholarly terms serve as contingent and provisional heuristic devices: both generating questions, and acting as a framework for exploring them. The point is not 'do they exist as such?' but 'what are they *useful* for?' Not as a political programme, or a fund-raising mechanism, or even as a means of defending vulnerable subjects, but as the framework within which research questions can be asked and explored. Most questions, as suggested by the hierarchically ordered scale above, have taken 'container' concepts of territory for granted: this is the way that the world is politically divided and ruled. But it follows that, in circumstances in which culture, knowledge and power are not contained within neatly bounded territorial units, it makes sense to look for alternative ways of conceptualizing space and different questions. Literary interactions, transfers of ideas, trading relationships or the movement of people and commodities prompt us to trace routes, flows, commodity chains or networks and to ask about obstacles in the path, friction or the nodes where people and processes converge. The existence of far-flung diasporic communities might cause us to recognize terrestrial archipelagos, and ask what links these separate islands and how they interact or not with the currents that surround them. Above all, we might ask about what borders do: when are they boundaries and when are they interfaces, defining rather than dividing areas? These are not new questions in East European Studies, but they suggest ways in which not just the content but the contours of the field might be reconceptualized.

How might the notion of 'with and without borders' be translated into the relations between academic cultures and communities, and help rethink the production of knowledge more generally? First, thinking of borders as interfaces as well as boundaries helps to reframe questions about the vexed relations between discipline and area. The disciplines and Area Studies operate according to different epistemologies, and they organize the production of knowledge differently. The assumptions and claims of the disciplines are rooted in an understanding of reality as structured according to the separate, independent domains of society, culture, politics and economics, changing over time. The nineteenth century conventionally framed and institutionalized each of these disciplinary domains within (and at the service of) the nation state and according to global hierarchies of power and prestige. This framework, though often challenged, has remained hegemonic. Area Studies, in contrast, takes concepts of space as the starting point for inquiry, and pursues problems that arise from the interaction of the disciplinary domains on the ground and in context. It is no accident that some interdisciplinary configurations have arisen from studying the complexity of area-based realities: for instance, the modern concept of 'political economy' as the 'continual and reciprocal relationship between the political and the economic' arose from the study of a particular time and place (inter-war Romania in its regional context).[48] Nor is it surprising that area-based knowledge has served as an important check on the validity and extent of disciplinary claims.[49] However, Area Studies has tended to articulate its insights in disciplinary or cross-disciplinary terms rather than engage in independent theory-building. This is now changing, driven by two impulses: attempts to chart the complexity of Area Studies' spatial frames, and attention to the entangled histories of Area Studies themselves. An awareness of the boundaries between area and discipline does not lead to one dissolving into the other; instead, it maintains a productive tension between their different perspectives.

A different set of borders and interfaces between academic communities involves the relations between here, there and elsewhere. What distinguishes or connects East European Studies as seen from the universities of Chicago, London, Berlin, Warsaw, Beijing and Hokkaido, all of which have Area Studies centres under that label? This raises a cluster of questions around the political dimensions of knowledge production, encompassing not only positionality – who studies whom and where – but also asymmetries in the legitimation, circulation and assimilation of knowledge. This is a more complex problem than that of the 'local' scholar and 'Western' expert. As noted above, the entangled genealogy of East European Studies renders this problematic; so, too, do the nesting ideologies of Eastness – and these complexities are mirrored, if not precisely reproduced, across other academic communities spanning global divides. Recognizing the politics of area knowledge thus requires recognizing multiple borders, competing hegemonies and a multidimensional distribution of power and legitimating authority. These criss-cross borders and intersecting interfaces make a simple reversal of perspective problematic: claiming centrality for one's own location in the production of knowledge simply produces new hierarchies.

But border crossing under such circumstances facilitates useful shifts in perspective. The prize is not just an awareness that there is more than one possible way of seeing the world (worthwhile in itself), but also the possibility of rethinking the politics of knowledge production. One such model might draw on Galin Tihanov's radical shift in perspective in examining the origins of modern literary theory in central and eastern Europe. He does not just challenge the notion of East/West 'lag', but displaces mono-directional models of influence or genealogy, proposing instead the concept of historically specific 'regimes of relevance' – based on the prevalent modes of literary consumption in a society at a particular time, whether for its social or political critique, its aesthetic qualities, as therapy, entertainment or a window into the world.[50] Such 'regimes of relevance' might offer a useful model for understanding how area studies work within and across academic cultures, depending on their mode of knowledge production: whether as an exercise of power, in the service of resistance and emancipation, driven by market-based utilitarianism, or as a search for alternatives. Cross-border collaboration, under such conditions, goes beyond essentialized positions of subject/object, foreign/indigenous, and allows us to think of academic agency in Area Studies more critically.

And, finally, the slogan of 'with and without borders' should encourage us to look more critically at other borders between academic communities. Despite widespread recognition that the world is not neatly subdivided into separate and autonomous areas, our academic institutions often act as though this were the case as far as Area Studies research initiatives, institutional structures and teaching programmes are concerned, with little cross-border communication or cooperation. This volume is in itself a welcome exception. Elsewhere, efforts are being made to systematize comparative Area Studies, taking methodological tools from comparative politics to develop a framework for comparing political phenomena within and across areas;[51] while transnational and transregional approaches have also fed into 'cross-area' studies, bringing the perspectives and structures of different Area Studies frameworks into useful contact.[52] But a critical Area Studies is also well placed to examine and problematize the institutional and intellectual borderlines between other fields: Global Studies, Migration Studies, Urban Studies, Borderland Studies, Oceanic Studies, to identify but a few. Each of these is constituted around a particular conceptualization of space and set of problems, but here, too, the communication between such fields is limited. Without dismantling the borders between such endeavours, a critical and reflexive Area Studies offers the opportunity to consider the understandings of space and process that underpin such approaches, and at the same time refine the notion of 'area' as a useful and flexible concept.

The critique of Area Studies in general, and East European Studies in particular, has led to calls for 'post-Area Studies' or Area Studies 'without borders' – the title of one of the conferences that generated this volume. Rethinking the borders that delimit our intellectual endeavours is necessary and valuable, particularly to the extent that it allows us to see what limits convention places on our efforts, and to transcend them. But, at the same time, Dziaczkowski's ironic images of a Europe 'without borders' serve as a reminder that the move to erase borders is not always emancipatory. Dziaczkowski's collages hint at the sedimentary and symbolic dimensions of East European borders; ignoring them is to devalue the experiences and perceptions of those whose lives and identities have been shaped by such borders. An Area Studies both 'with and without borders' is needed to do justice to the complex reality of lived experience and its scholarly study.

Notes

1. Jan Dziaczkowski, *Kolaże*, ed. K. Hordziej (Kraków, 2013).
2. I use 'Eastern Europe' here as the term for the academic or geo-political construct and mental map; 'eastern Europe' for an unmarked geographical space. 'East European Studies' designates the institutional framework for academic study of Eastern Europe (how Eastern Europe has been framed in a particular context determines whether this includes study of Russia or the Soviet Union).
3. F. B. Schenk, 'Eastern Europe', in Diana Mishkova and Balázs Trencsényi (eds), *European Regions and Boundaries: A Conceptual History* (New York, 2017).
4. Larry Wolff, *Inventing Eastern Europe. The Map of Civilization on the Mind of the Enlightenment* (Stanford, 1994).
5. See, e.g., M. Confino, 'Re-inventing the Enlightenment: Western Images of Eastern Realities in the Eighteenth Century', *Canadian Slavonic Papers*, 36.3–4 (1994): 505–522.
6. See, e.g., R. M. Dainotto, *Europe (in Theory)* (Durham, NC, 2007); B. Struck, *Nicht West – nicht Ost. Frankreich und Polen in der Wahrnehmung deutscher Reisender zwischen 1750 und 1850* (Göttingen, 2006); H. Kliemann-Geisinger, 'Mapping the North: Spatial Dimensions and Geographical Concepts of Northern Europe', in K. K. Povlsen (ed.), *Northbound: Travels, Encounters, and Constructions 1700–1830* (Aarhus, 2007).
7. H. Lemberg, 'Zur Entstehung des Osteuropabegriffe im 19. Jahrhundert. Vom "Norden" zum "Osten" Europas', *Jahrbücher für Geschichte Ost-Europas*, 33 (1985): 48–81.
8. E. Adamovsky, *Euro-Orientalism. Liberal Ideology and the Image of Russia in France* (Oxford, 2006).

9 Halford Mackinder, 'The Geographical Pivot of History', *Geographical Journal*, 23 (1904): 421–437.
10 Milica Bakić-Hayden, 'Nesting Orientalisms: The Case of Former Yugoslavia', *Slavic Review*, 54.4 (1995): 917–931; W. Bracewell, 'The Limits of Europe in East European Travel Writing', in W. Bracewell and A. Drace-Francis (eds), *Under Eastern Eyes: A Comparative Introduction to East European Travel Writing on Europe* (Budapest, 2008).
11 T. Zarycki, *Ideologies of Eastness in Central and Eastern Europe* (New York, 2014).
12 P. Bugge, 'The Use of the Middle: Mitteleuropa vs. Střední Evropa', *European Review of History – Revue européenne d'Histoire*, 6.1 (1999): 15–35.
13 Maria Todorova, *Imagining the Balkans* (Oxford, 1997).
14 Diana Mishkova, 'Academic Balkanisms: Scholarly Discourses of the Balkans and Southeastern Europe', in R. Daskalov, Diana Mishkova, Tchavdar Marinkov and Alexander Vezenkov (eds), *Entangled Histories of the Balkans*, 4 ('Concepts, Approaches, and (Self-)Representations') (Leiden, 2017): 44–114.
15 See Diana Mishkova and Balázs Trencsényi (eds), *European Regions and Boundaries: A Conceptual History* (New York, 2017), especially the chapters by B. Trencsényi ('Central Europe'), F. B. Schenck ('Eastern Europe') and S. Troebst ('European History').
16 George Schöpflin and Nancy Wood (eds), *In Search of Central Europe* (Cambridge, 1989).
17 Charles Gati, 'East-Central Europe: The Morning After', *Foreign Affairs*, 69.5 (1990/91): 129–145.
18 See, e.g., Daniel Chirot (ed.), *The Origins of Backwardness in Eastern Europe: Economics and Politics from the Middle Ages Until the Early Twentieth Century* (Berkeley, CA, 1989); Catherine Evtuhov and Stephen Kotkin (eds), *The Cultural Gradient: The Transmission of Ideas in Europe, 1789–1991* (Lanham, MD, 2003); A. Melegh, *On the East–West Slope: Globalization, Nationalism, Racism and Discourses on Central and Eastern Europe* (Budapest, 2006).
19 For recent iterations of these arguments, Ian Klinke, 'Area Studies, Geography and the Study of Europe's East', *The Geographical Journal*, 181.4 (2015): 423–426; Gareth Dale, Katalin Miklóssy and Dieter Segert (eds), *The Politics of East European Area Studies* (London, 2016).

20 A good study on these lines is D. Engerman, *Know Your Enemy: The Rise and Fall of America's Soviet Experts* (Oxford, 2009), as well as the essays in David Szanton (ed.), *The Politics of Knowledge: Area Studies and the Disciplines* (Berkeley, CA, 2004).

21 Michael Burleigh, *Germany Turns Eastwards: A Study of Ostforschung in the Third Reich* (Cambridge, 1988); Ingo Haar, 'German Ostforschung and Anti-semitism', in Ingo Haar and Michael Fahlbusch (eds), *German Scholars and Ethnic Cleansing 1919–45* (New York, 2004); see also Ian Kershaw, '"Working Towards the Führer": Reflections on the Nature of the Hitler Dictatorship', *Contemporary European History*, 2.2 (1993): 103–118.

22 Ian Roberts, *History of the School of Slavonic and East European Studies, 1915–1990* (London, 1991), 43, 48; Maurice Pearton, 'The History of SSEES: The Political Dimension', *The Slavonic and East European Review*, 71.2 (1993): 287–294.

23 Engerman, *Know Your Enemy*, 261–285. Memoirs touching on the politics of official intelligence manipulation are revealing in this respect: see, e.g., Melvin Goodman, *Whistleblower at the Central Intelligence Agency* (San Francisco, 2017).

24 Barry M. Katz, *Foreign Intelligence: Research and Analysis in the Office of Strategic Services, 1942–1945* (Harvard, MA, 1989).

25 See, e.g., David C. Engerman, 'Social Science in the Cold War', *Isis*, 101 (2010): 393–400, and for more recent examples, Keith Brown (ed.), *Transacting Transition: The Micropolitics of Democracy Assistance in the Former Yugoslavia* (Bloomfield, CT, 2006).

26 See, e.g., Maria Zadencka, Andrejs Plakans and Andreas Lawaty (eds), *East and Central European History Writing in Exile 1939–1989* (Leiden, 2015).

27 For instance, the Polish-born Sovietologists Richard Pipes, Roman Szporluk, Seweryn Bialer and Zbigniew Brzezinski.

28 Richard Clogg, *Greek to Me: A Memoir of Academic Life* (London, 2018), p. 120.

29 On Halecki and his influence, see Stefan Troebst, 'Meso-regionalizing Europe: History Versus Politics', in Jóhann Páll Árnason and Natalie Doyle (eds), *Domains and Divisions of European History* (Liverpool, 2010).

30 Galin Tihanov, 'Why Did Modern Literary Theory Originate in Central and Eastern Europe? (And Why Is It Now Dead?)' *Common Knowledge*, 10.1 (2004): 61–81.
31 Anthropology between western and eastern scholarship provides a good example for this last point; see, inter alia, the debates in P. Skalnik (ed.), *A Post-Communist Millenium [sic]: The Struggles for Sociocultural Anthropology in Central and Eastern Europe* (Prague, 2002); M. Buchowski, 'Intricate Relations Between Western Anthropologists and Eastern Ethnologists', *Focaal – European Journal of Anthropology*, 63 (2012): 20–38; Hana Červinková, Michał Buchowski and Zdenek Uherek (eds), *Rethinking Ethnography in Central Europe* (London, 2015).
32 On political science and policy relevance in Sovietology, Engerman, *Know Your Enemy*, p. 255; on post-colonial/post-socialist relations, S. Chari and Katherine Verdery, 'Thinking Between the Posts: Postcolonialism, Postsocialism, and Ethnography After the Cold War', *Comparative Studies in Society and History*, 51.1 (2009): 6–34.
33 Roberts, *History*, p. 54.
34 Katz, *Foreign Intelligence*, p. xii.
35 M. Garber, *Academic Instincts* (Princeton, 2001), pp. 53–54.
36 See especially Ellen Comisso and Brad Gutierrez, 'Eastern Europe or Central Europe? Exploring a Distinct Regional Identity', in Szanton (ed.), *The Politics of Knowledge*, pp. 262–312, for a survey of the issues as they appeared in the early 2000s.
37 Among the most influential were Wolff, *Inventing Eastern Europe*; Todorova, *Imagining the Balkans*; also Iver Neumann, *Uses of the Other: 'The East' in European Identity Formation* (Manchester, 1999) and others.
38 See, e.g., W. Bracewell and Alex Drace-Francis, 'Southeastern Europe: History, Concepts, Boundaries', *Balkanologie*, 3.2 (1999): 47–66.
39 e.g., on east European images of Europe, W. Bracewell and A. Drace-Francis (eds), *Under Eastern Eyes: A Comparative Introduction to East European Travel Writing on Europe* (Budapest, 2009); or of the West, György Péteri (ed.), *Imagining the West in Eastern Europe and the Soviet Union* (Pittsburgh, PA, 2010).
40 S. Huntington, *The Clash of Civilizations and the Remaking of World Order* (New York, 1996); R. Bideleux and I. Jeffries, *A History of Eastern Europe* (London, 1998, 2nd edn 2008).

41 Mishkova and Trencsényi (eds), *European Regions*, is an invaluable survey of the history and use of regional concepts in Europe that makes this point by default.
42 Grigore Pop-Eleches, 'Pre-communist and Communist Developmental Legacies', *East European Politics and Societies*, Special Issue: Whither Eastern Europe? Changing Approaches and Perspectives on the Region in Political Science, 29.2 (May 2015): 391–408; see also M. Beissinger and S. Kotkin (eds), *Historical Legacies of Communism in Russia and Eastern Europe* (Cambridge, 2014).
43 See Valerie Bunce, 'Should Transitologists Be Grounded?', *Slavic Review*, 51.1 (1995): 111–127; Terry Lyn Karl and Philippe Schmitter, 'From an Iron Curtain to a Paper Curtain: Grounding Transitologists or Students of Postcommunism?', *Slavic Review*, 54.4 (1995): 965–978; and Valerie Bunce, 'Paper Curtains and Paper Tigers', *Slavic Review*, 54.4 (1995): 979–987 for the key exchanges.
44 The conference of the Genealogies of Memory project, 'Regions of Memory: A Comparative Perspective on Eastern Europe', held in Warsaw, 2012, explicitly problematized the spatial framework of memory studies (conference report at http://hsozkult.geschichte.hu-berlin.de/tagungsberichte/id=4715&view=pdf (accessed 8 February 2018)); U. Blacker, A. Etkind and J. Fedor (eds), *Memory and Theory in Eastern Europe* (Basingstoke, 2013) gives a good sampling of the debates. On genocide, Timothy Snyder's *Bloodlands* (London, 2010) prompted debate about the choice of the Soviet Union and Nazi Germany as the primary units of comparison (and Snyder's lack of attention to other perpetrators, as well as other parallel cases of genocide in the region), and the specificity of an East European space of violence, as against a post-imperial borderland zone of genocide from the Baltic through the Black Sea to the eastern Mediterranean, as argued by Aviel Roshwald, *Ethnic Nationalism and the Fall of Empires: Central Europe, Russia and the Middle East, 1914–1923* (London, 2001).
45 Marcel Cornis-Pope and John Neubauer (eds), *History of the Literary Cultures of East-Central Europe*, 4 vols (Amsterdam, 2004–2010).
46 Roumen Daskalov, Diana Mishkova, Tchavdar Marinkov and Alexander Vezenkov (eds), *Entangled Histories of the Balkans*, 4 vols (Leiden, 2013–2017).

47 Alexander Vezenkov, 'Entangled Geographies of the Balkans: The Boundaries of the Region and the Limits of the Discipline', *Entangled Histories of the Balkans*, 4 (Leiden, 2017), 115–256, makes this case particularly cogently.

48 Henry Roberts, *Rumania: Political Problems of an Agrarian State* (New Haven, CT, 1951), p. vii; cited (and the point about the concept of political economy made) in Joseph Rothschild, 'Henry L. Roberts and the Study of the History and Politics of East Central Europe', in Dennis Deletant and Harry Hanak (eds), *Historians as Nation-builders: Central and South-east Europe* (Basingstoke, 1988), pp. 206–215.

49 For an excellent example, see Zoran Milutinović's critique of Pascale Casanova's interpretation of international literary space as constituted by the 'great consecrating nations' of the West. By showing that writing from a geo-political periphery (Kiš's Belgrade) does not equate to writing from the periphery of world literary space and time, he reveals the way that Casanova (inadvertently?) re-maps the literary world according to the criteria of economic and political power: Zoran Milutinović, 'Territorial Trap: Danilo Kiš, Cultural Geography, and Geopolitical Imagination', *East European Politics and Societies*, 28.4 (2014): 715–738.

50 Tihanov, 'Why Did Modern Literary Theory Originate in Central and Eastern Europe?'

51 Matthias Basedau and Patrick Köllner, 'Area Studies, Comparative Area Studies, and the Study of Politics: Context, Substance, and Methodological Challenges', *Zeitschrift für Vergleichende Politikwissenschaft*, 1.1 (2007): 105–124; and see now also Ariel I. Ahram, Patrick Köllner and Rudra Sil (eds), *Comparative Area Studies: Methodological Rationales and Cross-regional Applications* (New York, 2018).

52 The ESRC-funded project 'Socialism Goes Global', examining second world/third world exchanges in different fields, including academic collaboration, is a good example of cross-area studies as history and as practice (http://socialismgoesglobal.exeter.ac.uk/). A comprehensive programme of rethinking Area Studies in a cross-area and transregional framework is to be found in Katja Mielke and Anna-Katharina Hornidge (eds), *Area Studies at the Crossroads: Knowledge Production After the Mobility Turn* (Basingstoke, 2016).

Bibliography

Adamovsky, E., *Euro-Orientalism. Liberal Ideology and the Image of Russia in France* (Oxford, 2006).

Ahram, Ariel I., Patrick Köllner and Rudra Sil (eds), *Comparative Area Studies: Methodological Rationales and Cross-regional Applications* (New York, 2018).

Bakić-Hayden, Milica, 'Nesting Orientalisms: The Case of Former Yugoslavia', *Slavic Review*, 54.4 (1995): 917–931.

Basedau, Matthias and Patrick Köllner, 'Area Studies, Comparative Area Studies, and the Study of Politics: Context, Substance, and Methodological Challenges', *Zeitschrift für Vergleichende Politikwissenschaft*, 1.1 (2007): 105–124.

Beissinger, M., and S. Kotkin (eds), *Historical Legacies of Communism in Russia and Eastern Europe* (Cambridge, 2014).

Bideleux, R., and I. Jeffries, *A History of Eastern Europe* (London, 1998, 2nd edn 2008).

Blacker, U., A. Etkind and J. Fedor (eds), *Memory and Theory in Eastern Europe* (Basingstoke, 2013).

Bracewell, W., and Alex Drace-Francis, 'Southeastern Europe: History, Concepts, Boundaries', *Balkanologie*, 3.2 (1999): 47–66.

Bracewell, W., and A. Drace-Francis (eds), *Under Eastern Eyes: A Comparative Introduction to East European Travel Writing on Europe* (Budapest, 2009).

Brown, Keith (ed.), *Transacting Transition: The Micropolitics of Democracy Assistance in the Former Yugoslavia* (Bloomfield, CT, 2006).

Buchowski, M., 'Intricate Relations Between Western Anthropologists and Eastern Ethnologists', *Focaal – European Journal of Anthropology*, 63 (2012): 20–38.

Bugge, P., 'The Use of the Middle: Mitteleuropa vs. Střední Evropa', *European Review of History – Revue européenne d'Histoire*, 6.1 (1999): 15–35.

Bunce, Valerie, 'Should Transitologists Be Grounded?', *Slavic Review*, 51.1 (1995): 111–127.

Bunce, Valerie, 'Paper Curtains and Paper Tigers', *Slavic Review*, 54.4 (1995): 979–987.

Burleigh, Michael, *Germany Turns Eastwards: A Study of Ostforschung in the Third Reich* (Cambridge, 1988).

Červinková, Hana, Michał Buchowski and Zdenek Uherek (eds), *Rethinking Ethnography in Central Europe* (London, 2015).
Chari, S., and K. Verdery, 'Thinking Between the Posts: Postcolonialism, Postsocialism, and Ethnography After the Cold War', *Comparative Studies in Society and History*, 51.1 (2009): 6–34.
Chirot, Daniel (ed.), *The Origins of Backwardness in Eastern Europe: Economics and Politics from the Middle Ages Until the Early Twentieth Century* (Berkeley, CA, 1989).
Clogg, Richard, *Greek to Me: A Memoir of Academic Life* (London, 2018).
Confino, M., 'Re-inventing the Enlightenment: Western Images of Eastern Realities in the Eighteenth Century', *Canadian Slavonic Papers*, 36.3–4 (1994): 505–522.
Cornis-Pope, Marcel, and John Neubauer (eds), *History of the Literary Cultures of East-Central Europe*, 4 vols (Amsterdam, 2004–2010).
Dainotto, R. M., *Europe (in Theory)* (Durham, NC, 2007).
Dale, Gareth, Katalin Miklóssy and Dieter Segert (eds), *The Politics of East European Area Studies* (London, 2016).
Dziaczkowski, Jan, *Kolaże*, ed. K. Hordziej (Kraków, 2013).
Engerman, D., *Know Your Enemy: The Rise and Fall of America's Soviet Experts* (Oxford, 2009).
Engerman, David C., 'Social Science in the Cold War', *Isis*, 101 (2010): 393–400.
Evtuhov, Catherine, and Stephen Kotkin (eds), *The Cultural Gradient: The Transmission of Ideas in Europe, 1789–1991* (Lanham, MD, 2003).
Garber, M., *Academic Instincts* (Princeton, 2001).
Gati, Charles, 'East-Central Europe: The Morning After', *Foreign Affairs*, 69.5 (1990/91): 129–145.
Goodman, Melvin, *Whistleblower at the Central Intelligence Agency* (San Francisco, 2017).
Haar, Ingo, 'German Ostforschung and Anti-semitism', in Ingo Haar and Michael Fahlbusch (eds), *German Scholars and Ethnic Cleansing 1919–45* (New York, 2004).
Huntington, S., *The Clash of Civilizations and the Remaking of World Order* (New York, 1996).
Karl, Terry Lyn, and Philippe Schmitter, 'From an Iron Curtain to a Paper Curtain: Grounding Transitologists or Students of Postcommunism?', *Slavic Review*, 54.4 (1995): 965–978.

Katz, Barry M., *Foreign Intelligence: Research and Analysis in the Office of Strategic Services, 1942–1945* (Harvard, MA, 1989).

Kershaw, Ian, '"Working Towards the Führer": Reflections on the Nature of the Hitler Dictatorship', *Contemporary European History*, 2.2 (1993): 103–118.

Kliemann-Geisinger, H., 'Mapping the North: Spatial Dimensions and Geographical Concepts of Northern Europe', in K. K. Povlsen (ed.), *Northbound: Travels, Encounters, and Constructions 1700–1830* (Aarhus, 2007).

Klinke, Ian, 'Area Studies, Geography and the Study of Europe's East', *The Geographical Journal*, 181.4 (2015): 423–426.

Lemberg, H., 'Zur Entstehung des Osteuropabegriffe im 19. Jahrhundert. Vom "Norden" zum "Osten" Europas', *Jahrbücher für Geschichte Ost-Europas*, 33 (1985): 48–81.

Mackinder, Halford, 'The Geographical Pivot of History', *Geographical Journal*, 23 (1904): 421–437.

Melegh, A., *On the East–West Slope: Globalization, Nationalism, Racism and Discourses on Central and Eastern Europe* (Budapest, 2006).

Mielke, Katja, and Anna-Katharina Hornidge (eds), *Area Studies at the Crossroads: Knowledge Production After the Mobility Turn* (Basingstoke, 2016).

Milutinović, Zoran, 'Territorial Trap: Danilo Kiš, Cultural Geography, and Geopolitical Imagination', *East European Politics and Societies*, 28.4 (2014): 715–738.

Mishkova, Diana, 'Academic Balkanisms: Scholarly Discourses of the Balkans and Southeastern Europe', in Roumen Daskalov, Diana Mishkova, Tchavdar Marinkov and Alexander Vezenkov (eds), *Entangled Histories of the Balkans*, 4 ('Concepts, Approaches, and (Self-)Representations'), (Leiden, 2017): 44–114.

Mishkova, Diana, and Balázs Trencsényi (eds), *European Regions and Boundaries: A Conceptual History* (New York, 2017).

Neumann, Iver, *Uses of the Other: 'The East' in European Identity Formation* (Manchester, 1999).

Pearton, Maurice, 'The History of SSEES: The Political Dimension', *The Slavonic and East European Review*, 71.2 (1993): 287–294.

Péteri, György (ed.), *Imagining the West in Eastern Europe and the Soviet Union* (Pittsburgh, PA, 2010).

Pop-Eleches, Grigore, 'Pre-communist and Communist Developmental Legacies', *East European Politics and Societies*, Special Issue: Whither Eastern Europe? Changing Approaches and Perspectives on the Region in Political Science, 29.2 (2015): 391–408.

Roberts, Henry, *Rumania: Political Problems of an Agrarian State* (New Haven, CT, 1951).

Roberts, Ian, *History of the School of Slavonic and East European Studies, 1915–1990* (London, 1991).

Roshwald, Aviel, *Ethnic Nationalism and the Fall of Empires: Central Europe, Russia and the Middle East, 1914–1923* (London, 2001).

Rothschild, Joseph, 'Henry L. Roberts and the Study of the History and Politics of East Central Europe', in Dennis Deletant and Harry Hanak (eds), *Historians as Nation-builders: Central and South-east Europe* (Basingstoke, 1988), pp. 206–215.

Schenk, F. B., 'Eastern Europe', in Diana Mishkova and Balázs Trencsényi (eds), *European Regions and Boundaries: A Conceptual History* (New York, 2017).

Schöpflin, George, and Nancy Wood (eds), *In Search of Central Europe* (Cambridge, 1989).

Skalnik, P. (ed.), *A Post-Communist Millenium [sic]: The Struggles for Sociocultural Anthropology in Central and Eastern Europe* (Prague, 2002).

Snyder, Timothy, *Bloodlands* (London, 2010).

Struck, B., *Nicht West – nicht Ost. Frankreich und Polen in der Wahrnehmung deutscher Reisender zwischen 1750 und 1850* (Göttingen, 2006).

Szanton, David (ed.), *The Politics of Knowledge: Area Studies and the Disciplines* (Berkeley, CA, 2004).

Tihanov, Galin, 'Why Did Modern Literary Theory Originate in Central and Eastern Europe? (And Why Is It Now Dead?)', *Common Knowledge*, 10.1 (2004): 61–81.

Todorova, Maria, *Imagining the Balkans* (Oxford, 1997).

Troebst, Stefan, 'Meso-regionalizing Europe: History Versus Politics', in Jóhann Páll Árnason and Natalie Doyle (eds), *Domains and Divisions of European History* (Liverpool, 2010).

Vezenkov, Alexander, 'Entangled Geographies of the Balkans: The Boundaries of the Region and the Limits of the Discipline', in Roumen Daskalov, Diana Mishkova, Tchavdar Marinkov and Alexander Vezenkov (eds), *Entangled Histories of the Balkans*, 4 (Leiden, 2017): 115–256.

Wolff, Larry, *Inventing Eastern Europe. The Map of Civilization on the Mind of the Enlightenment* (Stanford, 1994).

Zadencka, Maria, Andrejs Plakans and Andreas Lawaty (eds), *East and Central European History Writing in Exile 1939–1989* (Leiden, 2015).

Zarycki, T., *Ideologies of Eastness in Central and Eastern Europe* (New York, 2014).

5

Disciplinarity, interdisciplinarity and the plurality of Area Studies: A view from the social sciences

Mark R. Beissinger

After the end of the Cold War, Area Studies programmes faced severe challenges, as government and foundations cut funding, universities came under financial pressures and academic departments came to place increasing value on theory and method rather than knowledge of place. These latter issues were particularly acute in the social sciences, where traditional Area Studies scholarship grew devalued and departmental hiring practices, in many cases, came to ignore area altogether. With the number of social scientists working in Area Studies dwindling, many Area Studies programmes faced the predicament of how to continue to function as multidisciplinary intellectual enterprises – at least if multidisciplinarity were understood to include the social sciences. Area Studies scholars frequently complained of the 'death' of Area Studies in the social sciences, expressing frustration over their inability to influence the ability of social science departments to hire Area Studies scholars.

I believe that such lamentations are premature. In this chapter I outline the ways in which Area Studies knowledge remains deeply implicated in social science research. But Area Studies as currently practised in the social sciences is significantly different from Area Studies as it was traditionally imagined during the Cold War (as an interdisciplinary enterprise aimed at a deepened understanding of place), or from Area Studies as it is currently practised in the humanities (focused on promoting a deepened knowledge of particular cultures). In short, what we have witnessed is not so much the 'death' of Area Studies in the social sciences as the emergence of multiple models of Area Studies that function parallel to one another, with each model serving different purposes. Area Studies in that sense needs to be treated as the plural noun that it is, in that what is often touted as a singular enterprise hides within it multiple purposes.

As I outline in this chapter, there are at least three models of organizing Area Studies knowledge: 1) the traditional area-driven model (Area Studies as a space for conversation between humanities and the social sciences to promote a deepened understanding of particular cultures or places); 2) discipline-driven Area Studies (an Area Studies that fosters research at the cutting edge of disciplinary knowledge); and 3) problem-driven Area Studies (the use of area knowledge to promote cross-area conversations around a particular problem). The social sciences have been involved in all three models (as have the humanities). As Area Studies serves multiple purposes, we need to think more imaginatively about how to achieve these multiple purposes and how Area Studies intersects with the variety of outcomes that we care about. In this chapter, I provide some ideas, based on my own experience as a long-time scholar and administrator working in Area Studies, about ways of achieving these outcomes. The quality of our knowledge about the world, the production of experts who can apply that knowledge and our ability to foster a citizenry capable of making informed decisions about the world all rest significantly on the health of multiple models of Area Studies and on the determination of governments and universities to ensure their continued vitality.

Three models of Area Studies in the production of knowledge

What are the intellectual foundations of Area Studies, and what should be the relationship of Areas Studies to disciplines and to multidisciplinary inquiry? These are questions that have occupied me throughout my professional career. I am a political scientist who works on the Eurasian region. Or perhaps I am a Eurasianist who works within the grammar of Political Science. I am not exactly sure. I have spent my entire academic career within a Political Science department and have taught courses within Political Science – some of which focus on the Eurasian region, some of which do not. I have won disciplinary awards, chaired a major Political Science department, mentored numerous Political Science scholars, hired and overseen the tenuring of many political scientists and handed out major awards within the Political Science discipline. But I have also been heavily involved in Area Studies throughout my career. I was trained as an Area Studies scholar at Harvard and founded an Area Studies centre at the University of Wisconsin-Madison. I have published in Area Studies journals and have taught Area Studies courses. And I served as President of the main North American Area Studies association in the Russian, East European and Eurasian Studies field. To complicate things further, my work has also strongly intersected with the work of sociologists and historians, I have often used sophisticated quantitative methods in my work alongside narrative and case study analyses and I have run an interdisciplinary institute whose purpose is to bring people together across disciplinary departments not only to study particular regions of the world, but also to address key issues that cut across both area and disciplinary boundaries. In general, when it comes to Area Studies, this kind of 'confusion' is a very good thing. It represents the ways in which Area Studies traverses the variety of boundaries by which we organize the production of knowledge and interpenetrates other forms of knowledge.

Traditional Area Studies as it developed after the Second World War – what I call the area-driven model of Area Studies – represented one such model of 'confusion' or interpenetration between area knowledge and the boundaries of knowledge production. It advertised itself as an interdisciplinary space for conversation across the humanities and social sciences as a way of producing a deepened understanding of particular cultures and places. But the aim of the area-driven model was less to produce interdisciplinary conversation than to train specialists literate in a variety of dimensions of the cultures and places with which they engaged through knowledge of their literature, culture, history, politics, economics, geography and so on. In the words of Japanese scholar Alan Tansman, the purpose of Area Studies, as traditionally understood, was to provide students with the skills to be able 'to know, analyze, and interpret foreign cultures through a multidisciplinary lens'.[1] Accordingly, Area Studies programmes were judged by the variety of disciplinary perspectives that they could offer to students concerning a specific region of the world. This was one of the key criteria used, for instance, by the US Department of Education Title VI programme in awarding grants and National Resource Center status to particular universities. Indeed, in the United States, part of what drove the rise of the traditional area-driven model was the possibility of gaining significant outside funding from government and foundations by demonstrating multidisciplinary 'coverage' of particular world regions, and area programme chairs often went to great lengths to lobby university administrations and disciplinary departments to enhance representation of their regions or replace departing faculty, precisely in order to meet the requirements of external funders.

As a way of training specialists thinking only about a specific culture or place, the area-driven model of Area Studies was extremely useful, and during its heyday it was used to produce a generation of area specialists for government and academia. However, it should be recognized that, on its own, it was often inadequate for the kinds of tasks that these individuals were asked to perform and usually needed to be combined with further professional or disciplinary training. Moreover, as a source of intellectual interaction, the area-driven model had severe limitations, as the humanities and the social sciences often spoke quite different languages, utilized profoundly different epistemologies and aimed to answer starkly different types of questions. History functioned as a kind of hinge discipline in its ability to engage with both the social sciences and humanities. But aside from conversations between social scientists and historians and between humanists and historians, it is not clear exactly how well the area-driven model was ever able to foster real intellectual engagement, even in its heyday in the 1950s and 1960s. In the Area Studies professional associations with which I am involved, there has never been a great deal of conversation between humanists and social scientists, as the two groups tend to gravitate towards separate tables.

The end of the Cold War and the professionalization of disciplines within academia presented severe challenges to the area-driven model of Area Studies. The traditional area-driven model continues to function, often at the undergraduate level in Area Studies majors and certificates, as well as in MA programmes aimed at training area-wise professionals and government officials. But a different model of area knowledge and its interpenetration with the boundaries of knowledge production emerged alongside the area-driven model, particularly within the social sciences: a discipline-driven model of Area Studies. Here, the production of knowledge was informed by area knowledge, but the purpose was not to produce a deepened knowledge of culture and place but rather to address better the broader theoretical issues salient within specific disciplines. This discipline-driven model of Area Studies has largely come to dominate scholarly interchange and doctoral training within the social sciences.[2] The result has been the emergence of a different model of Area Studies within the social sciences that aims to further social scientific knowledge rather than produce a deepened knowledge of particular cultures and places. In contrast to the area-driven model, which viewed itself in opposition to social science methods and generalization, the discipline-driven model sees area knowledge as critical to the development of social science theory.

With the rise of rational choice in the 1980s and 1990s (particularly within Political Science), the demise of Area Studies within Economics (which has come to imagine itself as a universal science with minimal regard to local circumstances) and the growing role of globalization (not only under the effects of neoliberalism, but also as an object of academic study), there were soundings about the imminent death of Area Studies within the social sciences in the 1990s.[3] Geography, supposedly, no longer mattered, and Area Studies was accused of the sin of being incapable of generating larger propositions and of failing to identify general processes unfolding in local circumstances.[4] Viewed in hindsight, those debates now seem overblown, caricatured and falsely dichotomized – as most of those who participated in them now recognize. Not only is it clear that, despite globalization, place and culture continue to matter (and, indeed, have sometimes manifested themselves with particular revenge); there is also significant value in knowledge of the local for understanding the general, particularly when one possesses the ability to place it in broader perspective.

Gradually, a new generation of area scholars representing a synthesis of social science training and area skills has emerged within a number of social science disciplines (economics being the only exception). Today, area knowledge remains a critical part of the production of social science knowledge (though some social scientists continue to downplay its contribution). Not only is area knowledge critical in helping social scientists identify the questionable (and often taken-for-granted) assumptions of general theories, but it also provides much of the empirical information that social scientists use to develop theories and test ideas, as a large proportion of social science research takes place within an area context. This is no less true for those social scientists who study their own society than it is for those studying other societies. (In the United States, those studying American politics are often jokingly referred to by those studying other societies as the most narrow of all Area Studies scholars.) There is no contradiction between outstanding social scientific work (including work using highly sophisticated quantitative methods) and Area Studies knowledge. Rather, the two are mutually complementary and reinforcing, and many of the most highly regarded works within social science have been carried out within an area setting, relying extensively on area knowledge in their analyses.[5]

For the positivist social scientist, Area Studies is not about knowledge of culture and space for its own sake, but rather about knowledge of 'context' – the set of circumstances or facts that surround a particular situation. In positivist terms, context is often viewed as a holder for the variety of local causal factors that one has not clearly specified or that one does not fully understand. Area knowledge is especially good for unpacking context, and in this respect it necessarily plays an important role in the production of social scientific knowledge. Let me be clear: within social science, area knowledge is not a substitute for social scientific method or research design. Simply knowing area context is not enough, and there is a great deal of Area Studies research and writing that social scientists rightly view as questionable from a social scientific point of view, given the absence of thinking through issues of methodology, research design, logic of inference, and scope conditions and generalizability. But simply knowing theory and method is grossly insufficient as well. Knowledge of context is critical if one is to get one's social science right, and many of the most egregious errors in social science research have to do with insufficient knowledge of context.

Context is closely intertwined with all social scientific method. An understanding of context is obviously critical for ethnographic and case-based research, which directly relies on knowledge of context in order to draw inferences. But it is equally critical for quantitative, formal and experimental work. In large-n statistical work, for instance, an absence of knowledge about context frequently leads to what social scientists refer to as measurement error (the mismeasurement of concepts) and specification error (omitting important variables that affect the outcome of interest) – errors that can invalidate findings. Indeed, for those fluent in both Area Studies and quantitative methods, these are the kinds of issues often examined in judging the quality of scholarship. Area scholars conversant with the language and purposes of rational choice know that the purpose of formal modelling is not to substitute for empirical research but rather to sharpen empirical research. Formal modelling is a purposeful oversimplification – not a description of reality – in order to think through the logics that might guide action under specific conditions (that is, the assumptions and payoff structures that modellers identify). It is not meant to be realistic, but to be stylized and stripped of all context except that which the modeller cares about. Rational choice generally attempts to describe the way that people would behave under particular assumptions were they to act rationally, not the way that people actually behave in reality. The best formal modellers recognize the limits of rationality, the importance of contextual factors other than those that they identify and the ways in which culture can establish rule-based behaviours that might violate self-interest. But area-trained social scientists have a great deal to contribute in terms of explaining why actual behaviour has or has not conformed to the modeller's predictions, isolating the critical aspects of context that the modeller may have misconstrued and identifying the limits of rationality. In some respects, the experimental fad in social science may be an even bigger challenge than rational choice to area knowledge. It pretends that one can isolate causal processes from their larger context through games or framing exercises conducted under controlled conditions (limiting the effects of other causal factors). But the most widely cited problems with experimental research have all been about context: the artificiality of the controlled environment in which many experiments are conducted, the inability of experiments to control completely for critical contextual variables affecting behaviour, and the ways in which context continues to shape the validity and applicability of findings beyond the experimental setting in which it was conducted. In short, all social science methods assume knowledge of context or make assumptions about context, and it is here that a discipline-driven Area Studies plays an important role in the production of social scientific knowledge.

As the discipline-driven model suggests, Area Studies knowledge need not be counter-posed to disciplinary research, but can complement and improve such research. Still, as one can also see from these examples, the knowledge requirements necessary for working as an Area Studies scholar within the social sciences have skyrocketed. In addition to the language and area skills necessary to be able to understand the contextual dimensions of research, extensive training in increasingly sophisticated methodologies and a deep knowledge of disciplinary theoretical literature have become indispensable. It is literally impossible to cover all of this in the typical social science doctoral training programme. What this means is that social science doctoral students interested in working on a world region often have a thinner Area Studies knowledge than was true of scholars trained in the past according to the area-driven model of Area Studies. But it also means that most social science graduate students working on a world region will necessarily come to graduate study already with their area skills largely in place, either from masters' programmes that work along the area-driven model or because they are recruited from the world region that they are studying. Both of these trends are evident in graduate student recruitment within doctoral programmes in social science departments.

There is yet a third model for Area Studies to traverse the boundaries by which we organize the production of knowledge: the problem-driven or thematic model. This model, which focuses analysis around a specific problem that transcends disciplinary and geographical inquiry, draws on the widespread practice of knowledge production within the sciences and engineering, where individuals with various expertise come together to 'solve' a problem. In the social sciences and humanities we generally do not 'solve' problems in the same way that engineers and scientists do. Rather, we seek explanation or understanding. But the problem-driven approach is one that has at times been applied within International Studies as well. Many of the subjects and problems that we study and care about are not confined by geography but appear in multiple settings around the world. Most of these same subjects and problems transcend discipline, contain multiple dimensions and have been studied from multiple angles, opening up the possibility for broad interdisciplinary and cross-area engagement in ways that generate new perspectives. This type of learning can be among the most exciting, as it brings together scholars working on similar issues in different spatial localities to share their understanding and experience, thereby helping each other to place their experience into context and generating insights that otherwise might not be obtained. The purpose of such a model is less to produce generalizable propositions than to produce among its participants a better understanding of how specific cases or aspects of a problem relate to broader human experience through comparison with similar phenomena. However, problem-driven engagement, like interdisciplinary engagement in general, has often been difficult to organize, most universities lack ways of incentivizing it, and it requires a high level of personal commitment among its participants. Within International Studies it tends to be promoted by interdisciplinary institutions that stand above any particular discipline or region. But it is not as prevalent as it should be, given the intellectual gains that it promises to deliver.

Area knowledge obviously plays a critical role in the problem-driven model, since it is area specialists who are able to bring to bear knowledge of specific problems in their particular manifestations, and it is area specialists who perhaps stand to gain most through conversation with those studying similar phenomena in other contexts. But the problem-driven model is not confined to area specialists, and indeed the cross-fertilization of ideas can come by bringing area specialists together with generalists studying particular problems from a broader perspective and can also be quite useful for both. The problem-driven model has been applied in both the social sciences and the humanities, and sometimes can bring scholars together across the social science–humanities divide. But it has had particular appeal for social scientists as a way of thinking about a broader swathe of cases for the phenomena they study and for gaining a larger perspective. It can also be an excellent forum for brainstorming purposes, for fostering collaborative research and for enhancing the training of graduate students.

However, the problem-driven model assumes the already existing presence of disciplinary and area knowledge on the part of its participants and is not a substitute for disciplinary or area training. Indeed, all three models of Area Studies should be understood as interdependent. Traditional Area Studies programmes cannot function effectively in providing needed social science Area Studies curriculum to undergraduates and masters' students without also engaging the discipline-driven model prevalent within the social sciences. And the discipline-driven model within the social sciences depends on the presence of individuals who have already gained area skills largely obtained through traditionally organized Area Studies undergraduate and masters' programmes.

Promoting the vitality of Area Studies within the social sciences

The problems confronting Area Studies in the social sciences differ in fundamental ways from the problems confronting Area Studies in the humanities. Reflecting their different purposes and epistemologies, the humanities and social sciences have been organized in radically different ways. In general, the humanities have been organized on area principles – largely around languages, families of world-cultures or regions of the world. They self-consciously recruit faculty on the basis of their knowledge of culture and place. But in the social sciences this is not the case. The area-driven model's traditional emphasis on deep knowledge of place and multidisciplinarity has long been in tension with the emphasis within the social sciences on theory, method and generalization. Indeed, all four of the major social science disciplines – Anthropology, Economics, Political Science and Sociology[6]– by and large do not recruit faculty on the basis of region, but rather on the basis of contribution to disciplinary knowledge. (Political Science is sometimes an exception, but increasingly Political Science departments have come to recruit without regard for country or region.) Even Anthropology, which generally does not subscribe to positivist epistemologies and which accords a central place in the discipline to the study of culture, tends not to recruit on the basis of region – due largely to the same prioritization of theory and method that has come to dominate in the other social sciences.

As disciplinary needs have come to assume priority, the representation of Area Studies scholars has sharply declined within social science departments. For example, one study based on a comparison of large-scale surveys of Area Studies scholars in professional Area Studies associations in the United States found that the representation of political scientists among those identifying as Area Studies specialists had halved between 1991 and 2014.[7] The effects on curriculum offered to students at the undergraduate and graduate levels have been profound. I recently chaired a university-wide strategic task force on revitalizing Area Studies at Princeton.[8] As part of our review, we examined trends in non-language Area Studies instruction across the university, classifying all courses credited by Princeton that contained at least 50 per cent of their content on the study of societies other than the United States and that primarily aimed to promote knowledge of a specific world area. We then examined these courses by the division of the university in which they are formally offered: social sciences, humanities, sciences or engineering. The data showed that, while the number of Area Studies courses in the humanities increased slightly from 2008 to 2014, the number of Area Studies courses in the social sciences declined dramatically during the same period. Thus, the overall number of Area Studies courses offered at Princeton in the humanities increased by 8 per cent, while the number of Area Studies courses taught in the social sciences declined by 38 per cent. Our data only went back to the 2008–2009 academic year, and we strongly suspected that this downward trend among Area Studies social science courses would appear even more pronounced were the data to be extended back further. Moreover, of the Area Studies courses classified as social science courses over this six-year period, 38 per cent were offered in the History department (and therefore likely to be more humanities-oriented than oriented towards the social sciences),[9] while another 22 per cent were offered in departments outside the social science departments (often, humanities departments or Area Studies programmes frustrated with the absence of social science area curriculum within the social science departments). In other words, not only had the number of Area Studies courses in the social sciences declined dramatically, but a majority of the 'social science' area curriculum was not even taught within the social science departments. This decline of Area Studies instruction within the social sciences at Princeton is a reflection of general trends associated with the professionalization of the social sciences. In particular, the problem inheres in the hiring process within social science departments, where the needs of Area Studies programmes and concerns for providing Area Studies curriculum for students are not held as high priorities. Demand for such instruction remains high among students; yet social science departments are increasingly unable to meet student interests in these areas, as other foci within these departments have taken priority over Area Studies.

But when one examines the Princeton data more carefully, one sees evidence of a looming humanities Area Studies problem as well. Thus, while the number of Area Studies humanities courses taught by full-time faculty at Princeton remained relatively steady over this period, what had increased in the humanities was the use of lecturers and visitors to teach Area Studies courses. The growing proportion of non-staff appointments and part-time employees in the humanities who are teaching Area Studies courses is also not a positive development for Area Studies and in some university settings threatens to undermine the quality of Area Studies education (in addition to raising issues of fairness of labour relations). So far at Princeton there has been no parallel in the humanities to the sharp decline of Area Studies curriculum that has taken place in the social sciences. But there are worries that such a decline could take place, though for very different reasons. The humanities today at most universities feel under threat due to declining numbers of majors, as students seek out more 'practical' undergraduate majors. Moreover, public and private universities are under economic pressures due to the rising costs of education and declining government support. Many universities have responded to the need to cut costs by merging humanities departments based on languages, families of world-cultures or regions of the world into larger, non-area units and hiring part-time instructors and non-tenure-track staff in place of tenure-track professors. This of course threatens the traditional area-driven model of Area Studies from a different direction. In some universities the combination of declining numbers of majors and economic pressures has already led to significant cutbacks in the humanities. In short, there is a crisis of Area Studies in the humanities; but it is being experienced unevenly across universities, and its full force has yet to be fully felt. Moreover, it is fundamentally different from the crisis of Area Studies in the social sciences. In the social sciences the challenge has largely been the declining representation of Area Studies scholars among full-time faculty, caused by departments failing to hire Area Studies specialists. In the humanities, the challenge has largely been a watering down of the quality of instruction and the erosion of the traditional organization of the humanities around area, caused by declining numbers of majors and the economic pressures pummelling universities.

Why should we be troubled by the decline of Area Studies curriculum offered in social science departments? There are multiple reasons for concern. First, knowledge of contemporary cultures, economics, politics and societies around the world is vital for governments trying to address the myriad challenges that pervade our world. A recent survey of 234 current and former senior US policy-makers found that policy-makers considered Area Studies knowledge — not theoretical social science works, mathematical models, large-n cross-national studies or policy analyses — to be the most important contribution that academic social scientists can bring to policy-making.[10] Indeed, as training of area specialists within the social sciences has declined, the governments of both the United States and the United Kingdom have noted shortages of expertise on critical regions of the world.[11] If courses are not being taught on societies other than one's own within the social science departments, then it will be extremely difficult to train the expertise that governments need to function effectively.

Second, Area Studies is central to the very purposes of a liberal arts education, and the absence of area curriculum in the social sciences means impoverishing the type of liberal arts education that social science students receive. Knowledge about foreign societies and cultures is necessary for the development of a student's critical faculties by challenging culturally based assumptions often taken for granted, illuminating alternative ways of thinking and instilling a healthy understanding of one's place in the world. True knowledge of self can only be obtained through knowledge of others, and participation in a globalized world requires a basic understanding of diverse cultures and an awareness of different perspectives. The decline of Area Studies curriculum in social science departments has meant that many social science students are not receiving exposure to ideas that might challenge taken-for-granted culturally based assumptions. The result is the production of narrow-minded, culturally biased citizens.

Third, the thinning of Area Studies within social science departments is concerning because such practices tend to be reproduced over time through the production and hiring of new doctoral students and scholars at universities. Today in the social sciences, graduate students who do not receive a deep disciplinary training stand little chance of breaking into a disciplinary hierarchy. But who will train tomorrow's professors with area expertise if Area Studies scholars are not represented in the ranks of social science departments? They simply will not be there, magnifying the problem inter-generationally. As a report on the state of Russian Studies in the United States recently concluded, 'The movement within political science away from devoting faculty lines to area specialists in general and Russia specialists in particular threatens to vitiate the ranks of political scientists studying Russia in the medium- to long-term as current generations of political science faculty who work on Russia retire and are not replaced by other Russia specialists.'[12]

Finally, most universities recognize the need for internationalization, but rarely do they recognize the need to nurture leadership for internationalization. Internationalization depends critically on the initiative of faculty, and a significant part of that initiative necessarily comes from Area Studies faculty in the humanities and social sciences. It is primarily Area Studies faculty in the humanities and the social sciences who develop global networks and partnerships, organize study abroad experiences and mentor students interested in contemporary issues in various regions of the world. By eliminating Area Studies social science faculty, a significant portion of university leadership for internationalization is also removed. Moreover, interdisciplinary Area Studies programmes often rely heavily on social science faculty for their leadership, since Literature departments are already organized on an area principle. Such programmes need social science faculty in order to function.

Of course, an alternative to hiring Area Studies scholars in disciplinary departments is to create a separate Area Studies department along the lines of the area-driven model and simply to separate completely the study of world regions from social science theory and methods. Due to continued frustration with the inattention of social science departments to the curricular needs of area programmes in the social sciences and the decline in the numbers of humanities majors, there has been a trend at some universities towards the conversion of language and literature departments into Area Studies departments. But this insular approach tends to produce a faux interdisciplinarity within the context of a single department and leads to the isolation of the study of world regions from social science theory and methodology. Such Area Studies departments tend to be highly factious, with social science faculty hired in these departments cut off from the production of doctoral students competitive on the academic market and from academic discourse within their own disciplines. Such an approach may address the issue of the absence of area curriculum at the university for some students. But it does it in a way that ghettoizes Area Studies still further, reinforcing the very problems it is meant to address.

Any effective effort to strengthen Area Studies social science curriculum must start with the process of hiring faculty within the social science departments, as, left on their own, social science departments will not prioritize the hiring of Area Studies scholars or the provision of Area Studies curriculum; they will follow their own narrow departmental interests and ignore the broader interests of Area Studies altogether. However, knowledge about the contemporary world is too important for producing knowledgeable citizens, for creating expertise in government, for internationalizing universities and for challenging often taken-for-granted assumptions to be left simply to the whims of disciplinary bureaucracies. If there is to be an Area Studies representation within social science departments, university-level intervention is required.

Recently, Princeton has been experimenting with one such intervention: stimulating social science departments to pursue a discipline-driven model of Area Studies as a strategy for revitalizing Area Studies within the social science departments. Essentially, departments that participate in the search process must commit half of a position towards the appointment, while the university, through its interdisciplinary International and Area Studies institute, supplies the other half. After the university administration determines the Area Studies priorities for the search, the social science departments have the opportunity to nominate their own preferred candidates to the International Studies institute on a competitive basis. Any appointment carries the requirement that, at a minimum, the newly hired faculty member annually teach an area-focused undergraduate course in order to provide students with needed Area Studies curriculum. Social science departments normally are averse to any suggestions by Area Studies programmes to hire specific scholars, seeing this as an attempt to impose less-qualified candidates (from the disciplinary point of view) onto them. But when the veto-point is reversed, and departments nominate individuals instead to International and Area Studies programmes on a competitive basis, the social science departments tend to view this as an opportunity rather than a trade-off – indeed, an opportunity at a steeply reduced price. Within its first two years of operation, this discipline-driven model for Area Studies appointments in the social sciences had successfully stimulated four different proposals from three different social science departments to hire outstanding Area Studies scholars, two of whom were selected by the International Studies institute and were hired. Even the Economics department, not known to make Area Studies appointments, expressed interest in the process. The experiment has successfully provided needed Area Studies curriculum where it had previously disappeared. At the same time, it has brought several top-ranked social science scholars to the university. These new hires have been active in developing new area-focused research centres, seminars for students abroad and exchanges with particular regions of the world. In short, what this experiment shows is that fundamentally there is no contradiction between outstanding social science and promoting Area Studies, and that university administrations interested in addressing the issue of the decline of Area Studies curriculum in the social sciences can easily do so if they design the incentives properly and are sufficiently committed.

Conclusion: The virtue of multiple models

There is a need to reflect upon the multiple purposes of Area Studies and of Area Studies institutions and the variety of ways in which area knowledge might transcend the boundaries of knowledge production. Indeed, there is great value in fostering multiple models of Area Studies and multiple types of Area Studies institutions that address specialized purposes.

A discipline-driven model of Area Studies can help facilitate the production of area-knowledgeable doctoral candidates and can aid in addressing the declining representation of Area Studies scholars and area curriculum within social science departments. Area Studies knowledge has something distinctive to contribute to social science in its ability to unpack 'context' and to hold theory and method accountable to reality. The divorce of Area Studies from social science would only impoverish social science, just as the divorce of Area Studies from the social sciences would serve to impoverish Area Studies as well. But the presence of Area Studies scholars in social science departments will not come about automatically; it takes creative ways of stimulating departments to hire area scholars, and it takes committed intervention from university administrations.

The traditional area-driven model of Area Studies as a space for a deepened knowledge of culture and place through multidisciplinary learning is no longer a sufficient basis for the development of Area Studies. But there is still plenty of need for the traditional area-driven model, particularly in training undergraduates and master degree students, and in providing area training for government, business and journalism. The area-driven model is most applicable for pre-professional training. Such programmes prepare students for work on a world region, but realistically only after receiving further professional training or graduate education. It potentially could also find a niche in post-professional education – that is, in imparting area knowledge to mid-career professionals about to embark upon work in a particular region, or in providing disciplinary doctoral students who have already completed their disciplinary training with the necessary language skills and area knowledge to be able to carry out fieldwork in a particular context. We have not yet structured international and Area Studies programmes in ways that might cater to the needs of either of these groups.

Finally, the problem-driven model of Area Studies represents an exciting alternative to the area-driven model as a way of organizing cross-disciplinary exchange that draws in significant part on area expertise. It can provide a venue for broadening perspectives among area scholars, fostering collaborative research and enhancing doctoral student training. But it requires a high level of personal commitment among its participants, and it assumes the robustness of both area-driven and discipline-driven models for it to function effectively. Indeed, all three models of ways that area knowledge might transcend the boundaries of knowledge production are symbiotic and synergetic.

In short, the promotion of confusion between Area Studies and the variety of boundaries by which we organize the production of knowledge is a worthy goal. The more confused we are about the boundaries between Area Studies and other modes of knowledge production, the more thoughtful and knowledgeable we will be about the forces that shape the world in which we live.

Notes

1 Alan Tansman, 'Japanese Studies: The Intangible Act of Translation', in David L. Szanton (ed.), *The Politics of Knowledge: Area Studies and the Disciplines* (Berkeley, CA, 2004), pp. 184–216.

2   While the discipline-driven model of Area Studies has been predominantly a phenomenon of the social sciences, it has had weaker echoes within the humanities as well, particularly as literary theory came to play a larger role within the humanistic sciences. The rise of postmodernist perspectives within the humanities complicated conversation between humanists and social scientists, and the critique of 'Orientalism' (the creation of knowledge for the exercise of geo-political power) and post-colonial theory represented strong attacks on the traditional Area Studies model, though for reasons of political bias rather than epistemology. See Edward W. Said, *Culture and Imperialism* (New York, 1993). In short, the attack on traditional Area Studies was not only a phenomenon of the social sciences.

3   Robert H. Bates, 'Area Studies and Political Science: Rupture and Possible Synthesis', *Africa Today*, 44.2 (1997): 123–131; Robert H. Bates, 'Area Studies and the Discipline: A Useful Controversy?', *PS: Political Science & Politics*, 30.2 (1997): 166–169; Chalmers Johnson, 'Preconception vs. Observation, or the Contributions of Rational Choice Theory and Area Studies to Contemporary Political Science', *PS: Political Science & Politics*, 30.2 (1997): 170–174.

4   Arjun Guneratne, *Area Studies, Regional Worlds: A White Paper for the Ford Foundation* (Chicago, IL, 1997), available at http://works.bepress.com/arjun_guneratne/2/ (accessed 26 February 2018); Wolf Schäfer, 'Reconfiguring Area Studies for the Global Age', in Saïd Amir Arjomand (ed.), *Social Theory and Regional Studies in the Global Age* (Albany, NY, 2014).

5   Economics is exceptional in this regard, though fields such as institutional economics, behavioural economics and development economics have often relied on area knowledge to underpin empirical or theoretical work. The discipline, however, has tended to downplay these relationships.

6   I classify History among the humanities, though, as noted earlier, History has traditionally straddled the humanities and social sciences, with some historians (for example, those interested in global history) being in closer conversation with social scientists and others in closer conversation with humanists. Increasingly, however, History as a discipline has moved closer to the humanities, with fields such as

quantitative historical analysis, social science history, diplomatic history and economic history growing marginalized within the discipline.
7 Laura Adams, 'The State of Area Studies: A Survey of Foreign Language and Area Studies Specialists in Higher Education', Paper presented at the conference on 'The Future of International and Foreign Language Studies: A Research Conference on National Needs and Policy Implications', 11–13 April 2014, Williamsburg, VA, available at http://www.wm.edu/offices/revescenter/globalengagement/internationalization/papers%20and%20presentations/lauraadamsfull.pdf (accessed 26 February 2018).
8 For a copy of the report, see Regional Studies Task Force, 'Revitalizing Regional Studies at Princeton', Princeton University (2016), available at http://www.princeton.edu/strategicplan/files/Task-Force-Report-on-Regional-Studies.pdf (accessed 26 February 2018).
9 History courses formally count as social science courses at Princeton.
10 Paul C. Avey and Michael C. Desch, 'What Do Policymakers Want from Us? Results of a Survey of Current and Former Senior National Security Decision Makers', *International Studies Quarterly*, 58.2 (2014): 227–246.
11 See Jason Horowitz, 'Russia Experts See Thinning Ranks' Effect on U.S. Policy', *The New York Times*, 6 March 2014; James Coomarasamy, 'UK Struggles with Language of Russian Diplomacy', *BBC News*, 16 March 2015; Charles King, 'The Decline of International Studies: Why Flying Blind Is Dangerous', *Foreign Affairs*, 94.4 (2015): 88–98.
12 Theodore P. Gerber, 'Russia-related Research and Graduate Training in the United States', *NewsNet*, 55.4 (2015): 2.

Bibliography

Adams, Laura, 'The State of Area Studies: A Survey of Foreign Language and Area Studies Specialists in Higher Education', Paper presented at the conference on 'The Future of International and Foreign Language Studies: A Research Conference on National Needs and Policy Implications', 11–13 April 2014, Williamsburg, VA. Available at http://www.wm.edu/offices/revescenter/globalengagement/internationalization/papers%20and%20presentations/lauraadamsfull.pdf (accessed 26 February 2018).

Avey, Paul C., and Michael C. Desch, 'What Do Policymakers Want from Us? Results of a Survey of Current and Former Senior National Security Decision Makers', *International Studies Quarterly*, 58.2 (2014): 227–246.

Bates, Robert H., 'Area Studies and Political Science: Rupture and Possible Synthesis', *Africa Today*, 44.2 (1997): 123–131.

Bates, Robert H., 'Area Studies and the Discipline: A Useful Controversy?', *PS: Political Science & Politics*, 30.2 (1997): 166–169.

Coomarasamy, James, 'UK Struggles with Language of Russian Diplomacy', *BBC News*, 16 March 2015.

Gerber, Theodore P., 'Russia-related Research and Graduate Training in the United States', *NewsNet*, 55.4 (2015): 1–3.

Guneratne, Arjun, *Area Studies, Regional Worlds: A White Paper for the Ford Foundation* (Chicago, IL, 1997), available at http://works.bepress.com/arjun_guneratne/2/ (accessed 26 February 2018).

Horowitz, Jason, 'Russia Experts See Thinning Ranks' Effect on U.S. Policy', *The New York Times*, 6 March 2014.

Johnson, Chalmers, 'Preconception vs. Observation, or the Contributions of Rational Choice Theory and Area Studies to Contemporary Political Science', *PS: Political Science & Politics*, 30.2 (1997): 170–174.

King, Charles, 'The Decline of International Studies: Why Flying Blind Is Dangerous', *Foreign Affairs*, 94.4 (2015): 88–98.

Regional Studies Task Force, 'Revitalizing Regional Studies at Princeton', Princeton University (2016), available at http://www.princeton.edu/strategicplan/files/Task-Force-Report-on-Regional-Studies.pdf (accessed 26 February 2018).

Said, Edward W., *Culture and Imperialism* (New York, 1993).

Schäfer, Wolf, 'Reconfiguring Area Studies for the Global Age', in Saïd Amir Arjomand (ed.), *Social Theory and Regional Studies in the Global Age* (Albany, NY, 2014).

Tansman, Alan, 'Japanese Studies: The Intangible Act of Translation', in David L. Szanton (ed.), *The Politics of Knowledge: Area Studies and the Disciplines* (Berkeley, CA, 2004), pp. 184–216.

6

Comparative Area Studies without comparisons: What can Area Studies learn from Comparative Literature?

Zoran Milutinović

For the purposes of writing this chapter, I polled several colleagues and it transpired that, as a PhD student many years ago, I had not been the only one struggling to find the appropriate answer to a question about my profession which would come up in small talk with kind and benevolent strangers:

> Q: What do you do?
> A: I am writing a PhD dissertation.
> Q: What is your PhD in?
> A: Comparative Literature.
> Q: And what do you compare?
> A (with an apologetic smile): Actually, we don't compare anything …
> Q: Oh, is that so? So what do you do?
> A (even more apologetically): Well, we do other stuff, but … it's complicated.

I envied a physicist friend, who was fortunate enough to be able to say, with a lascivious smile on his face, that his dissertation dealt with *friction*, as this would immediately lead the conversation into a less inquisitive and more light-hearted direction (such as 'are there many jokes at the conferences you attend?'). For my part, I gradually learned to reply that my dissertation was on the metatheatrical aspects of plot structures, or on postmodern hermeneutical protocols, or with other similar conversation killers, and to immediately turn the tables by retaliating with 'and what do you do?', hoping that the stranger would come up with an answer simpler than mine. For how to explain that my academic discipline, although having 'comparative' in its name, rarely, if ever, compares anything? That it deals with a huge number of questions, covers enormous ground and deploys a potentially unlimited number of methods, yet it leaves the impression of not being about anything in particular, and of not insisting on doing whatever it may be doing in a specific manner? Moreover, that despite the rapid growth it has experienced in the last hundred years – measured in terms of newly opened academic programmes, newly established journals and book series and the sheer number of new publications which claim to belong to it – Comparative Literature has from the very beginning perceived itself as a discipline in crisis and at regular intervals declared its own death? Being in crisis, at the very edge of extinction, yet perpetually reconstituting its object, reinventing its methods or appropriating those created in other fields of knowledge, and thus surviving, growing, *thriving* – all this seems to be the mode of existence of Comparative Literature. Instead of fortifying its borders and fighting for a terrain over which it would have the exclusive right to rule, Comparative Literature delights in ignoring borders, and in seizing – ever so temporarily – territories ruled by others. Thus it constantly reinvents itself, redefining the answer to the question of what knowledge is worth possessing, and what the best ways of obtaining it are. Admittedly, this is not an answer appropriate for small talk with kind strangers: it may be better to honestly admit that, since you missed the last annual convention of your professional association, you are not quite sure if your discipline is still what it was when you last checked. Your peers may have already packed their bags and set up camp elsewhere.

My thesis is that Area Studies scholars should stop worrying, and learn from Comparative Literature to love their place among other fields of knowledge. Protean forms of academic inquiry are no less respectable than constant and fortified ones. If one's field of inquiry changes each time one asks a different question, and this brings about a new conceptuality, different methods and altered relations to other fields, this is all for the best – provided that the question points in the right direction.

Area Studies and Comparative Literature have occasionally been linked to one another in the past. Gayatri C. Spivak, for example, in her book *Death of the Discipline* – as the title indicates, one of those periodic post mortems for Comparative Literature, which conclude that the discipline has ceased to exist on the grounds that it does not look like it used to be a decade previously – defends the claim that Area Studies and Comparative Literature can and should work together.[1] In the context of reinventing her own discipline, Spivak calls for closer links between the humanities and social sciences in general, and for Comparative Literature and Area Studies in particular. Comparative Literature, she maintains, can supplement Area Studies, mitigate 'the arrogance of Area Studies where it retains the imprints of the Cold War'[2] and offer as its dowry what was 'the best of the old Comparative Literature: the skill of reading closely in the original'.[3] What is more, 'Comparative Literature supplemented by area studies' can transcend its traditional textual focus and begin to speak to us about questions and issues that concern us not only as readers of literature, but as human beings with varying ethnic, cultural, national, political and gender identities.[4] Thus, ironically, two academic fields, one of them constantly concerned with its own survival, and the other admittedly made redundant by the forces of globalization and by the end of the Cold War, could revitalize each other and perhaps forge an amalgam which would put forth what is the best in each. The purpose of this amalgam of Comparative Literature and Area Studies would be – to resort to a somewhat old-fashioned expression and to avoid reducing the problem only to the fiscal aspects of academic policies – to know the world outside its Western, Euro-American core.

At the time that Spivak voiced her call for mutual fertilization between Comparative Literature and Area Studies, much of what she proposed had already been taking place, and it seems safe to claim that one part of her proposition has been accepted. In its earliest periods, Comparative Literature had only European literatures as its normative horizon. It was created by scholars who would, in addition to their own, typically know three major European languages, which would bring their claims to a level of generality unattainable by those who studied only one national literature – again, typically their own. The tacit assumption was that only three or four similar and interconnected literary traditions could stand for literature as such. This hardly covered all European languages – there are more than forty of them – let alone global literary production in languages spoken and written in all other continents; yet, the sample languages were always only European. 'At the disciplinary core of Comparative Literature has always been the idea of Europe', maintains Mitsuhiro Yoshimoto; 'I would even venture to argue that Comparative Literature is less a discipline of literature than a type of Area Studies, a counterpart to East Asian Studies, Middle Eastern Studies, Latin American Studies, etc.'[5]

Area Studies, by contrast, although retaining the same tacit European normative horizon, were always the study of the non-Western (non-European and North American) world. Academic programmes in European Studies, together with the accompanying academic infrastructure, came into being only recently, and when they did it was specifically as a study of the political, economic and legal aspects of the European Union, and not as an academic equivalent of East Asian or Middle Eastern Studies. Thus, Spivak's proposal could aim at the way Area Studies and Comparative Literature can supplement or complement one another: Comparative Literature would add the missing area to the catalogue of existing Area Studies, and thus not only fill the cartographic gap but also supply its own specific disciplinary insights (to which we will have to return later).

However, the Eurocentric normative dimension of Comparative Literature was hardly as indisputable at the beginning of the twenty-first century as it had been during preceding decades. Since the 1980s, the rise of post-colonial studies has been one of the two most important academic developments – the other being gender studies – which transformed the profile of all of the humanities and a significant section of the social sciences. Although post-colonial studies is a research field and not a discipline, its earliest disciplinary base, its very place of origin, was Comparative Literature, and this is where the pressure exercised by the ideas, concepts and aims of post-colonial studies has been felt most. The leading promoters of post-colonial studies – including Spivak herself – spearheaded the transformation of Comparative Literature so successfully that at the present time it is difficult to say where the former ends and the latter begins. A large part of work carried out in Comparative Literature today can be easily categorized as belonging to post-colonial studies; the part that cannot is certainly made to feel uneasy for ignoring this development. Post-colonial concepts and ideas by their very existence compel even those who would prefer to continue their work as if nothing had happened in Comparative Literature since the 1980s to refrain, at the very least, from assumptions and conclusions characteristic of the older periods in our discipline's history. The (West) European normative horizon is either gone altogether, or made to appear insufficient, anachronistic or plain wrong. This is certainly a major achievement for a discipline which from the very beginning claimed to address the totality of human literary production; the price it had to pay for this success was a certain loss of a recognizable disciplinary profile. This loss – as all losses always are – is experienced as a crisis.

The old, traditional Area Studies were also affected by the development of the post-colonial studies agenda. While Comparative Literature had the advantage of being able to recognize it as one of its earliest aims, and to shake off the burden of the European normative horizon as a temporary, undesired and unavoidable phase – now overcome by the results of globalization, such as the migration of scholars, the smoother flow and availability of information and closer links between distant parts of the world – Area Studies had nothing similar to rely on. The loss of normativity seemed detrimental to it: for example, for several decades the notion of modernization served as the conceptual axis around which practitioners of Area Studies organized their research. Modernization was understood as Westernization, which reduced everything deemed non-modern and non-Western to objects 'defined and grasped only in terms of [their] relationship to the West', as Timothy Mitchell put it.[6] The West was posed, claims Mitchell, as 'a model that cannot be replicated faithfully' (p. 164), and historical itineraries, political forces and cultural phenomena were included in the paradigmatic area studies narrative only in order to measure an area's suitability to, or divergence from, the narrative of Western modernity.[7] Thus, all other parts of the world were 'made to appear as particular instances of the universal stories told in and about the West', concludes Mitchell.[8] When this normative horizon began to crumble under the pressure coming from various directions, including the post-colonial studies agenda, the core narrative was lost: instead of as a Western export, modernity is nowadays better understood if seen as a continual constitution and reconstitution of a multiplicity of cultural programmes, as Eisenstadt proposed;[9] mistaking modernization for Westernization means assuming a priority of origin over process, of geography over history, Lewis and Wigen claimed:[10] the Western understanding of Western modernity is based on a particular historical and intellectual tradition that cannot claim universal validity, and the same (universal) idea can take different shapes in different places and historical contexts, as Chakrabarty maintained.[11] With the loss of the conceptual axis, the normative horizon enshrined in it was gone as well, and what was left tended to become fragmented into millions of pieces impossible to put together: without a paradigmatic story and the normative horizon to guarantee it, what exactly should we look for when examining areas?

Thus, Comparative Literature would not only supply the missing – European or Western – area and fill in the gap on the map, but would also bring a salutary, non-normative approach. There are many reasons to believe that this is easier said than done. Much work on dismantling this normative horizon has already been done in other disciplines that contribute to the Area Studies project, as the quotes from the previous paragraph testify: my sources were two historians, two geographers and a political scientist, and a list of similar quotes could be extended if the prescribed length of this chapter allowed it. Other disciplines do not need Comparative Literature to tell them that the old normative horizon only distorts the picture, as they can find evidence for this in their own libraries. Losing this horizon is an imperative if Area Studies are to continue their existence; yet, its disappearance is experienced as a crisis.

Comparative Literature could also contribute – as one of the disciplines that jointly carries out Area Studies research – its own disciplinary insight into the areas. Here, however, Comparative Literature stands for literary studies in general, as national literary studies cannot be excluded as unnecessary here. Spivak puts this question very precisely: 'How can I, as a reader of literature, supplement the social sciences?' – that is, as a literature specialist, but not necessarily as a Comparative Literature scholar.[12] This is a difficult question to answer, not least because the tradition of thinking about literature offers contradictory views, and because other disciplines have their own take on the benefits of knowing something about the literature written in an area. The easiest answer is the least satisfactory: areas 'have' their cultures – of which literature is not just a part, but the very centre – just as they have rivers and mountains, religions, histories and institutions; knowledge of an area cannot be complete without knowing what people have thought, written and read. At times, the usefulness of literature is somewhat more emphasized: Friedrich Engels claimed that he learned a lot about capitalism by reading Balzac's novels, and in our time Thomas Piketty praises both Balzac and Jane Austen for their insights into economic processes. Historical novels sometimes offer popular interpretations of a nation's history, but no historian would base their research on them; historical novels are more significant for studying popular interpretations of history, which tend to guide people in their choices, decisions and allegiances more than academic historiography ever will. The core of the problem, however, is that *literary works of art* rarely, if ever, reflect the reality of historical, political or economic processes: even if they claim to do so, they are always works of fiction and the imagination, which are not bound by any laws of accurate representation. Moreover, only a small fraction of literature even pretends to do so. Poetry certainly does not, plays only occasionally and indirectly, and novels and stories more often, but by no means always. And to make things even more complicated, literature requires interpretation, and this depends on our possessing at least some basic disciplinary knowledge: a line spoken by a character in a play does not have the same meaning and significance as the same sentence found in a political programme, but relies on often very complex literary semantics, and can mean the exact opposite of what it means elsewhere. But the most problematic way of including the study of literature in the Area Studies agenda is the tendency of treating literature as *national allegory*. The creator of this label was Fredric Jameson, who claimed that all texts written in the third world 'are necessarily ... allegorical, and in a very specific way they are to be read as ... national allegories'.[13] The first world has undergone the radical split between the poetic and the political, or the private and the public, claimed Jameson, and its literature has become the preserve of the former. 'Third-world texts, even those which are seemingly private and invested with a properly libidinal dynamic – necessarily project a political dimension in the form of national allegory: *the story of the private individual destiny is always an allegory of the embattled situation of the public third-world culture and society*.'[14] In his criticism of this thesis, Aijaz Ahmad, Indian literary theorist and poet, wrote the following: 'I was born in India and I write poetry in Urdu, a language not commonly understood among US intellectuals. So I said to myself: "*All? ... necessarily?*" It felt odd.'[15] Western literature is 'all' and 'necessarily' about the poetic and private, while the rest – also 'all' and 'necessarily' – always write only about the public and political, about their embattled nations, regardless of what the actual text may be about. No love poetry for the third world, then. However, Jameson is certainly right in one respect: this really is how non-Western literature is very often read and interpreted in the context of Area Studies, and sometimes even in other academic contexts in Western academia, and if a particular poem, play or novel cannot be easily interpreted as a national allegory, it is deemed to be of no interest for Area Studies whatsoever. The results of such interpretations are, quite understandably, of little value: if one approaches *all* third-world texts with the assumption that they are *necessarily* about embattled nations, one will find in them only what one has put there oneself. Third-world texts will be able only to reflect back to us our own assumptions and projections, and what they may really be saying about people's lives, experiences, histories, hopes and dreams will remain unknown.

Yet, literary theory offered several different and even conflicting answers to the question 'what do we learn from literature about reality and history?' The debate on representation, or reference or *mimesis*, has from the very beginning been one of the central topics in literary theory. Plato's *Republic* and Aristotle's *Poetics*, literary theory's founding texts, initiated the long discussion about the relationship between literature on the one hand, and history and reality on the other. Closer to our own time, and in a century that witnessed a proliferation of different theoretical approaches to literature, two major directions crystallized: the conventionalists or formalists, who claimed that any reference to reality is only an illusion, a result of *semiosis* or a product of literary conventions; if novels and stories ever refer to anything, it is not to reality, but to other novels and stories. The opposite camp, the contextualists of various persuasions, believe that every text has its own context, which may be purely literary, as the conventionalists insist, but may also be extra-literary: historical, social, cultural and political. This context can be the dominant ideology of a specific time and space – as various Marxist schools of thought claimed, disagreeing about the content of this concept all along;[16] or structures of feeling, a concept created by Raymond Williams in order to refer to a set of perceptions, values and norms characteristic of a group of people in a specific historical period, and best materialized in art forms;[17] or the poetics of culture, as New Historicism maintains, understood as a network of various discourses that circulate in a society and become sedimented in literary texts.[18]

Aside from both camps, one branch of phenomenology assigns literature a role much more important than just 'reflecting', 'recording' or 'allegorizing': it maintains that, whatever else stories may achieve, they also create a meaningful society and make possible an ethical sharing of the common world, as opposed to the merely common physical environment. Telling a story is a communicative act through which a society establishes what it means to be human, to be a saint or a hero, honourable or happy, or to live with others, and this act constructs tacit, background understandings, which to all members of a society seem natural and universal.[19] Or, to put it differently: individuals become members of a particular society if they share the same tacit background understandings. These are preserved in, and communicated by, society's stories, which point to them, or present them to us, usually without precise and explicit definitions. Inspired by Heidegger's reinterpretation of the notion of the world – not the totality of entities, but the web of meanings that construct our self-understanding and the understanding of everything else around us – phenomenology sees cultures as the totality of significance that we share with one another: 'the world is always the one that I share with Others', as one of Heidegger's most memorable theses goes.[20] Cultures prescribe normative patterns of interpretation and conduct through their languages: different worlds can be intersubjectively shared only if they are articulated in languages, which bear and transmit tacit pre-understandings of something or other. We share a meaningful world because it has already been previously linguistically articulated: we get to know it not through innocent and fresh perception, but through becoming accustomed to the ways everything in the world has been previously understood and interpreted. Language records and stores these pre-understandings in its most developed forms, in speech genres such as paradigmatic story, habitual everyday expression and proverb, and literary genres such as myth, epic, history, folktale, romance, confession, prayer, chronicle, essay, novel, poem, play, newspaper article and so on. These genres not only offer an unrivalled opportunity to examine the worlds – webs of meanings – sedimented in languages, but also make it possible to see how these worlds come into being through contradictions, paradoxes, ambiguities and uncertainties, and develop through processes of narration and symbolization in such a manner that the level of conceptualization is rarely achieved, and yet a specific world still emerges. Understanding a particular world – a historical one, such as the medieval world, or a synchronic one, such as the Chinese world – is only possible if one is familiar with the background understandings this world's language creates, stores and communicates to its speakers, and thus binds them in a society. They become members of the same collectivity if they share these meanings, and strangers and foreigners if they do not. Hence, the language genres we are accustomed to calling 'literature' are not studied in the context of area studies only because areas have literatures as they have rivers and mountains – rivers and mountains become a particular area, distinguishable from another, when alongside them a specific tradition of storytelling takes root. *Traditio*, or handing down, passing on to a new generation a set of intersubjectively shared webs of meaning, created in and by the language genres listed above, is what can also be seen as a definition of an area.

The study of literature is the study of these speech and literary genres. It is *not only* about intersubjective articulation of a world through language, as it approaches these language genres from many different perspectives, but it does also include that. There is no other humanities discipline which has developed such sophisticated tools for the close reading of cultural texts, spoken or written, in the original language, as the study of literature. It is the most natural, necessary and unavoidable basis of Area Studies, and it is quite understandable that the first Area Studies academic programmes developed in the early twentieth century from *language and literature* academic programmes, as they still do evolve in this direction in our time. If the question is 'how can the study of literature complement Area Studies?', the simple answer is – by doing what it has been doing so far, through close readings of cultural texts in the original language, and uncovering the pre-understandings of the world into which all members of a culture are initiated, and through this initiation taught to share a world and be bound together into a society.

However, this is not all. This justifies the place the study of literature has among other humanities and social sciences in the Area Studies project, but hardly convinces Area Studies scholars that they should stop worrying and learn from Comparative Literature to love their place among other fields of knowledge.

One of the negative starting points in this process of convincing should be the rejection of what I will tentatively name the *quest for essences*. Area Studies are reproached for failing to fully integrate various academic disciplines around a common thread. Such an integration, we are told, would result in the production of a full, complete, total presentation of an area. The assumption behind this reproach is that everything in a given area fits seamlessly together with everything else: the object under study is animated by a perfect coherence and integration, which Area Studies fail to translate into a logically coherent and integrated representation. At the core of this coherence and integration is an assumed, but not yet brought to daylight, essence of the area under study, which radiates into various aspects of reality and which must be present and detectable in them. Our academic disciplines deal with these various aspects, but they continue to analyse and explain them more or less independently of one another. As a result, instead of the essence of the Middle East, of this specific 'middleeasterness' which makes this area different from, say, Southeast Asia and 'southeastasianess' hidden deep beneath the phenomenal surface, we are only given a set of perhaps true, accurate, well-founded and evidenced insights, which still fail to describe the essence. Logic, coherence and integration must be proper to reality, it is assumed. If our account of an area consists of various elements that do not coherently fit together – though they do not necessarily contradict each other, as they may not fit simply because various disciplines approach it with interests in various processes, temporalities and elements belonging to different orders – and does not point to the essence proper to it, we have already failed to give a true account of it. For, as Hegel put it, the true is the whole.[21] The whole is guaranteed by an essence.

There is nothing anyone can raise against interdisciplinarity, save that interdisciplinarity is a very difficult thing to do. What goes under this label in many academic journals and publishers' lists is more often than not an application of the concepts, methods and interpretative protocols of one discipline in the 'section of reality' normally entrusted to another discipline. Sometimes it brings forward unexpected and valuable insights; sometimes it misses the point altogether, as we all know all too well. This is not a reason to stop trying, but neither is the challenge of being interdisciplinary effectively a good reason to look down upon the second-best and less glamorous multidisciplinary endeavours. The latter can be unsynchronized, out of step and incoherent, as they do not assume that logic, coherence and integration are proper to reality. Universal suffrage, liberal democracy, high modernism in arts and sophisticated intellectual culture, on the one hand, and appalling levels of illiteracy and infant mortality, underdeveloped agrarian economy and minimal capital accumulation, on the other, are not supposed to be the emanation of the same essence, yet they sometimes come together. The account which points to this would have to be based on contingencies, different temporalities, discontinuities, contradictions, breaks and reversals; if nothing fits in with anything else, and the object under study does not seem to be animated by a perfect coherence and integration, but rather is incapable of being translated into a logically coherent and integrated representation, it might be better to stay closer to what one sees and can truthfully describe than to continue the quest for essences and reproach the method for insufficient interdisciplinary integration. Perhaps there are no essences, just contingent and contradictory processes: the whole is the false, as Adorno put it.[22]

Closely related to the quest for essences is the *obsession with purity*. It comes in various guises: firstly as a variant of the quest for (areal) essences, which by definition must be pure and uncontaminated by features belonging to others; secondly, as a methodological and disciplinary purity, which demands that every sphere of academic enquiry should have its own clearly demarcated domain and a method appropriate to it, and deems everything else a breach of disciplinary protocol and a methodological eclecticism, which *ipso facto* bears only invalid results. However, even before the twentieth-century globalizing cultural, political and economic processes irreversibly destroyed any uncontaminated areal purities – if they ever existed as such – the reality of inter-areal relations was *creolization* rather than a jealous guarding of some putative areal purity. This does not mean that globalization and the processes that preceded it obliterated all areal distinctions and specificities: globalization, as many other historical processes, produces contradictory results, dismantling some borders while simultaneously creating new ones, homogenizing and differentiating, integrating and disintegrating at the same time. Area specificities are preserved in the unpredictable results of creolization, which are never simple sums or regular syntheses of all elements involved, but incalculable and contingent hybrids brought about by unending permeation and, as a reaction which it provokes, attempts at purification. But a lot more important is the question of disciplinary and methodological purity, often raised in discussions about Area Studies. This kind of purity is the legacy of late nineteenth- and early twentieth-century academic divisions, of the heroic period of the social sciences' and humanities' attempts to establish themselves as clearly distinct entities, and to divide human reality into domains appropriate to each of them. This process was far more complex than today's common departmental conflicts over resources and 'land grabbing', and to a certain extent the opposite of it, as it concerned each discipline's self-understanding and the search for their appropriate and unique methods: the point was not to appropriate what may have been the domain of other disciplines, but to exclude any reference to what might be others' territory, and to focus on one's own specific and unique interest and method. Literary studies, for example, strove to disregard everything that could have been deemed 'external' to literature, such as the social relations represented in a novel, as these belonged to Sociology, or ideas advocated, as these were the domain of Philosophy, or discussions regarding characters' emotions and motivations, as this was what Psychology dealt with, or the historical circumstances of the period represented, and of the time authors lived in, as these were better understood by History. What remained was the pure essence of literature, *literariness* in the terminology of Russian Formalists, or rhetoric in Anglo-American New Criticism, or structures of signification in various versions of structuralism. One of the main promoters of the term *literariness*, Roman Jakobson, famously claimed that traditional literary studies – the late nineteenth-century positivistic, historical, social or 'philosophical' criticism – behaved as policemen who came to the crime scene and, instead of arresting the criminal, arrested everything and everyone present.[23] Consequently, only a method that gave an account of *literariness*, rhetoric or structures of signification could be relied upon to preserve the purity of the object under study. Although Marxism and psychoanalysis, however marginal and suspect they may have been in literary studies, offered an alternative to methodological purity, a good two-thirds of the twentieth century witnessed ever more sophisticated efforts to devise a pure approach – to something, such as literature, that can hardly be isolated and purified from other human interests, such as history, politics, ideas and psychology. The last third of the century, however, brought about a plethora of *impure* methods, often borrowed from other humanities and social science disciplines, or sometimes resulting from the modifications and adaptations these methods acquired during their long trajectories through various disciplines: for example, New Historicism, developed in the 1980s, hybridized Foucault's discourse theory developed on the ruins of structuralism's purity, with the social interests of the *Annales* School in historiography, and Clifford Geertz's 'thick description' method, itself an adaptation of New Criticism's practice of a *close reading* of literary texts to phenomena studied by Cultural Anthropology. How very impure – created to be able to simultaneously address texts, language, culture and history, this method would certainly fail the test of 'what is your unique object and your method appropriate to it', to which Area Studies are sometimes subjected.

The moral of this story is not only that the disciplinary focus on essences and purity should be abandoned, as most disciplines engaged in Area Studies loudly advertise their anti-essentialism and openness to methods and theories developed in other disciplines – up until the point that the discussion turns to Area Studies, when the usual reproach regarding the lack of a clearly defined object and an appropriate method makes itself heard again. The point is rather to recognize how Comparative Literature successfully dealt with similar objections. In what follows, I will point out some similarities and certain differences between Comparative Literature and Area Studies, and put forward the thesis that the object of Area Studies is not readily available, but constructed in the process of research, and is dependent on it – that Area Studies should assume a metaphorical rather than metonymical modus operandi, and that its methodological uncertainties are not a shameful insufficiency, but a source of strength.

To a certain extent, Comparative Literature can also be viewed as a field composed of disciplines, which are various national literatures.[24] This is an imperfect analogy, as national literatures, although dividing human reality into distinct entities – such as French or German literature – still share the effort of defining the exact object of their common interest, borrow theoretical concepts and approaches from each other and labour towards the same aim: understanding the anthropological constant of human groups producing oral and written texts considered to be literary, and distinct from non-literary language use. But the analogy is instructive in the sense that Comparative Literature is in the same position regarding its component 'disciplines' as Area Studies are regarding their components: what is it that Comparative Literature can give us, that is not already given by the sum total of its disciplines? Instead of collecting, rearranging and ordering the knowledge already present in national literatures, after several decades of trying to define its specific and unique object – among which at some point featured connections and influences between national literatures, migrations of motives, plots and so on – Comparative Literature became a testing ground for methodological and theoretical innovation, to the extent that all theoretical work became routinely classified as its natural 'subject'. This was not entirely accurate, as much theoretical discussion was still carried out within the scope of individual national literatures, but the fact that whatever was produced under the label 'theory' became instantly recognized as 'comparative' points to the fact that there was a free, unoccupied space between and above national literatures, which Comparative Literature was to fill progressively. The nature of this theoretical production was interdisciplinary by its very nature: beginning in the 1950s and 1960s, linguistic structuralism was appropriated by literary studies and transformed into a universal interpretative method suitable for all the humanities and some social sciences as well, thus reversing the process of disciplinary purification and confirming the claim that approximately every fifty years the humanities and social sciences agree on the need for having one universal method (the rise of structuralism occurred half a century after the demise of positivism, which at the beginning of the twentieth century played this role). In the 1970s and 1980s, Derrida's and Foucault's post-structuralism became almost hegemonic humanities and social science methods, reaching as far as legal studies and archaeology, and at the turn of the century the study of identities pioneered in Comparative Literature – gender, sexuality, race, meta-geography and so on – permeated almost all corners of academic inquiry. True, the impulses always came from somewhere else, be it a Swiss linguist whom linguistics quickly abandoned, or from the two French philosophers not taken seriously by Philosophy departments, but Comparative Literature still served as a laboratory and testing ground where various theoretical impulses were developed into fully-fledged theories with far-reaching implications, impossible for other academic disciplines to ignore. Comparative Literature became the theoretical laboratory for the humanities and social sciences thanks to, firstly, literature's ability to absorb and represent our shared experience of being human in all its varieties and dimensions, and secondly, by what Gadamer refers to as the *linguisticality* of this experience, the key meta-topic of the most important currents in twentieth-century philosophy, which made literature, the language art, a suitable domain for intellectual innovation, and which recognized language as the basis for theorizing.[25] With each and every theoretical turn, the object of Comparative Literature changed: there was not *an* object, natural, finished and hidden, waiting to be subjected to our investigation as soon as we devised the appropriate method to approach it. Rather, the object(s) came into being as the result of *questions asked*, that is, methods and theories that animated those methods. Thus, Comparative Literature became not the sum of knowledge stored in national literatures, nor a space in which their specific achievements could be interconnected and compared, but a generator of questions which, it turned out, concerned them all, and demanded to be addressed, but could not initially be asked in any one of them. National literatures are limited by what is their primary and natural object: the canon of works to be read, commented upon, analysed, and thus preserved and transmitted within a larger whole, which is the life of a nation. They can, and have been able to, pay their tribute to the open set of questions regarding literary interest as such, which is generated by Comparative Literature – if prompted from the outside – but they do not usually generate such questions themselves. These questions, such as my example of exploring tacit, background understandings hidden in languages and literary genres that serve as language repositories, are normally beyond their focus: if a national literature specialist begins to ask the question of different background understandings, it means that she has already stepped out of her domain and has become a comparatist.

Area Studies should assume a similar position with regard to their component disciplines. They should not try to be a sum total of all disciplinary knowledge about an area – which is a fine thing, normally called 'an encyclopaedia of …', but not a very dynamic field of academic inquiry – or even imagine themselves as the mortar connecting disciplinary bricks into a larger whole. Area Studies should generate questions that no single discipline concerned with an area can ask, focused as they are on objects established by tradition and verified by practice. These questions can arise only if Area Studies are to change their understanding of interdisciplinarity, which is at present limited to asking a question arising from the framework and interests of one discipline, and requiring all other disciplines to provide their contributions to fleshing out the answer. To be able to do this, Area Studies must abandon the quest for their proper object, which can only lead back to the search for essences of areas, or expose Area Studies as inferior to the disciplines which do not have such concerns. The proper object(s) of Area Studies will appear, or keep appearing in different shapes and forms, as a result, not as a starting point: the object(s) will be brought about by various methods with which we approach an area, or various contexts in which we place it/them, and various questions we ask about it/them. The object of Area Studies will be revealed as knowledges that we could not have acquired by approaching an area from the perspectives of the disciplines studying it. Not being a discipline, Area Studies have the right to enjoy their protean nature, to delight in the impurity of their methods and results and to reject the demand to offer their knowledge as *a whole*: a whole in this context can only be imagined as 'an encyclopaedia of', neatly fitting and covering everything, guided by a pure method and letting an essence shine through – an impossible demand, which has been generating all the complaints about Area Studies' unfulfilled promises.

In this respect, the insights offered by Area Studies should be metaphorical rather than metonymical. Disciplines offer metonymical knowledge: a history of the Middle East tells us a part of what could and should be known about an area. It is assumed that there is a lot more to be known about the Middle East, but the discipline of History gives us only *pars pro toto*. The promise of Area Studies, we are told, was that they would be able to devise a method with which to put all these parts together and offer us a total, integrated knowledge of an area. Yet, all Area Studies seem to have been able to do is offer us several parts, all originating in various disciplines and sitting uncomfortably – in a non-integrated fashion – next to each other. The synthesis is missing; the specific object of Area Studies – as opposed to the specific objects of the disciplines involved in the project, which are not questionable – never appeared, not to speak of a distinct Area Studies method.

A metaphorical model of knowledge, on the contrary, would abandon all pretence that a total, integrated knowledge is possible: even disciplines can claim to be offering their knowledges as total and integrated entities only if compared with even less totalizing ventures, such as Area Studies. Examined individually, all disciplinary knowledge tends to be far from a whole – neatly fitted and all-encompassing – however pure the method and integrated the results: there is no Middle Eastern history book which professes to cover everything that could be imagined as Middle Eastern history; the 'part' all of them offer is only a part of the part. While a metonym, taken in this sense, rests on an assumed (spatial) overlap between a part and the whole, and on at least partial identification, a metaphor does not: it is based on dissimilarity between entities, which often belong to different orders (*love*, an emotion, and *rose*, a physical object). However, this dissimilarity reveals an unexpected, fresh and new connection between two things: by transferring, or carrying over – *metapherein* in Greek – a thing from one order to another, in which we choose to find its equivalent, a metaphor puts it into a new context in which its new dimension, feature or characteristic is revealed. And it is always only one dimension, feature or characteristic, never a presumed totality: what metonymy achieves by *extension*, pretending to cover the thing totally, metaphor substitutes with *intensity* of insight. Metaphorical insights are temporary, as metaphors wear off, and also partial, but in a different way: while metonymic knowledges are always revealed as insufficient horizontally (spatiality and extension), metaphorical knowledge does not promise any horizontal coverage, for it works vertically. Also, such a model of inquiry should never promise any kind of total comprehension: a succession of metaphoric insights never crystallizes into anything resembling total knowledge.

Is it, then, still a model of knowledge worth striving for?

I am fully aware that offering an example for such a model of inquiry can only deflate the description I proposed above; one would prefer to keep it as general as possible, leaving the reader to think of examples closest to its requirements, or even to imagine fictional ones. However, an example, however imperfect, cannot be denied here; although while writing this description I did not have in mind Edward W. Said's *Orientalism*, it can serve as an illustration as good as any, having the advantage of being widely known and exemplifying many – although by no means all – characteristics one would want to see in productive and successful Area Studies' *metaphorical* works. We do not need to engage in recasting the debate about the shortcomings of *Orientalism* here; both Said's empirical errors and theoretical inconsistencies have been discussed at length.[26] For my purposes, however, neither empirical errors nor theoretical shortcomings devalue its main achievement. This book, despite its limitations, pointed to the several important practices of Area Studies: it demonstrated how we construct an area, how interests limit or distort cognition and interpretation of it, and how *impure* supposedly pure disciplinary knowledge can be. In the process, Said successfully cleared away the debris that blocked the way to the question: what is the Middle East as an area? He did not offer an answer, let alone a total knowledge of the area or of its essence; his rhetorical and theoretical exaggerations – especially the claim that Middle East specialists *misrepresent* the area – often screen off what is truly valuable in this book: it shows that for Middle Eastern Studies, there is not an object, natural, finished and hidden, but that their object appears as the result of questions asked. 'How should we rule them?' is one of these questions, which made the object appear in the specific form for the authors Said is interested in. Said achieved this by thinking metaphorically: he equated the Middle East, a geographic and historical area, with phenomena of a different order, such as sexuality and madness, as presented by Foucault. 'The Middle East is like sexuality', the simile goes; it is not a naturally given, but a discursively constructed object. He thus revealed the similarities in dissimilar phenomena: his object, or the object of Area Studies in *Orientalism*, is not the Middle East, but the ways of constructing it, and his method does not belong to any of Area Studies' component disciplines, but to Foucault's interdisciplinary genealogical perspectivism, created at the intersection of Philosophy, History, Sociology and Linguistics. This he achieved not by following a prescribed disciplinary or even Area Studies protocol, which define the object and the method, but by asking a simple question: why do people in power, or close to it, in Western societies say such things about the Middle East? Both the object of his investigation, and the method he used, followed from it. If *Orientalism* belongs to the corpus of Area Studies, and I hope everyone agrees that it does, then Area Studies were ever so temporarily redefined, moved and recreated by this book. Their object was reconstituted, and their method reinvented: Area Studies reinvented themselves, redefined the answer to the question of which knowledge is worth possessing and what the best ways of obtaining it are. Despite its many shortcomings, *Orientalism* is a landmark book. It is difficult to imagine anyone working in Area Studies in our time approaching an area without Said peering over their shoulder. It was followed by a number of works that specified, modified, furthered and improved Said's object and method, until they – as pretty much everything else in our academic environment – became a petrified set of claims beyond dispute, a dogma our undergraduates learn early on and never bother to question. All metaphors wear off eventually. Nevertheless, it permanently changed the profile of Area Studies by showing what unorthodox things can be done with it.

Orientalism is written from a non-disciplinary perspective, and it may be more than just a coincidence that its author's disciplinary background was Comparative Literature. He was not a Middle East expert, which to an extent explains the number of empirical errors he made, and he had a strong emotional and political investment in the matter, which perhaps accounts for the theoretical inconsistencies that would otherwise have been obvious to such a superior theoretical mind as his was, had he been able to approach his subject without such investment. However, another kind of investment was more important here: Said's, and Comparative Literature's in general, investment in theory. For many years, before setting out to write *Orientalism*, Said worked on introducing European literary and cultural theory to Anglo-American audiences, and was one of Foucault's principal American promoters.[27] My point is not that Area Studies should look up to Comparative Literature for its theoretical inspiration – although the latter has offered its services to anyone who cared to listen – but that Area Studies could assume the same position with regard to academic disciplines contributing to the Area Studies project: to become not a sum total of areal knowledges, but a meta-discipline that inspires disciplinary efforts, a field of theoretical innovation and experimentation in which questions are asked, conceptual vocabularies proposed and new perspectives tested. This would also mean not only that Area Studies must accept being in a state of permanent crisis – metaphors, as we know, wear off quickly and new ones must be proposed all the time – but that Area Studies should strive to permanently subvert themselves, to undermine whatever threatens to become an orthodoxy in terms of Kuhn's normal science. Not having a method, always looking for its proper object and being in a perpetual state of methodological uncertainty in this context should be understood not as a shameful insufficiency, but as a source of strength and the main prerequisite of Area Studies' existence. This kind of uncertainty is what has made Comparative Literature survive, grow and thrive, reinvent itself and reconstitute its object(s). It could do the same for Area Studies. The best hope for Area Studies is that one day this will become a shorter name for the Theory of Area Studies. Their triumph will be announced the moment young Area Studies PhD students begin to find it difficult to give a simple answer to the question 'what is your PhD in', and decide to say briefly – 'it's complicated'.

Notes

1. Gayatri Chakravorty Spivak, *Death of a Discipline* (New York, 2003).
2. Ibid., p. 70.
3. Ibid., p. 6.
4. Ibid., p. 72.
5. Mitsuhiro Yoshimoto, 'Questions of Japanese Cinema: Disciplinary Boundaries and the Invention of the Scholarly Object', in M. Miyoshi and H. D. Harootuinian (eds), *Learning Places. The Afterlives of Area Studies* (Durham and London, 2002), Kindle edition, location 8561.
6. Timothy Mitchell, 'Deterritorialization and the Crisis of Social Science', in A. Mirsepassi, A. Basu and F. Weaver (eds), *Localizing Knowledge in a Globalizing World. Recasting the Area Studies Debate* (Syracuse, NY, 2003), p. 163.

7 Ibid., p. 164.
8 Ibid., p. 167.
9 S. N. Eisenstadt, 'Multiple Modernities', *Daedalus*, 129.1 (2000): 1–29.
10 Martin W. Lewis and Kären E. Wigen, *The Myth of Continents. A Critique of Metageography* (Berkeley, 1997), p. 101.
11 Dipesh Chakrabarty, *Provincializing Europe. Postcolonial Thought and Historical Difference* (Princeton, 2007).
12 Spivak, *Death of a Discipline*, p. 37.
13 Fredric Jameson, 'Third-World Literature in the Era of Multinational Capitalism', *Social Text*, 15 (1986): 69.
14 Ibid., p. 69 (italics in the original).
15 Aijaz Ahmed, *In Theory. Classes, Nations, Literatures* (London and New York, 1992), p. 96. See also Michael Sprinker, 'The National Question: Said, Ahmad, Jameson', *Public Culture*, 6 (1993): 3–29.
16 David Hawkes's *Ideology* (London, 1996) and Michèle Barrett's *The Politics of Truth. From Marx to Foucault* (London, 1992), in addition to Terry Eagleton's popular *Ideology. An Introduction* (London, 1991), offer good overviews of both the concept itself and its use in literary studies.
17 Raymond Williams, *The Long Revolution* (London, 1971), p. 64.
18 Although New Historicism avoided producing explicit and systematic theoretical accounts, Catherine Gallagher's and Stephen Greenblatt's *Practicing New Historicism* (Chicago and London, 2000) offers the closest equivalent to a manifesto of New Historicism.
19 Charles Taylor develops phenomenology's – Heidegger's and Gadamer's – position on background understandings and conceptual schemes in 'Understanding the Other: A Gadamerian View on Conceptual Schemes', in J. Malpas, U. Arnswald and J. Kertscher (eds), *Gadamer's Century. Essays in Honor of Hans-Georg Gadamer* (London and Cambridge, MA, 2002), pp. 279–297.
20 Martin Heidegger, *Being and Time*, trans. by J. Macquarrie and E. Robinson (Oxford and Cambridge, MA, 1997), p. 155.
21 G. W. F. Hegel, *Phenomenology of Spirit*, trans. by A. V. Miller (Oxford, 1977), p. 11.
22 Theodor W. Adorno, *Minima Moralia. Reflections from Damaged Life*, trans. by E. F. N. Jephcott (London, 2002), p.50.
23 One of my teachers at the University of Belgrade, the late Svetozar Petrović, ironized this stance by maintaining that a scholar such as

Jakobson attempted to arrest the crime itself instead of the criminal, and that, when it comes to crime and criminals, arresting an eyewitness or two would not be such a bad idea.

24 I am following the convention, admittedly confusing for non-specialists, of referring to 'the study of national literature' and 'the study of comparative literature' – the proper names for the disciplines – as 'national literature' and 'Comparative Literature', respectively.

25 Having both the (human) world and self-understanding is possible due to our having language; our experience of the world and ourselves is always and only linguistic, to the extent that 'being that can be understood is language' (Hans-Georg Gadamer, *Truth and Method* (London, 1989), p. 474).

26 Robert Irwin's *For Lust of Knowledge. The Orientalists and Their Enemies* (London: Penguin, 2006) is focused on Said's empirical errors, and rewrites the history of the field in order to expose them. Irwin also sums up the most important arguments in criticism of Said's theoretical model and list the most important contributions to it. A brief overview of theoretical criticism of *Orientalism* is offered also in Bill Ashcroft and Pal Ahluwalia, *Edward Said. The Paradox of Identity* (London and New York, 1999), pp. 74–86.

27 Especially in *Beginnings: Intention and Method* (New York, 1975) and *The World, the Text, and the Critic* (Cambridge, MA, 1983).

Bibliography

Adorno, Theodor W., *Minima Moralia. Reflections from Damaged Life*, trans. by E. F. N. Jephcott (London, 2002).
Ahmed, Aijaz, *In Theory. Classes, Nations, Literatures* (London and New York, 1992).
Ashcroft, Bill, and Pal Ahluwalia, *Edward Said. The Paradox of Identity* (London and New York, 1999).
Barrett, Michèle, *The Politics of Truth. From Marx to Foucault* (London, 1992).
Chakrabarty, Dipesh, *Provincializing Europe. Postcolonial Thought and Historical Difference* (Princeton, 2007).
Eagleton, Terry, *Ideology. An Introduction* (London, 1991).
Eisenstadt, S. N., 'Multiple Modernities', *Daedalus*, 129.1 (2000): 1–29.

Gadamer, Hans-Georg, *Truth and Method* (London, 1989).
Gallagher, Catherine, and Stephen Greenblatt, *Practicing New Historicism* (Chicago and London, 2000).
Hawkes, David, *Ideology* (London, 1996).
Hegel, G. W. F., *Phenomenology of Spirit*, trans. by A. V. Miller (Oxford, 1977).
Heidegger, Martin, *Being and Time*, trans. by J. Macquarrie and E. Robinson (Oxford and Cambridge, MA, 1997).
Irwin, Robert, *For Lust of Knowledge. The Orientalists and their Enemies* (London, 2006).
Jameson, Fredric, 'Third-World Literature in the Era of Multinational Capitalism', *Social Text*, 15 (1986).
Lewis, Martin W., and Kären E. Wigen, *The Myth of Continents. A Critique of Metageography* (Berkeley, 1997).
Mitchell, Timothy, 'Deterritorialization and the Crisis of Social Science', in A. Mirsepassi, A. Basu and F. Weaver (eds), *Localizing Knowledge in a Globalizing World. Recasting the Area Studies Debate* (Syracuse, NY, 2003).
Said, Edward W., *Beginnings: Intention and Method* (New York, 1975).
Said, Edward W., *The World, the Text, and the Critic* (Cambridge, MA, 1983).
Spivak, Gayatri Chakravorty, *Death of a Discipline* (New York, 2003).
Sprinker, Michael, 'The National Question: Said, Ahmad, Jameson', *Public Culture*, 6 (1993): 3–29.
Taylor, Charles, 'Understanding the Other: A Gadamerian View on Conceptual Schemes', in J. Malpas, U. Arnswald and J. Kertscher (eds), *Gadamer's Century. Essays in Honor of Hans-Georg Gadamer* (London and Cambridge, MA, 2002).
Williams, Raymond, *The Long Revolution* (London, 1971).
Yoshimoto, Mitsuhiro, 'Questions of Japanese Cinema: Disciplinary Boundaries and the Invention of the Scholarly Object', in M. Miyoshi and H. D. Harootuinian (eds), *Learning Places. The Afterlives of Area Studies* (Durham and London, 2002).

7

Rethinking Area Studies: Figurations and the construction of space

Claus Bech Hansen

Since the end of the Cold War, Area Studies disciplines as traditionally conceptualized, organized and taught at universities have been subject to worldwide debates. Charged with notions of ethnocentrism, methodological obsoletism and for creating fixed geographical 'areas', solidifying regimes of (Western) hegemony, Area Studies has been described as unsuitable for the study of the modern world, processes related to globalization and the increasing mobility of people, goods and ideas. In Germany the debates have resulted in numerous self-reflexive 'rethinking' initiatives and corresponding funding lines sponsored by government and research agencies such as the German Ministry for Research and Education and Deutsche Forschungsgemeinschaft.

In this chapter, I discuss how figurational sociology can serve as a fruitful interlocutor for rethinking Area Studies in the twenty-first century. I draw on recent relational theories in the social sciences and related disciplines as well as the findings from the research network Crossroads Asia to shed light on interdependencies between actors and structures under the condition of globalization. I will show how Norbert Elias's figurational sociology can be used in Area Studies, and I will bring it into an interdisciplinary dialogue with recent theories on space and mobility in a world marked by a collapse in time and space. I will argue that Elias's figurations constitute a powerful tool that can enable us to better understand socially constructed translocal contexts, spatial arrangements, positionality and epistemic regimes, as well as the compound interrelations between structures and action in today's globalized world.

Area Studies and Crossroads Asia

The interdisciplinary research network Crossroads Asia was launched in 2011 to tackle the question of how to conduct and position Area Studies disciplines in the twenty-first century. Preceding the project's foundation was a long-drawn-out debate over the means and ends of Area Studies at German universities.[1] The debate reached a critical point with a report by the German Council for Science and Humanities (Wissenschaftsrat) in 2006. The report concluded that 'the process of globalization on the one hand, and the consequential increasing consolidation of cultural and regional identities on the other, have led to a growing interest in regional-specific expertise'.[2] Given the increasing need to provide expert knowledge to policy-makers in times of globalization, the report argued that 'the currently existing range of regionally defined disciplines must also in the future be preserved and structurally strengthened'.[3] The report thus concluded that area-specific knowledge appeared more urgent than ever in a globalized world. In hindsight its projections have been proven right, in so far as while globalization may tie the world closer together, national, cultural, economic interests and differences persist, underlining the need for area-specific knowledge.

Contrary to other countries, the deliberations during the early 2000s over the future of Area Studies in Germany revitalized Area Studies disciplines and institutes. Funding agencies have supported a series of interdisciplinary Area Studies projects that seek to rethink, reform and redress Area Studies disciplines for the twenty-first century, as well as to better link them to 'systematic' disciplines such as political science, sociology and human geography. It was hoped that this would increase student and policy-maker interest and better integrate output into overarching theory and methodology debates.[4] Overall the funding opportunities have strengthened the quality of Area Studies research in Germany and made available crucial knowledge for policy-makers, suggesting that, rather than attempts to strangle Area Studies through budget cuts, universities and funding agencies would be well advised to instead push for a constructive rethinking process.

A cooperation of seven partners over a project period of six years, Crossroads Asia was founded following a call from the German Ministry of Science and Education and has consisted of two funding periods (2011–2014 and 2015–2016, respectively).[5] In the name of interdisciplinarity, the project gathered researchers from the Social and Political Sciences, Human Geography, Linguistics, Social Anthropology and History. It was consciously decided to disrupt traditional notions of territorial areas such as Central Asia or Eurasia by researching an area that has traditionally been marked by high mobility and exchange of people, goods and ideas, a territory spanning from the Aral Sea to China's Xinjiang province on an east–west axis and from Kazakhstan to India on a north–south one.

Broadly organizing its research around Norbert Elias's concept of figurations and the intricate web of interdependencies shaping the social world, Crossroads Asia's initial funding period focused on mobility in the three thematic areas – *development, conflict* and *migration* – and devised a series of empirical studies in seven interrelated work packages.[6] While keeping Elias's figuration as the overarching conceptual framework, the second funding period aimed at analysing the empirical findings of the first phase around the themes *figurational construction of space, follow the figuration* and *reflexivity*, as a means to contribute theoretically and methodologically to the revitalization of Area Studies.[7]

On the following pages, I will briefly introduce Norbert Elias's figurational sociology. This will provide a basis for the subsequent discussion of recent advances in the social sciences and related disciplines, many of which have not only sparked critique of Area Studies disciplines but also brought to light a series of challenges that pertain to Area Studies. In a second part, I will examine more specifically how Elias's theory can be implemented in research focusing on space and mobility, while at the same time highlighting some of the areas in which Elias's work can benefit from the inclusion of more recent scholarly work to strengthen figurational sociology methodologically and theoretically.

Figurations in times of globalization

In recent years, the theories of the German sociologist Norbert Elias have gained considerable traction in social sciences and humanities. His holistic approach, insisting on drawing on a variety of disciplines (for example, Sociology, Psychology and History) in order to meaningfully analyse and understand the development of human society, appears to suit well a science arena characterized by a growing demand for interdisciplinarity in a world that is becoming increasingly global, intertwined and interdependent. Central to Elias's theory is the concept of figurations prominently described in his seminal work *The Civilizing Process* and later in *Was ist Soziologie*. Elias understands figuration as a dynamic web of interdependencies characteristic of human society, into which every human being is born, and which form and impact individual agency.[8] According to figurational sociology, societies are made up of such networks of human interdependencies, which tie agents to one another. To successfully understand the essence of societies, we must, says Elias, examine the interdependencies that glue individuals to one another in society and perceive of these as figurations.[9] In his day the incorporation of actor- and structure-centred disciplines in Elias's approach aimed at overcoming what he saw as a faulty division between the individual and society first and foremost in the theories of disruption championed by Talcott Parson.[10] Hence, Elias argued, a separation between actors and the structures of the social world they inhabit would fail to explain the bonds between humans that allow them to make up a society in the first place and, by extension, the processes of development that societies go through.[11]

The interdependencies conceptualized by Elias are not merely related to socio-economic or political interdependencies. Elias defines the interdependencies making up figurations with analytical finesse, conceiving of them as varied in nature to include affective elements such as emotions, fear and superiority, while also covering the social, economic and spatial realms of human interaction.[12] Elias understands figurations as interrelated and complex, so that changes in one 'corner' of a figuration may (but need not) influence interdependencies in another. By necessity, then, figurations can be analytically extended vertically and hierarchically across planes, levels and scales in human society, potentially generating ever larger and encompassing figurations.[13]

Elias's figurational paradigm has been criticized for remaining logically weak due to its expansive nature.[14] There is some truth to the critique, especially on a purely theoretical level, for how does one delimit interdependencies that arguably encompass every human being? The critique resembles a general problem of chaos theory (butterfly effect) and causality chains, and seems to me a critique that could be extended to all meta-theories concerned with explaining the development of human society. Moreover, I am not convinced that it must provide methodological or even theoretical contradictions in the operationalization of figurational sociology. It belongs to the core practice of any research to follow and delimit evidence of interdependencies and causality to a conceivable whole that draws a border between logical extremes and comprehensible evidence from the social world under the conscious premise of the researcher's own positionality.[15] In the Crossroads Asia project this was achieved by using mobile methods captured in the phrase 'follow the figuration' – an inductive approach, using empirical evidence to follow and navigate figurational dynamics as a means to explore further the extent of figurations.[16] This approach is rooted in Elias's processual understanding of development and pursued by defining middle range concepts to macro-level theorization.[17] Figurational sociology is meaningful only under this precondition.

Abstracting from the theoretical level, Elias famously analogized figurations to games or dances:

no one will imagine a dance as a structure outside the individual or as a mere abstraction. The same dance figurations can certainly be danced by different people but without a plurality of reciprocally oriented and dependent people, there is no dance ... just as the small dance figurations change – becoming now slower, now quicker – so too, gradually, or more suddenly, do the large figurations which we call societies.[18]

The analogy to a dance does not equal its essentialization. The point Elias intends to bring across is that the structure of and the agents participating in a dance are interdependent and that changes can by consequence affect the entire figuration. By underlining the dynamism of a dance, Elias alerts us to the processual nature of the social world and offers a methodology that allows us to analyse the processes of human interdependencies and the contexts (structures) in which they develop.[19]

The basic principles of Elias's figurational sociology, with its aim to bridge the gap between functional and strategic analyses, stand at the beginning of a debate that still marks the social sciences. Some scholars even see him as the initiator of a 'relational turn'.[20] Scholars have sought to provide theoretical and methodological tools allowing us to overcome the dichotomous view of structures and agency and analytically perceive them as mutually constituent of the social world.[21] Holistic theories based on relational approaches have been developed by scholars such as Anthony Giddens (structuration theory),[22] Bob Jessop (strategic-relational theory),[23] Pierre Bourdieu and Loïc Wacquant (reflexive sociology)[24] and Jürgen Habermas (communicative rationality).[25] All of these theories have sparked further questions and the debate is unlikely to be concluded any time soon.

The advances of the structure–agency debate have been part of and influenced by various new-isms and turns in critical social sciences and humanities: the spatial, non-human and Anthropocene turns, as well as post-structuralism, new institutionalism and transnationalism, are all signs of this process. They have changed our understanding of the social world and brought new points of view into the scholarly arena, which have challenged the existing epistemic regimes, methodology and theorization.[26] In reference to Area Studies disciplines, the cultural turn,[27] spatial turn[28] and post-structuralism[29] have been particularly influential, and have fostered concepts such as transnationalism,[30] transregionalism and regional orders,[31] scale[32] and translocality,[33] signalling that scholars go beyond specific national and regional containers and eschew 'methodological nationalism'.[34]

The altered view on the social world as well as the globalizing condition have led scholars to question the role of nation states and traditional conceptualizations of society. John Urry,[35] Manuel Castells[36] and Arjun Appadurai[37] have been particularly influential and each produced seminal works that have shaped views on mobility, interconnectivity and networks in the age of globalization. Urry argues for a reconsideration of 'the state' as traditionally conceived of in sociology because of the high levels of mobility of resources, knowledge and people in the globalizing world, which crucially influences not only the way we experience everyday life and act in it, but also the 'traditional' borders of state and society. In other words, the role of the state has dramatically altered, making it a regulator rather than an arbiter of change.[38] In a similar vein, Castells argues for a reconceptualization of society to suit the information age, in which it is increasingly the flows between (worldwide) networks and networked spaces that direct it.[39] Finally, Appadurai has shed light on the global from the local and the Global Now with its disrupted patterns of social relations that may upset identities and boundaries by creating new spaces, famously captured in his *scapes* typology.[40]

Further scholarship focused on these questions has sparked vivid discussions about the constituents of space, place, locality and positionality, and their relevance in an ever more interconnected world.[41] For what are the properties of the nation states, for instance, when distance, borders and time collapse through increasing mobility and technological advances connecting distant localities anywhere in the world, or when nation states begin to lose power to networked 'global cities'[42]? What repercussions does it have for the spaces we inhabit, their location and the institutions that order them?

The rising emphasis on trans-isms should not lead to the belief that 'space' is inconsequential. Henri Lefebvre, perhaps the most prolific writer on space, held that 'social space is constituted neither by a collection of things or an aggregate of (sensory) data, nor by a void packed like a parcel of various contents'.[43] Space is constructed, defined and delimited by the people and institutions acting within or in regard to it. Hence, 'social space serves as an important frame of reference for social positions and positioning and ... determines everyday practices, biographical employment projects, and human identities, simultaneously pointing beyond the social context of national societies'.[44] At the heart of these spatial considerations stands the basic acknowledgement that, while the traditional institutions ordering the space we live in are undergoing change (for example, nation state), human beings are always products of and act within concrete places; they are woven into a web of spatially defined relations, dependencies and boundaries.[45]

We see this in Appadurai's Global Now as well, which is characterized by simultaneous, yet opposing, forces: we observe a de-territorialization of space, while place and space continue to impact people's lives and opportunities. This alludes to Ron Martin's remark that 'globalization may well have eliminated *space*, but it has by no means undermined the significance of location, of *place*',[46] precisely because the spatialization of networks needs concrete places.[47] In short, global and local factors merge in communities around the world, a circumstance eloquently captured by the concept 'glocal'.[48]

The debates on space, place, scale, mobility and networks have altered our view on Area Studies and pushed for a self-reflexive rethinking process of their means and ends. Nevertheless, the explicit aim to factor into analyses the many variables of an ever more complex reality does provide considerable methodological challenges.[49] With its emphasis on the various dimensions of interdependencies, Elias's figurational sociology can function as a fruitful interlocutor. Given its methodological premise, Elias arguably anticipated some of the fundamental processes of today's social reality that add further substance to recent structure–agency debates by equipping us with tools to analyse the link between agents and structures at different levels and scales. Much like the TPSN approach's understanding of Territories, Places, Scales and Networks (TPSN) as 'mutually constitutive and relationally intertwined dimensions of sociospatial relations',[50] figurational sociology, too, bridges the gap between these dimensions. However, contrary to the TPSN approach, figurational sociology has the advantage that it provides a strong conceptual framework that inherently holds high levels of flexibility by promoting a processual analysis of sociospatial relations in their different dimensions as dynamic interdependencies across time and space. Moreover, with Elias we can uncover the underlying forces that generate the very territories, places, scales and networks on an ontological level, allowing us to navigate the intertwined dimensions of agency and structure making up reality.

Space, mobility and figurational sociology

Discussions on the challenges of conventional Area Studies disciplines to account for the influences of globalization are complex. Broadly speaking, scholars argue that considerations should encompass, first, a self-reflexive approach to epistemology and the production of knowledge.[51] Secondly, Area Studies scholars should devote increasing attention to the relational interplay between space, structures and action and vigilantly implement methodological and theoretical sophistication that retains a high level of flexibility and avoid simple quantifications of a compound social reality. Thirdly, with research continuously challenging common notions of space and areas as impervious to change, we must strive to understand better how spatial boundaries are generated despite being perforated and negotiated through everyday practices. In the subsequent sections, I will discuss how Elias's figurational sociology can be operationalized to suit various dimensions of Area Studies. Given spatial constraints, I will limit my discussion to examples referring to space and mobility, whereby

I will try to push the borders of Elias's initial figurational sociology by considering advances in the social sciences and related disciplines, which can serve as a source of inspiration for Area Studies in the twenty-first century.

The figurational construction of space

A core critique directed at Area Studies disciplines is based on a dual interconnected argument relating to the history of Area Studies and the artificial, constructed nature of their subject matter. The former rightfully contends that Area Studies institutes were by and large products of imperial interest of domination, as they arose during the era of European empires and following the Second World War in the United States (and the Soviet Union). The latter holds that Area Studies arbitrarily divided the world into regions based on Othering processes, developed often for the purpose of political and economic domination or Cold War alliances.[52] 'Areas are not facts but artefacts', says Appadurai rightly, 'built on our interests and our fantasies as well as on our needs to know, to remember, and to forget.'[53] Areas and Area Studies reflect an academic and political process of 'making sense of' the social world, a process that must undergo rigid critical examination not only of the epistemological underpinnings we use but also of our own stance – our positionality – in it. We need to ask 'ourselves what it means to internationalize any sort of research before we apply our understandings to the geography and regions'.[54] Areas of the world are, in other words, social constructions, and critical self-reflexive Area Studies should at the very least be aware of the 'geography of knowing' they are informed by and push towards a broader, more inclusive practice to produce knowledge.[55]

As social constructions, areas are imagined communities and share this property with nations, borders and social space on a more general level.[56] Notions of spatial objectivities and subjectivities more specifically are 'social space' that is always 'already imagined, made, moulded (*zugerichtet*), appropriated or discerned from the point of view of gain and development';[57] they are not given, natural entities but the product of processual space–time entanglements, (imagined) cognitive maps that are negotiated through communicative action, producing spatialities.[58] Moreover, if areas and space – both defining pillars of Area Studies disciplines – are mere constructions, produced by research as 'a practice of imagination', that have little ontological foundation, what is the basis for Area Studies and what could an adequate reply be?

Elias's figurational sociology does not constitute a ready-made paradigm to overcome this question, but it does provide an approach that can assist Area Studies scholarship. For while today's spatial theorization goes far beyond Elias's considerations, space did hold a prominent place in his figurational deliberations. Discussing the relationship between structure and subject, Elias notes that 'social systems, in which structure is recursively implicated ... comprise the situated activities of human agents, reproduced across time and space'.[59] Space provides the situation for agents to act and to reproduce structures. So, while space clearly matters to Elias, he leaves it up to us to discern its distinguishing properties. Actors are situated in specific contexts and these contexts are, if we follow his civilizational theorem, shaped by the processual development of society. Further, Elias would say that the civilizational development can be read through figurations such as a dance where the structures of the game only become meaningful through individual action and vice versa.[60] Elias clearly did heed spatial considerations by awarding context a pre-eminent role in generating figurations but, given the lack of clarification, only by inference (and by leaning on other theoreticians) may we arrive at a plausible figurational understanding of space.

Following Ludger Pries's and Henri Lefebvre's notion of space as a social construction influences not only the lifeways and practices of individuals and communities, but also identities and social hierarchies.[61] Understood in relational terms, space reflects structures and action, and it generates and changes them in a convoluted process of interdependencies. We can exemplify this by adopting a spatial lens to Elias's 'football match': the stadium encloses a spectacular space that opposing fan groups fill with life and symbols; rules and social hierarchies determine fan seating; the space is filled with recognizable songs and rhythms – elements constitutive of a football match but in and of themselves elements of little meaning. Equally, the game itself – the pitch, the rules, the players, referees, age and skill – all these elements only carry meaning through the participation of the individual players who act and react within the space and its structures. These in turn are generated only through action, revealing the interdependencies of the figuration.[62] In other words, we can reasonably argue that figurations are arbiters of spatiality.[63]

Figurational sociology proves useful to unlock the organization, appropriation and properties of spatiality. In fact, incorporating spatial considerations into figurational sociology not only allows us to shed light on spatial aspects of figurations, leading to a better understanding of their constitution, but it also enables us to show figurational aspects of space, providing additional insights into its formation and constitution. Self-reflexive, critical Area Studies research can use the combination of spatial theory and figurational sociology as one avenue that does not delimit space to certain areas, hermetically closed off to the world and recalcitrant to change.[64] Instead, it focuses on the ontological level, which sheds light onto the manifold dimensions of structures, space and human action that can unearth contingent developments by examining interdependencies. We may reasonably term this the 'figurational construction of space'.

Research from the Crossroads Asia network has probed analysis into the figurational construction of space and provided instructive results. Drawing on empirical findings from studies of cross-border trade between Kyrgyzstan, Kazakhstan and Xinjiang and on education migration in Gojal, Pakistan and Kumaon, India, Alff and Benz tentatively contend that the analysis of space must be relational, processual and constructivist.[65] Centring their figurational analysis on actors, relationality and translocality, they read place as an arena for interactions of differently positioned actors; understand territory as a marker towards governance of clearly delimited areas; use networks to underline connectivity of all space; argue that positionality is inherently relational and power laden; and, finally, see mobility to be about the embodied practice of movement which includes the meanings, ideologies or representations associated with the mobility of people, objects, ideas and so on.[66] As a result, they show how space, place, identity and power are appropriated, disrupted and negotiated in various localities, resulting in changes in figurations such as university environments. As a result, in their reading, agency contests religious symbols and changes the norms (structures) that conventionally rule university environments so that the contestation ultimately empowers female students.[67]

Research on ethno-political figurations and their reflections in spatialities have yielded equally instructive results. In her analysis of China's Xinjiang Uyghur population, Agnieszka Joniak-Lüthi focuses on an ethnically defined figuration to exemplify how spatial layering has been subject to change due to demographic government policies.[68] Traditionally constituting the ethnic majority in the region, increasing migration of Han Chinese to Xinjiang has led to new hierarchies of power in various domains. These become evident through the altered spatial layering, resulting from new spatial practices and language, which essentially marginalize the traditional Uyghur spatialities, revealing how we can read power, development and the dynamic of figurations in space.[69]

Figurationally speaking, studies on space, identity and power are helpful to understand contingencies inherent in the dynamic of interdependencies. Changes in figurations bear the potential to change other parts of the same or different figurations. The examples mentioned here not only provide evidence to this effect and alert us to the need for careful inductive analysis as a means to understand the 'stuff' of the social world and the spatialities it consists of. They also give an inkling of the complex entanglements between human action, structures, space, power and time, to name but a few of the factors that influence spatialities. Figurational sociology provides an approach that allows us to deconstruct processes that are part of a dynamic, interdependent, multi-layered reality in constant negotiation between different actors and their (spatio-)structural constraints. This negotiation process occurs continuously and may be rooted in local, translocal or glocal interdependencies, made possible through the partial collapse of time in the information age.

Mobility and migration

Mobility is the flow of humans, goods, ideas and resources among networks, as well as the effects arising from these flows; it is movement, and it appears when a contextually determined potential for movement is activated through mobilizational dynamics, which could, for example, take the form of migration, exchange in ideas across virtual and material space, trade in material or immaterial resources, or upward or downward social mobility, habitually resulting in further mobilization processes.[70] Inherent in mobility are forces that can disrupt existing orders by perforating the social constructions of space, power and identity.

Scholars have shown that implementing Elias's figurational sociology to analyse mobility can yield instructive results,[71] and neither motion nor mobility are in and of themselves anything new to figurational sociology. Elias factored in the influence of mobility both explicitly and implicitly in developing key concepts such as mobile figurations, interdependency chains, figurational dynamics and power balances. Indeed, Elias's analogies to dances or football games clearly show the importance of movement to figurations, where influences in any given figuration at one level may influence interdependencies within the same figuration or lead to changes at other scales and spatial contexts within broader figurations.

Although mobility was an inherent part of Elias's figurational theory, he never seriously elaborated on it with the conceptual finesse and sophistication of more recent research. Urry's 'social as mobility', Castells' 'flows' and Appadurai's 'theory of rupture' all consider mobility to be one of the primary forces of modern society capable of altering its conventional pillars and borders.[72] All borders – political or imagined – are permeable and porous; mobility engenders movement that sifts through them, giving rise to exchange and change. Against the background of Elias's dance analogy, we might say with Urry that mobility not only introduces novel movements but, on a fundamental level, bears the potential to alter the very rules of the dance through its influence on figurational dynamics. For, according to Urry, diverse mobilities in today's world result in complex intersections in all areas of social reality that are characterized by an element of unpredictability, continuously disrupting and changing it. What is more, society is not only directed by social entities between humans, but includes inhuman components (think here, for example, of climate change) so that 'societies are necessarily hybrids'.[73]

Undoubtedly, Elias would agree with Urry's hybrid society. Elias explained at length his processual understanding of 'development' of society and described his *Civilizing Process* as a study that approaches personality and social structures, not as fixed entities, 'but as changing, and as interdependent aspects of the same long-term development'.[74] In Elias's understanding, then, societies are in constant development, trapped in flux, so to speak. And even if he did not describe mobility as an arbiter of change, it is fair to assume that he considered interdependencies receptive to change through mobility inside or outside any given figuration, potentially altering its mobile dynamics. Hence, Elias commented that one of the forces underlying all *intended* interactions of human beings is their *unintended* interdependence.[75] Mobility, then, must be understood as an influence factor to any given figuration (economic, spatial, cultural, emotional, etc.), which can cause changes and disruptions that are not only unintended but may also be undesired.[76]

The influence of mobility can be traced in almost any society throughout history. Through mobility languages change, (imported) economic structures upend societies, and discoveries of natural resources can fundamentally alter societies. In his study of the Wakhi of Gojal in Gilgit-Baltistan, Andreas Benz highlights how the changes in education, employment, income and financial resources have in part turned on its head the social stratification of local society: 'former "lower-class" families [which] participated from the very beginning in migration strategies and had the chance to advance socially through education and job-income, while some former "upper-class" families have missed the chance'. Migration and the mobility of ideas have resulted in social position in today's Gojal being less determined by 'family origin (class) and agricultural resources (irrigated land, livestock) and instead on formal education, knowledge, skills, and professional careers'.[77] Interpreted as a figuration, the alteration of conventional class-based structures among the Wakhi people ushered in a new period of socio-cultural interdependencies, a change likely to materialize further, as the knowledge of possibilities spread through society. Moreover, agency altered the structures of social interdependencies, inciting change in the nature and dynamic of the figuration.

Equally compelling evidence of the influence that migratory groups have on societies and communities through their movement is seen across the world.[78] But migratory mobility has many facets: Madeleine Reeves has shown that migration for the purpose of labour or education is often realized against the immobility of members of a solidarity group.[79] Other research has shown that 'movers' habitually land in a mobilization 'trap', where the host society deprives them of upward mobilization, while, paradoxically, upward social mobility of the immobilized is achieved nonetheless through remittance payments.[80] Finally, mobility is not a resource accessible to all groups of society. Despite huge migration waves, predominantly between rural and urban environments such as in China, the majority of the earth's population is trapped in immobility, restrained from movement by insufficient economic means, political structures, conflicts and so on. This is not to say that locally fixed figurations are not subject to change, but that change is less rapid and occurs through other kinds of mobility, such as state-sponsored mobility of resources or the forceful imageries of the virtual world.[81] Nevertheless, the quest for improving one's livelihood is cumbersome and its success chances are dependent on mobility being accompanied by concrete possibilities of social mobility, whereby imaginaries of mobility outcomes are particularly powerful.[82]

Adopting a figurational lens on migration as a form of mobility of people and/or knowledge from A to B, we might say that it may bring change to figurations – be it through economic possibilities (for example, remittances, economic investment), human and social capital (for example, education, ideas, networks), the exchange of ideas and goods, mobile groups the dynamics of figurations.[83] Figurational disruptions can materialize through the changes in traditional family structures and cultural particularities, behavioural properties, taste, ideology and preferences.[84] However, migrants might also provoke changes in larger figurations on community or state levels. Such change can occur through the activities of return-migrants or through diaspora groups.[85] Migrants not only become constituents of change in existing figurations; they can spark the development of new figurations often based on their shared migratory experience. Central Asian labour migrants in Moscow, for example, have established well-functioning ethno-cultural figurations that assist in providing social security, housing and jobs, which influence home and destination countries. Conversely, migrant networks based on common experience often persist among migrant returnees in home countries.[86]

One needs to emphasize that mobility and movement are not independent variables. Despite the challenges that nation states face against the backdrop of undermining forces such as mobility, states and governments possess extraordinary powers to influence social, economic and geographic mobility potentials. This has been seen time and again, for example, through the influence of the Iron Curtain and persists in several authoritarian regimes today, which – in the hope of keeping out influences that could destabilize the regimes – often invest enormous resources in obstructing the movement of people and goods. In Turkmenistan, for example, where the government ferociously tries to curb the movement of its people and their exchange with the outside world, the dreams and imaginations about the world among the youth are undergoing fundamental change. Eloquently captured in a statement by a young Turkmen blogger, this change is reflected in their mental maps: 'the main difference between [the older] and the younger generation is the way they perceive the world. While for the young people Turkmenistan is the entire world, for the older ones it is the former Soviet Union, where they were born and grew up.'[87] States, in other words, still possess the power to curtail interdependencies of figurations.

Thematically and analytically, mobility and figurational sociology provide powerful tools for Area Studies research. They enable us to break the conceptual strait-jacket generated by epistemic regimes and socially constructed boundaries and borders, which have often been reproduced uncritically. Furthermore, mobility writ large not only allows us to discover new relationships and dynamisms of interdependencies; it also allows us to push the conceptual boundaries of figurations. For, in processual engagement with mobility through mobile methods, we encounter the changing nature of figurations and their translocality as they travel across vast distances through the entanglements of the virtual and the non-virtual world. Moreover, the time–space collapse that we experience in our increasingly globalized and hybrid world adds to the complexity of figurational dynamics, and mobility provides a research avenue by which we can better understand these dynamics and the influence they exert on the relationship between agency and structure.

Area Studies in the twenty-first century

The twenty-first century has put enormous pressure on Area Studies disciplines worldwide. On the one hand, there is a demand (and need) for increased knowledge about areas and regions of the world as we grow closer. On the other hand, globalization releases forces that are said to undermine the very regions, the knowledge about which is in demand. Based on insights from the Crossroads Asia project as well as broader reflections from Area Studies related research, in this chapter I have made an argument for using Norbert Elias's figurational sociology as a means to strengthen Area Studies research theoretically and methodologically. This can help Area Studies research meet the demands of changing academic and political environments, while retaining the flexibility and diversity so crucial to innovative Area Studies research. Figurational sociology is undoubtedly but one of many possible entry points to rethink Area Studies, but I hope to have demonstrated that it can inspire Area Studies research, which helps us break with the simple reproduction of epistemic regimes and revitalize discussions on space and mobility. The chapter is meant to contribute to a growing body of literature on rethinking Area Studies and invite critical reflection not only on the way we conduct Area Studies research and engage in knowledge production but also on how we can make sense of the many forces and relational (inter-)dependencies that influence our everyday lives, our agency and the institutions we create to order our social reality. This requires a review of some of Elias's core terms in light of innovative research, which give us an inkling of how figurations form and change in a world that seems more complex, fast-paced and smaller than it did in Elias's days. Nevertheless, while inherently accepting the ephemeral nature of its findings given its insistence on hybridity, figurational sociology provides a flexible methodological toolset for combining micro-level empirical findings with meso- and macro-level theorization for the revitalization of Area Studies in the twenty-first century.

Notes

1   Matthias Middell, 'Area Studies Under the Global Condition. Debates on Where to Go with Regional or Area Studies in Germany', in Matthias Middell (ed.), *Self-Reflexive Area Studies*, Global History and International Studies 5 (Leipzig, 2013), 7–58; Anna-Katharina Hornidge and Katja Mielke, 'Crossroads Studies: From Spatial Containers to Studying the Mobile', *Middle East – Topics & Arguments*, 4 (May 2015): 13–19.

2   Wissenschaftsrat, 'Empfehlungen Zu Den Regionalstudien (Area Studies) in Den Hochschulen Und Außeruniversitären Forschungseinrichtungen', July 2006, p. 5.
3   Ibid., p. 29.
4   Hornidge and Mielke, 'Crossroads Studies'.
5   Partners in the first phase included Zentralasien-Seminar der Humboldt-Universität zu Berlin, Geographisches Institut U Cologne, Asien-Orient-Institut/Department of Ethnology U Tübingen, Institut für Ethnologie Ludwigs-Maximilians-University, Zentrum Moderner Orient (ZMO), Institut für Orient- und Asienwissenschaften (IOA) and Zentrum für Entwicklungsforschung (ZEF) for Bonner Asien Zentrum of U Bonn, Centre for Development Studies (ZELF)/Institut für Geographische Wissenschaften at the Free University Berlin. In the second phase, Bonn International Center for Conversion joined the project instead of the Geographisches Institut U Cologne and Asien-Orient-Institut/Department of Ethnology U Tübingen.
6   The project website provides a full overview of work packages: 'Crossroads Asia', available at www.crossroads-asia.de/crossroads-asia.html (accessed 23 November 2016); Norbert Elias, *The Civilizing Process: Sociogenetic and Psychogenetic Investigations*, rev. edn (Oxford and Malden, MA, 2000). On Norbert Elias's concept of figuration: Norbert Elias, *Was ist Soziologie?* (Munich, 1970).
7   Second phase projects were: 1) 'How to speak conflict' – Konfliktualität in sprachlicher Kommunikation; 2) Mobilität im mobilisierten Raum: Interaktion von autochthoner Bevölkerung und Kolonialmacht in der mittelasiatischen Frontierregion; 3) Menschen im Zwischenraum: Umgang mit erzwungender Immobilität in Kabul; 4) Spatial production and identity negotiations along Xinjiang's roads; 5) Sozialräumliche Transformation von Handelsorten und Zielorten der Bildungsmigration: Die relationale Konstituierung des Lokalen; 6) 'Re-bordering' in Kaschmir: Aushandlung von Räumen und Staatlichkeit in umstrittenen Grenzregionen; 7) The Crossroads Perspective: a fundament for Crossroads Studies? 'Crossroads Asia'.
8   Elias, *The Civilizing Process*; Elias, *Was ist Soziologie?*
9   Elias, *Was ist Soziologie?*, p. 151.

10 See here in particular the postscript from 1968 in Elias, *The Civilizing Process*, pp. 449–484.
11 Elias, *Was ist Soziologie?*, p. 151.
12 Ralf Baumgart and Volker Eichener, *Norbert Elias zur Einführung*, 4th edn (Hamburg, 2013), pp. 113–123.
13 Eric Dunning and Jason Hughes, *Norbert Elias and Modern Sociology* (London, 2012), pp. 52–56.
14 Derek Layder, 'Social Reality as Figuration: A Critique of Elias's Conception of Sociological Analysis', *Sociology*, 20.3 (August 1986): 367–386.
15 Peter A. Jackson, 'Spatialities of Knowledge in the Neoliberal World Academy. Theory, Practice and 21st Century Legacies of Area Studies', Crossroads Asia Working Paper Series (Bonn, 2015).
16 George E. Marcus, 'Ethnography in/of the World System: The Emergence of Multi-sited Ethnography', *Annual Review of Anthropology*, 24 (January 1995): 95–117; Mark-Anthony Falzon, *Multi-sited Ethnography: Theory, Praxis and Locality in Contemporary Research* (Farnham, 2012); see also Ghassan Hage, 'A Not so Multi-sited Ethnography of a Not so Imagined Community', *Anthropological Theory*, 5.4 (December 2005): 463–475; Hornidge and Mielke, 'Crossroads Studies'.
17 Robert K. Merton, 'On Sociological Theories of the Middle Range', in *Social Theory and Social Structure* (New York, 1949), pp. 39–53.
18 Elias, *The Civilizing Process*, p. 482.
19 Martin Sökefeld, 'Crossroads Asia and the State: Anthropological Perspectives. Paper Presented at the 5th International Crossroads Asia Conference, Bonn, September 22–23, 2016', *Crossroads Asia Working Papers*, no. 35 (2016).
20 Dunning and Hughes, *Norbert Elias and Modern Sociology*, p. 3.
21 The structure–agency dualism is not the only form of dualist debates in sociology. Eric Dunning and Jason Hughes, for example, count materialism versus idealism, social statics versus social dynamics, and synchronic studies versus diachronic studies (ibid., 8). Claus Bech Hansen, 'The Crossroads Perspective', Crossroads Asia Concept Paper Series (Bonn, 2017), available at https://tinyurl.com/yaupbv75.
22 Anthony Giddens, *The Constitution of Society: Outline of the Theory of Structuration* (Berkeley, 1984).

23 Bob Jessop et al., 'Institutional Re(turns) and the Strategic–Relational Approach', *Environment and Planning A*, 33.7 (July 2001): 1213–1235.
24 Pierre Bourdieu and Loïc J. D. Wacquant, *An Invitation to Reflexive Sociology* (Chicago, 1992).
25 Jürgen Habermas, *The Theory of Communicative Action* (Boston, 1984); Jari I. Niemi, 'Jürgen Habermas's Theory of Communicative Rationality: The Foundational Distinction Between Communicative and Strategic Action', *Social Theory and Practice*, 31.4 (2005): 513–532.
26 Hornidge and Mielke, 'Crossroads Studies'; Walter D. Mignolo and Madina V. Tlostanova, 'Theorizing from the Borders Shifting to Geo- and Body-politics of Knowledge', *European Journal of Social Theory*, 9.2 (May 2006): 205–221; Ramón Grosfoguel, 'Epistemic Racism/Sexism, Westernized Universities and the Four Genocides/Epistemicides of the Long Sixteenth Century', in Marta Araújo and Silvia Rodríguez Maeso (eds), *Eurocentrism, Racism and Knowledge* (London, 2015), pp. 23–46; Aníbal Quijano, 'Coloniality and Modernity/Rationality', *Cultural Studies*, 21.2–3 (March 2007): 168–178.
27 Michael Lackner and Michael Werner, *Der Cultural Turn in Den Humanwissenschaften. Area Studies Im Auf- Oder Abwind Des Kulturalismus?*, ed. Programmbeirat der Werner Reimers Konferenzen, vol. 2, Schriftenreihe Suchprozesse Für Innovative Fragestellungen in Der Wissenschaft (Bad Homburg, 1999); Doris Bachmann-Medick, *Cultural Turns: Neuorientierungen in den Kulturwissenschaften* (Reinbek bei Hamburg, 2007).
28 Henri Lefebvre, *The Production of Space* (Oxford and Malden, MA, 1992); Bob Jessop, Neil Brenner and Martin Jones, 'Theorizing Sociospatial Relations', *Environment and Planning D: Society and Space*, 26.3 (June 2008): 389–401; Doreen Massey, *For Space* (London, 2005); Edward W. Soja, *Postmodern Geographies: The Reassertion of Space in Critical Social Theory* (London and New York, 1989); Helga Leitner, Eric Sheppard and Kristin M. Sziarto, 'The Spatialities of Contentious Politics', *Transactions of the Institute of British Geographers*, 33.2 (April 2008): 157–172.
29 Peter A. Jackson, 'Mapping Poststructuralism's Borders: The Case for Poststructuralist Area Studies', *Sojourn: Journal of Social Issues in Southeast Asia*, 18.1 (2003): 42–88.
30 Nina Glick Schiller, Linda Basch and Cristina Szanton Blanc, 'From Immigrant to Transmigrant: Theorizing Transnational Migration',

Anthropological Quarterly, 68.1 (1995): 48–63; Sidney W. Mintz, 'The Localization of Anthropological Practice from Area Studies to Transnationalism', *Critique of Anthropology*, 18.2 (June 1998): 117–133; Gayatri Chakravorty Spivak, *Outside in the Teaching Machine* (New York, 1993).

31 'Tagungsbericht: Area Studies Revisited. Transregional Studies in Germany, 13.02.2009–14. 02.2009 Berlin', *H-Soz-Kult* (30 May 2009), available at www.hsozkult.de/conferencereport/id/tagungsberichte-2625 (accessed 1 July 2019); Nadine Godehardt and Oliver W. Lembcke, 'Regionale Ordnungen in Politischen Räumen. Ein Beitrag Zur Theorie Regionaler Ordnungen', *GIGA Working Paper*, 124 (2010).

32 Paolo Novak, 'Tracing Connections and Their Politics', in Henryk Alff and Andreas Benz (eds), *Tracing Connections: Explorations of Spaces and Places in Asian Contexts*, 1st edn (Berlin, 2014); Willem van Schendel, 'Geographies of Knowing, Geographies of Ignorance: Jumping Scale in Southeast Asia', *Environment and Planning D: Society & Space*, 20.2002 (2002): 647–668.

33 Ulrike Freitag and Achim Von Oppen, *Translocality: The Study of Globalising Processes from a Southern Perspective* (Leiden and New York, 2009).

34 Andreas Wimmer and Nina Glick Schiller, 'Methodological Nationalism, the Social Sciences, and the Study of Migration: An Essay in Historical Epistemology', *The International Migration Review*, 37.3 (2003): 576–610.

35 John Urry, *Sociology Beyond Societies: Mobilities for the Twenty-First Century* (London, 2002).

36 Manuel Castells, *The Rise of the Network Society: The Information Age: Economy, Society, and Culture Volume I*, 2. 2009 (Chichester, West Sussex and Malden, MA, 1996).

37 Arjun Appadurai, *Modernity at Large: Cultural Dimensions of Globalization* (Minnesota, 1996); Arjun Appadurai, 'Grassroots Globalization and the Research Imagination', *Public Culture*, 12.1 (January 2000): 1–19; Arjun Appadurai, *The Future as Cultural Fact: Essays on the Global Condition* (London and New York, 2013).

38 Urry, *Sociology Beyond Societies*; Mimi Sheller and John Urry, 'The New Mobilities Paradigm', *Environment and Planning A*, 38.2 (February 2006): 207–226.

39 Castells, *The Rise of the Network Society*; Eric Sheppard, 'The Spaces and Times of Globalization: Place, Scale, Networks, and Positionality', *Economic Geography*, 78.3 (July 2002): 307–330. See also: Claus Bech Hansen, 'Mastering the Current. Studying Central Asia in the 21st Century', in Susan Hodgett and Patrick James (eds), *Necessary Travel. New Area Studies and Canada in Comparative Perspective* (Washington, DC, 2018).

40 Appadurai, *Modernity at Large*. See also Hansen, 'The Crossroads Perspective'.

41 Leitner, Sheppard and Sziarto, 'The Spatialities of Contentious Politics', p. 158.

42 Saskia Sassen, *The Global City: New York, London, Tokyo* (Princeton, NJ, 1991).

43 Lefebvre, *The Production of Space*, p. 27.

44 Ludger Pries, *Migration and Transnational Social Spaces* (Aldershot, UK and Brookfield, VT, 1999), p. 26.

45 Appadurai, *Modernity at Large*; Klaus Segbers, 'Vom (Großen) Nutzen Und (Kleinen) Elend Der Komparatistik in Der Transformationsforschung', in Ulrich Menzel (ed.), *Vom Ewigen Frieden Und Vom Wohlstand Der Nationen* (Frankfurt am Main, 2000), pp. 493–517; Martin W. Lewis and Kären Wigen, *The Myth of Continents: A Critique of Metageography* (Berkeley, 1997).

46 Ron L. Martin, 'The New Economic Geography of Money', in Ron L. Martin (ed.), *Money and the Space Economy* (Hoboken, NJ, 1999), pp. 15–16.

47 Crossroads Asia Working Group Migration, 'Crossroads Asia Through the Lens of Mobility and Migration: A Conceptual Approach [with Postscript]', Crossroads Asia Working Group Migration (2012/2014), Crossroads Asia Concept Paper Series (Bonn, 2012, 2014), p. 11, available at www.crossroads-asia.de/veroeffentlichungen/concept-papers/concept-paper-migration.html (accessed 1 July 2019); Cilja Harders, 'Dimensionen Des Netzwerkansatzes – Einführende Theoretische Überlegungen', in Roman Loimeier (ed.), *Die Islamische Welt Als Netzwerk. Möglichkeiten Und Grenzen Des Netzwerkansatzes Im Islamischen Kontext* (Würzburg, 2000), p. 28.

48 Roland Robertson, 'Glocalization: Time-Space and Homogeneity-Heterogeneity', in Mike Featherstone, Scott Lash and Roland Robertson

(eds), *Global Modernities* (London, 1995), pp. 25–44. See also Sheppard, 'The Spaces and Times of Globalization', p. 308; Hansen, 'Mastering the Current', n.p.

49   Jessop, Brenner and Jones, 'Theorizing Sociospatial Relations'.
50   Ibid., p. 389.
51   Hansen, 'The Crossroads Perspective', p. 2.
52   Chris Burgess, 'The Asian Studies "Crisis": Putting Cultural Studies into Asian Studies and Asia into Cultural Studies', *International Journal of Asian Studies*, 1.1 (January 2004): 125; Cynthia Chou and Vincent Houben, 'Introduction', in Cynthia Chou and Vincent Houben (eds), *Southeast Asian Studies: Debates and New Directions*, IIAS/ISEAS Series on Asia (Singapore and Leiden, The Netherlands, 2006), pp. 1–22.
53   Arjun Appadurai, 'Grassroots Globalization and the Research Imagination', *Public Culture*, 12.1 (January 2000): 1–19, p. 8.
54   Ibid., p. 9.
55   van Schendel, 'Geographies of Knowing, Geographies of Ignorance: Jumping Scale in Southeast Asia'.
56   Benedict R. Anderson, *Imagined Communities: Reflections on the Origin and Spread of Nationalism* (London, 1983).
57   Ludger Pries, *Die Transnationalisierung Der Sozialen Welt: Sozialräume Jenseits von Nationalgesellschaften*, 1. Aufl, Edition Suhrkamp 2521 (Frankfurt am Main, 2008), 81. Author's translation.
58   Peter L. Berger and Thomas Luckmann, *The Social Construction of Reality: A Treatise in the Sociology of Knowledge* (Garden City, NY, 1966); Hubert Knoblauch, *Kommunikationskultur: die kommunikative Konstruktion kultureller Kontexte* (Berlin and New York, 1995); Hubert Knoblauch, 'Diskurs, Kommunikation und Wissenssoziologie', in Reiner Keller et al. (eds), *Handbuch sozialwissenschaftliche Diskursanalyse* (Wiesbaden, 2001), pp. 207–224; Hubert Knoblauch, 'Grundbegriffe und Aufgaben des kommunikativen Konstruktivismus', in Reiner Keller, Jo Reichertz and Hubert Knoblauch (eds), *Kommunikativer Konstruktivismus Theoretische und empirische Arbeiten zu einem neuen wissenssoziologischen Ansatz* (Wiesbaden, 2013), pp. 25–48; Reiner Keller, 'Kommunikative Konstruktion und diskursive Konstruktion', in Reiner Keller, Jo Reichertz and Hubert Knoblauch (eds), *Kommunikativer Konstruktivismus. Theoretische und empirische Arbeiten zu einem neuen wissenssoziologischen Ansatz* (Wiesbaden, 2013), pp. 69–96.

59 Quoted from Dunning and Hughes, *Norbert Elias and Modern Sociology*, p. 176.
60 Elias, *Was ist Soziologie?*, p. 155.
61 Pries, *Migration and Transnational Social Spaces*, p. 26; Lefebvre, *The Production of Space*, p. 27.
62 Elias, *Was ist Soziologie?*, p. 155.
63 I follow Lefebvre's distinction between space as a 'natural space' and spatiality as the production of social space: Lefebvre, *The Production of Space*, pp. 1–67.
64 Edward W. Soja, 'Taking Space Personally', in *The Spatial Turn: Interdisciplinary Perspectives*, ed. Barney Warf and Santa Arias, Routledge Studies in Human Geography 26 (London and New York, 2009), 11–35.
65 Henryk Alff and Andreas Benz, 'The Multi-dimensionality of Space: Challenging Spatial Bias in the Production of Places', 5th International Crossroads Asia Conference: Area Studies' Futures, ZEF, University of Bonn, 23 September 2016, available at http://tinyurl.com/zosmh55 (accessed 1 July 2019). Alff's and Benz's conceptualization draws on John Agnew's threefold view on place as locale, location and a sense of place. John A. Agnew, *Place and Politics: The Geographical Mediation of State and Society* (Boston, 1987), pp. 25–47.
66 Alff and Benz, 'The Multi-dimensionality of Space'.
67 Alff and Benz, 'The Multi-dimensionality of Space'.
68 Agnieszka Joniak-Lüthi, 'Xinjiang's Geographies in Motion', *Asian Ethnicity*, 16.4 (October 2015): 428–445; Judd Kinzley and Agnieszka Joniak-Lüthi, *Territory, Border, Infrastructure – Imagining and Crafting National Borderlands in Twentieth Century China*, Crossroads Asia Working Paper No. 36, Crossroads Asia Working Paper Series, No. 36 (Bonn, 2016).
69 Joniak-Lüthi, 'Xinjiang's Geographies in Motion', pp. 437–440. Agnieszka Joniak-Lüthi exemplifies this change through the tomb-shrine of Qirmish Ata, which once served as an important Muslim spatial marker on the Silk Road and a testimony to Uyghur identity. Located in a unique natural environment, the tomb is decayed in a distant corner of what is today known as the Park of Mysterious Trees (Han Chinese), which serves as a tourist attraction.
70 Urry, *Sociology Beyond Societies*, p. 2.

71 See, for example, Crossroads Asia Project; see also Dunning and Hughes, *Norbert Elias and Modern Sociology*; V. J. H. Houben and Mona Schrempf (eds), *Figurations of Modernity: Global and Local Representations in Comparative Perspective, Eigene Und Fremde Welten* (Frankfurt and New York, 2008); Tim Newton, 'Elias, Organisation and Ecology', in Ad van Iterson et al. (eds), *The Civilized Organization: Norbert Elias and the Future of Organization* (Amsterdam, 2002), pp. 189–204.

72 Urry, *Sociology Beyond Societies*; Sheller and Urry, 'The New Mobilities Paradigm'; Manuel Castells (ed.), *The Network Society: A Cross-cultural Perspective* (Cheltenham, UK and Northampton, MA, 2005); Appadurai, *Modernity at Large*.

73 Urry, *Sociology Beyond Societies*, p. 15.

74 Elias, *The Civilizing Process*, p. 452.

75 Quoted in Newton, 'Elias, Organisation and Ecology', p. 194; Richard Kilminster, 'Structuration Theory as World-view', in Christopher G. A. Bryant and David Jary (eds), *Giddens' Theory of Structuration: A Critical Appreciation* (London and New York, 1991), p. 101.

76 An often-cited example of the negative impact of unintended interdependence is that of car use. Drawing on Zygmunt Bauman, Richard Newton rightfully describes how cars were intended to deliver unheard-of personal mobility, but in accomplishing it the corollary was traffic jams, air and noise pollution, etc., as consequences of the unintended interdependence of millions of 'autonomous' car users: Newton, 'Elias, Organisation and Ecology', p. 194; Zygmunt Bauman, *Thinking Sociologically* (Oxford and Cambridge, MA, 1990), p. 188.

77 Andreas Benz, 'Multilocality as an Asset – Translocal Development and Change Among the Wakhi of Gojal, Pakistan', in Henryk Alff and Andreas Benz (eds), *Tracing Connections: Explorations of Spaces and Places in Asian Contexts*, 1st edn (Berlin, 2014), p. 132.

78 Claus Bech Hansen and Markus Kaiser, 'Transnational Practices and Post-Soviet Collective Identity', in Günther Schlee and Alexander Horstmann (eds), *Difference and Sameness as Modes of Integration: Anthropological Perspectives on Ethnicity and Religion* (New York; Oxford, 2017), pp. 133–38. Stephen Adaawen, *Reflections on Migration Dynamics in Northern Ghana from the 'Crossroads Perspective'*, Crossroads Asia Working Paper Series, No. 32 (Bonn, 2016); Douglas S. Massey,

Worlds in Motion: Understanding International Migration at the End of the Millennium (Oxford and New York, 1998); Stephen Castles and Mark J. Miller, *The Age of Migration: International Population Movements in the Modern World* (Basingstoke and New York, 2009); Pries, *Migration and Transnational Social Spaces*; Wimmer and Schiller, 'Methodological Nationalism, the Social Sciences, and the Study of Migration'; Boris Nieswand, *Theorising Transnational Migration: The Status Paradox of Migration* (London, 2011).

79 Madeleine Reeves, 'Staying Put? Towards a Relational Politics of Mobility at a Time of Migration', *Central Asian Survey*, 30.3-4 (December 2011): 555–576.

80 Ronald Skeldon, 'Going Round in Circles: Circular Migration, Poverty Alleviation and Marginality', *International Migration*, 50.3 (June 2012): 43–60.

81 J. K. W. Hill and P. Nehls, *In the Lap of the Mountains: The Irrigation Systems of Ladakh's Farming Communities*, Documentary (2015); Joe Hill, 'The Role of Authority in the Collective Management of Hill Irrigation Systems in the Alai (Kyrgyzstan) and Pamir (Tajikistan)', *Mountain Research and Development*, 33.3 (2013): 294–304.

82 Thomas Kern, *Soziale Bewegungen: Ursachen, Wirkungen, Mechanismen* (Wiesbaden, 2008). For this latter point, see the work of Arjun Appadurai; for example, Appadurai, *The Future as Cultural Fact*. See also United Nations Children's Fund and REACH, 'Children on the Move in Italy and Greece', Geneva, 2017, pp. 30–40.

83 Eckhard Dittrich and Heiko Schrader, '*When Salary Is Not Enough...*': *Private Households in Central Asia* (Berlin, 2015).

84 Adaawen, *Reflections on Migration Dynamics in Northern Ghana from the 'Crossroads Perspective'*.

85 Changes of human figurations are, Elias notes, influenced by the possibility of any given generation to pass on their experiences to subsequent generations as learned societal knowledge. The accumulation of knowledge is in itself a bearer of alterations in human cohabitation and changes of the human figurations (translation by CBH). Norbert Elias, *Die Höfische Gesellschaft: Untersuchungen Zur Soziologie Des Königtums Und Der Höfischen Aristokratie*, 3rd edn, Soziologische Texte, 54 (Darmstadt, 1977), 26.

86 Markus Kaiser and Michael Schönhuth, *Zuhause? Fremd? Migrations- und Beheimatungsstrategien zwischen Deutschland und Eurasien* (Bielefeld, 2015).
87 Cited in Christopher Schwartz, 'The Relics of 1991: Memories and Phenomenology of the Post-Soviet Generation', in Sevket Akyildiz and Richard Carlson (eds), *Social and Cultural Change in Central Asia: The Soviet Legacy*, Central Asia Research Forum (London and New York, 2014), p. 198.

Bibliography

Adaawen, Stephen, *Reflections on Migration Dynamics in Northern Ghana from the 'Crossroads Perspective'*, Crossroads Asia Working Paper Series, No. 32 (Bonn, 2016).

Agnew, John A., *Place and Politics: The Geographical Mediation of State and Society* (Boston, 1987).

Alff, Henryk, and Andreas Benz, 'The Multi-dimensionality of Space: Challenging Spatial Bias in the Production of Places', 5th International Crossroads Asia Conference: Area Studies' Futures, ZEF, University of Bonn, 23 September 2016, available at http://tinyurl.com/zosmh55 (accessed 1 July 2019).

Anderson, Benedict R., *Imagined Communities: Reflections on the Origin and Spread of Nationalism* (London, 1983).

Appadurai, Arjun, *Modernity at Large: Cultural Dimensions of Globalization* (Minnesota, 1996).

Appadurai, Arjun, 'Grassroots Globalization and the Research Imagination', *Public Culture*, 12.1 (January 2000): 1–19.

Appadurai, Arjun, *The Future as Cultural Fact: Essays on the Global Condition* (London and New York, 2013).

Bachmann-Medick, Doris, *Cultural Turns: Neuorientierungen in den Kulturwissenschaften* (Reinbek bei Hamburg, 2007).

Bauman, Zygmunt, *Thinking Sociologically* (Oxford and Cambridge, MA, 1990).

Baumgart, Ralf, and Volker Eichener, *Norbert Elias zur Einführung*, 4th edn (Hamburg, 2013).

Benz, Andreas, 'Multilocality as an Asset – Translocal Development and Change Among the Wakhi of Gojal, Pakistan', in Henryk Alff and Andreas

Benz (eds), *Tracing Connections: Explorations of Spaces and Places in Asian Contexts* (Berlin, 2014).

Bourdieu, Pierre, and Loïc J. D. Wacquant, *An Invitation to Reflexive Sociology* (Chicago, 1992).

Burgess, Chris, 'The Asian Studies "Crisis": Putting Cultural Studies into Asian Studies and Asia into Cultural Studies', *International Journal of Asian Studies*, 1.1 (January 2004): 121–136.

Castells, Manuel, *The Rise of the Network Society: The Information Age: Economy, Society, and Culture Volume I*, 2.2009 (Chichester, West Sussex; Malden, MA, 1996).

Castells, Manuel (ed.), *The Network Society: A Cross-cultural Perspective* (Cheltenham, UK and Northampton, MA, 2005).

Castles, Stephen, and Mark J. Miller, *The Age of Migration: International Population Movements in the Modern World* (Basingstoke and New York, 2009).

Chou, Cynthia, and Vincent Houben, 'Introduction', in *Southeast Asian Studies: Debates and New Directions*, ed. by Cynthia Chou and Vincent Houben, IIAS/ISEAS Series on Asia (Singapore and Leiden, The Netherlands, 2006), 1–22.

Dunning, Eric, and Jason Hughes, *Norbert Elias and Modern Sociology* (London, 2012).

Elias, Norbert, *The Civilizing Process: Sociogenetic and Psychogenetic Investigations*, rev. edn (Oxford and Malden, MA, 2000).

Elias, Norbert, *Was ist Soziologie?*, 12.2014 (Munich, 1970).

Elias, Norbert, *Die Höfische Gesellschaft: Untersuchungen Zur Soziologie Des Königtums Und Der Höfischen Aristokratie*, 3rd edn, Soziologische Texte; 54 (Darmstadt, 1977).

Falzon, Mark-Anthony, *Multi-sited Ethnography: Theory, Praxis and Locality in Contemporary Research* (Farnham, 2012).

Freitag, Ulrike, and Achim Von Oppen, *Translocality: The Study of Globalising Processes from a Southern Perspective* (Leiden and New York, 2009).

Giddens, Anthony, *The Constitution of Society: Outline of the Theory of Structuration* (Berkeley, 1984).

Godehardt, Nadine, and Oliver W. Lembcke, 'Regionale Ordnungen in Politischen Räumen. Ein Beitrag Zur Theorie Regionaler Ordnungen', *GIGA Working Paper*, 124 (2010).

Grosfoguel, Ramón, 'Epistemic Racism/Sexism, Westernized Universities and the Four Genocides/Epistemicides of the Long Sixteenth Century', in

Marta Araújo and Silvia Rodríguez Maeso (eds), *Eurocentrism, Racism and Knowledge* (London, 2015), 23–46.

Habermas, Jürgen, *The Theory of Communicative Action* (Boston, 1984).

Hage, Ghassan, 'A Not so Multi-sited Ethnography of a Not so Imagined Community', *Anthropological Theory*, 5.4 (December 2005).

Hansen, Claus Bech, 'The Crossroads Perspective', Crossroads Asia Concept Paper Series (Bonn, 2017), available at https://tinyurl.com/yaupbv75 (accessed 1 July 2019).

Hansen, Claus Bech, 'Mastering the Current. Studying Central Asia in the 21st Century', in Susan Hodgett and Patrick James (eds), *Necessary Travel. New Area Studies and Canada in Comparative Perspective* (Washington, DC, 2018).

Hansen, Claus Bech and Markus Kaiser, 'Transnational Practices and Post-Soviet Collective Identity', in Günther Schlee and Alexander Horstmann (eds), *Difference and Sameness as Modes of Integration: Anthropological Perspectives on Ethnicity and Religion* (New York; Oxford, 2017).

Harders, Cilja, 'Dimensionen Des Netzwerkansatzes – Einführende Theoretische Überlegungen', in Roman Loimeier (ed.), *Die Islamische Welt Als Netzwerk. Möglichkeiten Und Grenzen Des Netzwerkansatzes Im Islamischen Kontext* (Würzburg, 2000).

Hill, J. K. W., and P. Nehls, *In the Lap of the Mountains: The Irrigation Systems of Ladakh's Farming Communities*, Documentary (2015).

Hill, Joe, 'The Role of Authority in the Collective Management of Hill Irrigation Systems in the Alai (Kyrgyzstan) and Pamir (Tajikistan)', *Mountain Research and Development*, 33.3 (2013): 294–304.

Hornidge, Anna-Katharina, and Katja Mielke, 'Crossroads Studies: From Spatial Containers to Studying the Mobile', *Middle East – Topics & Arguments*, 4 (May 2015).

Houben, V. J. H., and Mona Schrempf (eds), *Figurations of Modernity: Global and Local Representations in Comparative Perspective, Eigene Und Fremde Welten* (Frankfurt and New York, 2008).

Jackson, Peter A., 'Spatialities of Knowledge in the Neoliberal World Academy. Theory, Practice and 21st Century Legacies of Area Studies', Crossroads Asia Working Paper Series (Bonn, 2015).

Jackson, Peter A., 'Mapping Poststructuralism's Borders: The Case for Poststructuralist Area Studies', *Sojourn: Journal of Social Issues in Southeast Asia*, 18.1 (2003): 42–88.

Jessop, Bob, 'Institutional Re(turns) and the Strategic–Relational Approach', *Environment and Planning A*, 33.7 (July 2001): 1213–1235.

Jessop, Bob, Neil Brenner and Martin Jones, 'Theorizing Sociospatial Relations', *Environment and Planning D: Society and Space*, 26.3 (June 2008): 389–401.

Joniak-Lüthi, Agnieszka, 'Xinjiang's Geographies in Motion', *Asian Ethnicity*, 16.4 (October 2015): 428–445.

Kaiser, Markus, and Michael Schönhuth, *Zuhause? Fremd? Migrations- und Beheimatungsstrategien zwischen Deutschland und Eurasien* (Bielefeld, 2015).

Kern, Thomas, *Soziale Bewegungen: Ursachen, Wirkungen, Mechanismen* (Wiesbaden, 2008).

Kilminster, Richard, 'Structuration Theory as World-view', in Christopher G. A. Bryant and David Jary (eds), *Giddens' Theory of Structuration: A Critical Appreciation* (London and New York, 1991).

Kinzley, Judd, and Agnieszka Joniak-Lüthi, *Territory, Border, Infrastructure – Imagining and Crafting National Borderlands in Twentieth-Century China*, Crossroads Asia Working Paper No. 36 (Bonn, 2016).

Lackner, Michael, and Michael Werner, *Der Cultural Turn in Den Humanwissenschaften. Area Studies Im Auf- Oder Abwind Des Kulturalismus?* ed. Programmbeirat der Werner Reimers Konferenzen, vol. 2, Schriftenreihe Suchprozesse Für Innovative Fragestellungen in Der Wissenschaft (Bad Homburg, 1999).

Layder, Derek, 'Social Reality as Figuration: A Critique of Elias's Conception of Sociological Analysis', *Sociology*, 20.3 (August 1986): 367–386.

Lefebvre, Henri, *The Production of Space* (Oxford and Malden, MA, 1992).

Leitner, Helga, Eric Sheppard and Kristin M. Sziarto, 'The Spatialities of Contentious Politics', *Transactions of the Institute of British Geographers*, 33.2 (April 2008): 157–172.

Lewis, Martin W., and Kären Wigen, *The Myth of Continents: A Critique of Metageography* (Berkeley, 1997).

Marcus, George E., 'Ethnography in/of the World System: The Emergence of Multi-sited Ethnography', *Annual Review of Anthropology*, 24 (January 1995).

Martin, Ron L., 'The New Economic Geography of Money', in Ron L. Martin (ed.), *Money and the Space Economy* (Hoboken, NJ, 1999).

Massey, Doreen, *For Space* (London, 2005).

Massey, Douglas S., *Worlds in Motion: Understanding International Migration at the End of the Millennium* (Oxford and New York, 1998).

Merton, Robert K., 'On Sociological Theories of the Middle Range', in *Social Theory and Social Structure* (New York, 1949).

Middell, Matthias, 'Area Studies Under the Global Condition. Debates on Where to Go with Regional or Area Studies in Germany', in Matthias Middell (ed.), *Self-Reflexive Area Studies*, Global History and International Studies 5 (Leipzig, 2013).

Mignolo, Walter D., and Madina V. Tlostanova, 'Theorizing from the Borders Shifting to Geo- and Body-politics of Knowledge', *European Journal of Social Theory*, 9.2 (May 2006): 205–221.

Mintz, Sidney W., 'The Localization of Anthropological Practice from Area Studies to Transnationalism', *Critique of Anthropology*, 18.2 (June 1998): 117–133.

Newton, Tim, 'Elias, Organisation and Ecology', in Ad van Iterson et al. (eds), *The Civilized Organization: Norbert Elias and the Future of Organization* (Amsterdam, 2002), pp. 189–204.

Niemi, Jari I., 'Jürgen Habermas's Theory of Communicative Rationality: The Foundational Distinction Between Communicative and Strategic Action', *Social Theory and Practice*, 31.4 (2005): 513–532.

Nieswand, Boris, *Theorising Transnational Migration: The Status Paradox of Migration* (London, 2011).

Novak, Paolo, 'Tracing Connections and Their Politics', in Henryk Alff and Andreas Benz (eds), *Tracing Connections: Explorations of Spaces and Places in Asian Contexts*, 1st edn (Berlin, 2014).

Pries, Ludger, *Migration and Transnational Social Spaces* (Aldershot, UK and Brookfield, VT, 1999).

Pries, Ludger, *Die Transnationalisierung Der Sozialen Welt: Sozialräume Jenseits von Nationalgesellschaften* (Frankfurt am Main, 2008).

Quijano, Aníbal, 'Coloniality and Modernity/Rationality', *Cultural Studies*, 21.2-3 (March 2007): 168–178.

Reeves, Madeleine, 'Staying Put? Towards a Relational Politics of Mobility at a Time of Migration', *Central Asian Survey*, 30.3-4 (December 2011): 555–576.

Robertson, Roland, 'Glocalization: Time-Space and Homogeneity-Heterogeneity', in Mike Featherstone, Scott Lash and Roland Robertson (eds), *Global Modernities* (London, 1995), pp. 25–44.

Sassen, Saskia, *The Global City: New York, London, Tokyo* (Princeton, NJ, 1991).

Schendel, Willem van, 'Geographies of Knowing, Geographies of Ignorance: Jumping Scale in Southeast Asia', *Environment and Planning D: Society & Space*, 20.2002 (2002): 647–668.

Schwartz, Christopher, 'The Relics of 1991: Memories and Phenomenology of the Post-Soviet Generation', in Sevket Akyildiz and Richard Carlson (eds), *Social and Cultural Change in Central Asia: The Soviet Legacy*, Central Asia Research Forum (London and New York, 2014).

Segbers, Klaus, 'Vom (Großen) Nutzen Und (Kleinen) Elend Der Komparatistik in Der Transformationsforschung', in Ulrich Menzel (ed.), *Vom Ewigen Frieden Und Vom Wohlstand Der Nationen* (Frankfurt am Main, 2000), pp. 493–517.

Sheller, Mimi, and John Urry, 'The New Mobilities Paradigm', *Environment and Planning A*, 38.2 (February 2006): 207–226.

Sheppard, Eric, 'The Spaces and Times of Globalization: Place, Scale, Networks, and Positionality', *Economic Geography*, 78.3 (July 2002): 307–330.

Skeldon, Ronald, 'Going Round in Circles: Circular Migration, Poverty Alleviation and Marginality', *International Migration*, 50.3 (June 2012): 43–60.

Soja, Edward W., 'Taking Space Personally', in Barney Warf and Santa Arias (eds), *The Spatial Turn: Interdisciplinary Perspectives*, Routledge Studies in Human Geography 26 (London and New York, 2009), 11–35.

Sökefeld, Martin, 'Crossroads Asia and the State: Anthropological Perspectives. Paper Presented at the 5th International Crossroads Asia Conference, Bonn, September 22–23, 2016', *Crossroads Asia Working Papers*, no. 35 (2016).

Spivak, Gayatri Chakravorty, *Outside in the Teaching Machine* (New York, 1993).

Urry, John, *Sociology Beyond Societies: Mobilities for the Twenty First Century* (London, 2002).

Wimmer, Andreas, and Nina Glick Schiller, 'Methodological Nationalism, the Social Sciences, and the Study of Migration: An Essay in Historical Epistemology', *The International Migration Review*, 37.3 (2003): 576–610.

Wissenschaftsrat, 'Empfehlungen Zu Den Regionalstudien (Area Studies) in Den Hochschulen Und Außeruniversitären Forschungseinrichtungen', July 2006.

Index

Abrahamsen, Rita 39–40
academic appointments 141–2, 144
Acharya, Amitav 19, 32
Adamovsky, Ezequiel 94
Adorno, Theodor W. 163
agency 55–6; *see also* structure-agency debates
Ahmad, Aijaz 158
Ahram, Ariel 27–8
Alff, Henryk 188–9
allegories, national 158
Annales School 165
anthropology 93–4, 139
'anything goes' principle 31
Appadurai, Arjun 33, 183–6, 190–1
area
 as a category of analysis 11
 concept and definition of 7, 53–4, 58–64, 98, 111, 116
area-driven model of Area Studies 131–3, 137, 141, 144–7
area-specific knowledge and skills 2, 114, 134, 137–9, 146–7, 177
Area Studies 1–17, 59–62, 79
 benefits from 8, 28, 32
 best hope for 173
 boundaries with other modes of knowledge production 147
 breadth of literature on 25
 comparative 116
 crisis in 21–3, 26, 141–2, 157, 173
 criticisms of 1–2, 7–8, 15, 20–3, 28, 32, 116, 169, 177, 179, 186
 current status of 1, 3, 19
 decline and resurgence of 19–23, 33, 140–3, 146
 different models of 12–13, 129–39
 discipline-driven 13–14
 as distinct from Comparative Literature 16
 evolutionary thought in 25–9
 future prospects for 15–16, 37–8, 194–5
 institutional aspect of 13
 lack of coherence and integration in 162–3
 locally-based 26
 multidisciplinary 34
 need for 33
 novel approach to 53, 77
 objects of 9, 169, 171
 problem-driven 13–14
 regarded as a social science 21
 rethinking and revitalization of 29, 139–46, 177–9, 195
 seen as a product of colonialism 26
 self-examination in 23–7
 'soft' methods in 28
 strengthening of 195
 threats faced by 6, 14, 129
 tools used in 194
 with and without borders 113, 116–17
Aristotle 159
Arnold, Matthew 30
Ash, Timothy Garton 64
asymmetrical multilateralism 66
Atlas, Pierre 36
Austen, Jane 157
authoritarian regimes 193

Balkan region 95, 111
Balzac, Honoré de 157
Barrow, J.D. 31
Basedau, Matius 28
Beissinger, Mark R. 6, 12–14, 130–1; *author of Chapter 5*
Benelux countries 70
Benz, Andreas 188–92

Bernhard, Michael 74
Bideleux, R. 109
'Blurring Genres' research network 36
Bohle, Dorothee 75
borders 76, 113–16
   between academic communities 116
   functions of 113
   as interfaces 113–14
   see also disciplinary boundaries
'borderlessness' 107–8
Bourdieu, Pierre 182
Bracewell, Wendy 4–5, 9, 11–12; *author of Chapter 4*
'BRIC' countries 70
Brzezinski, Zbigniew 4, 102
Bulletin of Concerned Asian Scholars 5
Burawoy, Michael 33
butterfly effect 181

Castells, Manuel 183, 190–1
Central Europe 9–10, 54, 57–79, 95, 98
Centrepoint building, London 91–2
Chakrabarty, Dipesh 2, 156
chaos theory 181
Chen, Kuan-hsing 26
Chicago University Oriental Institute 3
China 188–9, 192
Chirot, Daniel 69
Chodakiewicz, Marek Jan 67, 72
Cieszyn Silesia 75
classical education 30
Clifford, James J. 33
climate change 191
Clogg, Richard 103
Cold War 2–4, 7, 12, 21–2, 26, 79, 91–3, 99, 102–3, 106, 129, 133, 177, 186
collective existence 78
Committee of Asian Studies 5
communism, fall of 74

Comparative Literature as a discipline 14–15, 152–7, 162, 166–8, 172–3
consolidation 55–6, 71–2
constructivism 53–4, 64, 78
contextual factors 136, 146
contextual holism 9–10, 34, 53, 58–62, 77, 79
   principles of 60
conversational scholarship 39
Cornis-Pope, Marcel 110
corruption 76
Cosmopolitan Area Studies 34
creolization 15, 164
cross-area studies 12–14, 28, 116
cross-disciplinary communication 147
Crossroads Asia research network 16, 177–81, 188, 194–5
cultural legacies 72–3
cultural values 65
culture in its fullest sense 32
culture-language areas 32–3
Czech Republic 74–5
Czechoslovakia 102

dance figurations 181–2, 190–1
Derrida, Jacques 167
détente 102
disciplinary boundaries and boundary-crossing 20–1, 36
disciplinary knowledge 5–8, 13, 114, 130, 138–9, 143, 158, 170–1
discipline-driven model of Area Studies 133, 136, 145–7
discourse, concept of 37
discourse theory 165
diversity, seeking for 32
Droit, Emmanuel 73
Duffield, Mark 32, 39
Dziaczkowski, Jan 91–2, 98, 107, 116

East-Central Europe 111
East European Studies 98–116
   crisis in 111

funding of 111–12
institutional 111
East Europeanness 112
Eastern Europe 11, 34, 68, 77, 93–9, 102, 109–10
Eastness 112, 115
Eisenstadt, S.N. 156
Elias, Norbert 16–17, 177–87, 190–1, 195
elite and *non-elite* actors 55–6, 66–7, 71–2, 78
'emic' approach 61–2
émigré scholarship 103–4
Engels, Friedrich 157
Engerman, David 101
Enlightenment thinking 93–4
essences of areas 162–5, 168–9
Esterházy, Péter 63
ethnography 33–4
'etic' approach 61
Eurasia 65–6
'Euro-Orientalism' 94–6
European integration 106
European Union 92, 154
'Europeanness' 93
evolutionary thought 25–9

Fanon, Franz 104
Feyerabend, Paul 31
figurational sociology 16–17, 177–90, 193–5
football matches 187–8, 190
Foucault, Michel 5, 37, 165, 167, 171–2
framing 11–12

Gadamer, Hans-Georg 5, 167
Garber, Marjorie 106
Gati, Charles 97
Geertz, Clifford 38, 61, 165
gender studies 154
genres 160–1
geographers 29
geo-politics 108
Germany 177–9
Gibson-Graham, Katherine 34

Giddens, Anthony 182
Global Encyclopedia of Informality 76
globalization 1–2, 13, 17, 22, 33, 133–4, 143, 153, 155, 164, 177–8, 183–5, 194
Gojal 191–2
Graham, Katherine 23
Graham, Loren 26–9
Greece 92, 96
Greskovits, Bela 75
Guha-Khasnobis, Basudeb 57
Gunst, Peter 69

Habermas, Jürgen 182
Habsburg Empire 76
Halecki, Oscar 103
Hansen, Claus Bech 16–17; author of Chapter 7
Hart, Gillian 33
Hegel, G.W.F. 162
Heidegger, Martin 160
Heryanto, Anson 26
Hill, Emma 38
historical ethnography 33
historical novels 157
historicism and historicizing 56–7, 60, 70–5, 78
Hodgett, Susan 7–8; author Chapter 2
Homo Sovieticus (HS) model 73–4
Hoover Institution, Stanford University 101
Horschelmann, Kathrine 34
Hozic, Aida 26
humanities 139
Hungary 10, 58, 68, 70, 72, 74, 102
Huntington, S. 109

imagined communities 186
imperialism 186
informality and informal practices 10, 58–60, 76–8
Inglis Review 31–2
interdisciplinarity 12–15, 25–6, 35, 79, 105–7, 111, 114, 131,

137–8, 143–4, 162–3, 167–8, 178–80
Intermarium 67–72, 79
International Relations 39–40
International Studies 137–8
internationalization 143, 186
interpretation 5
introspection 24

Jackson, Peter 32–3
Jacobson, Roman 104, 165
Jameson, Fredric 158
Jeffries, I. 109
Jessop, Bob 182
Johnston, Ron 24
Joniak-Lüthi Agnieszka 189
Jung, Dietrich 21–2, 38–9

Kagan, Jerome 30–1
Kanbur, Ravi 57
Kantor, Jean Michel 26–9
Karl, Terry Lyn 55, 71
Kay, Rebecca 34
Kazakhstan 188
Kissinger, Henry 4
knowledge of subject content 135
knowledge production, politics of 114–15
Köllner, Patrick 28
Kristeva, Julia 104
Kubik, Jan 9–10, 16, 34; *author Chapter 3*
Kuhn, Thomas 173
Kundera, Milan 64–5
Kyrgyzstan 188

Lambert, Richard 20–1
language skills 6
Leavis, F.R. 30
Ledeneva, Alena 76
Lefebvre, Henri 184, 187
legacies of different types 71–3, 76, 78, 109
Levi-Strauss, Claude 104

Lewis, Martin W. 156
liberal arts education 142
linguisticality 167
List, Friedrich 63
literary studies 157–61, 164–7
literatures, national 166, 168
Liverpool University 105
local perspectives 8
localism 57
Lukács, Georg 104

McFaul, Michael 55
Mackinder, Halford 95
Małowist, Adam 68
Marcus, George 34
Marcuse, Herbert 104
Martin, Ron 184
Marxist thinking 103, 159
measurement error 135
memory 57, 73–5, 78
Merriam-Webster Dictionary 72
meta-disciplines 16
metaphorical models of knowing 169–71
metonymic knowledge 170–1
Middle Eastern Studies 22, 171
Milutinović, Zoran 14–15; *editor and author of Chapters 1 and 6*
Mishkova, Diana 95
Mitchell, Timothy 3, 155–6
Mitteleuropa 63, 67, 79
mixed-methods research 27–8
mobility 190–4
modelling, purpose of 135–6
modernity and modernization 106, 156
multiculturalism 25
multidisciplinarity 15, 34, 106–7, 129–32, 139, 163
multilateralism 66

nation states 183
Naumann, Friedrich 63
Nazi regime 73

neo-liberal economic reforms 75
networks 55–8
   building of 9
   and relationism 64–70
Neubauer, John 110
New Historicism 159, 165
NicCrath, Mairead 38

obscurantism 23
Oldfield, Jonathan 34
Orientalism 25, 37, 95
Orientalism (book) 108, 170–2
Ostrom, Elinor 23, 57
'otherness' and 'othering' 112, 186
Ottoman Empire 94

Pares, Bernard 105
Parsons, Talcott 180
Partsch, Josef F.M. 63
Pascal, Blaise 5
periphery, *interface* and *external* types of 70
phenomenology 159–60
Philby, Kim 4–5, 101
philosophes 93
Piketty, Thomas 157
Piłsudski, József 68
Plato 159
Podraza, Antoni 63
Poland and Polishness 10, 54, 58, 61, 68–75
Pop-Eleches, Grigore 109
populism 72
Porębski, Mieczysław 54
positionality 186
positivism 20–1, 134–5
post-Area Studies 116
post-colonial studies 154–6
post-communist transition 58, 61, 109
postmodernism and postmodernity 23, 25
post-structuralism 33, 167
Pries, Ludger 187

Prime, Geoffrey 4–5, 101
Princeton University 3, 14, 140–1, 145
problem-driven Area Studies 130, 137–8, 147
professionalization 133, 140–1
purity, *methodological* and *disciplinary* 163–9
Putin, Vladimir 111

Rafaele, Vincente 21, 35
rational choice theory 8, 22–3, 135–6
Rausch, Anthony 26
Reeves, Madeleine 192
'regimes of relevance' 115
regionalism 57
relationism 9, 55–6, 60, 77
   and networks 64–70
remittances 192
Research Excellence Framework (REF) 112
research questions 113
'revolving door' between government and academia 101–2
Rokkan, Stein 70
Romania 114
Russell, David 24
Russia and Russian Studies 65–6, 70, 94, 143

Said, Edward 4, 24–5, 29, 37, 108, 170
scale 10, 57, 60, 78
Schierenbeck, Isabell 35
Schmitter, Philippe 55, 71
School of Oriental and African Studies (SOAS), London 3
School of Slavonic and East European Studies (SSEES), London 3, 100, 102–3, 105
'scientist', first use of the term 30
self-examination 23–7
self-identity 10
'semi-periphery' concept 68–9
Sharma, Miriam 26

Slovakia 74
Snow, C.P. 30
social analysis 27
social construction 186–7, 194
social scientific method 135–6, 140, 167
Somer, Murat 36
space, theory and analysis of 187–9
specification error 135
Spivak, Gayatri C. 14, 153–5, 157
Stanford University 101
state socialism 57–8, 74–6
Stenning, Alison 34
story-telling 159–60
structuralism 167
structure–agency debates 182–7; see also agency
Switzerland 70
symbolic interactionism 54
symmetrical bilateralism 65–6
Szanton, David 5

Tansman, Alan 132
Tessler, Mark 22
theory
    development of 8
    evolution of 29
    investment in 172
'thick' description 165
third-world texts 159
Thomas Theorem 54, 62
Tihanov, Galin 115
'Title VI' programme 132
Todorov, Tzevtan 104
Todorova, Maria 95
Tolstrup, Jacob 66
TPSN (Territories, Places, Scales and Networks) approach 185

'traditional' Area Studies 131–2, 138–41, 146, 155, 177
trans-disciplinarity 21
transition, study of 55
Turkish Studies 36
Turkmenistan 193–4

Ughur population 189
university environments 189
Urry, John 183, 190–1
Urwin, Derek 70

Vance, Cyrus 102
Visegrád (V4) countries 68, 75

Wacquant, Lois 182
Wakhi people 191–2
Wallerstein, Immanuel 68–9, 77–8, 104
Wang, Ban 26
Weber, Max 38–9
Wellek, René 104
West-centrism 109
Whelan, Robert 30
White, Gregory 22
Wigen, Kären E. 156
Williams, Raymond 159
Wisconsin-Maddison, University of 131
Wolff, Larry 93–4

Xinjiang 188–9

Yoshimoto, Mitsuhiro 154

Zarycki, Tomasz 69–70

www.ingramcontent.com/pod-product-compliance
Lightning Source LLC
Chambersburg PA
CBHW052040300426
44117CB00012B/1898